Jimmy Collins

ALSO BY CHARLIE BEVIS
AND FROM MCFARLAND

Doubleheaders: A Major League History (2011)

*The New England League:
A Baseball History, 1885–1949* (2008)

*Sunday Baseball: The Major Leagues' Struggle to
Play Baseball on the Lord's Day, 1876–1934* (2003)

*Mickey Cochrane:
The Life of a Baseball Hall of Fame Catcher* (1998)

Jimmy Collins
A Baseball Biography
Charlie Bevis

McFarland & Company, Inc., Publishers
Jefferson, North Carolina, and London

LIBRARY OF CONGRESS CATALOGUING-IN-PUBLICATION DATA

Bevis, Charlie, 1954–
    Jimmy Collins : a baseball biography / Charlie Bevis.
       p.   cm.
    Includes bibliographical references and index.

    ISBN 978-0-7864-6359-6
    softcover : acid free paper ∞

    1. Collins, Jimmy, 1870–1943. 2. Baseball players — United States — Biography. I. Title.
GV865.C6436B48 2012
796.357092—dc23
[B]   2012014898

BRITISH LIBRARY CATALOGUING DATA ARE AVAILABLE

© 2012 Charlie Bevis. All rights reserved

No part of this book may be reproduced or transmitted in any form or by any means, electronic or mechanical, including photocopying or recording, or by any information storage and retrieval system, without permission in writing from the publisher.

On the cover: Jimmy Collins, 1899 (photograph by Elmer Chickering)

Manufactured in the United States of America

McFarland & Company, Inc., Publishers
  Box 611, Jefferson, North Carolina 28640
    www.mcfarlandpub.com

Contents

Preface 1

1. Businessman in a Baseball Uniform 5
2. Policeman's Son 10
3. Ballplayer in Buffalo 19
4. Sold to Boston, Loaned to Louisville 31
5. Boston's Third Baseman 40
6. Temple Cup Series and All-America Tour 49
7. Long-Ball Hitter 58
8. Fielding Wizard 64
9. Players Union Representative 71
10. Jump to the American League 78
11. Rookie Manager 88
12. Soft-Spoken Leadership 98
13. Champions of the American League 106
14. The First World Series 114
15. Spring Training in Macon 123
16. Another Championship Season 129
17. Clash with Boston Ownership 140
18. Minor League Magnate 147

19. Manager Absent Without Leave	151
20. Making Sense of "It"	164
21. Playing for Mack in Philadelphia	171
22. Back to the Minor Leagues	177
23. Real Estate Mogul	189
24. Muny League President	197
25. Hall of Fame Selection	208
26. Legacy to Baseball	213
Chapter Notes	223
Bibliography	232
Index	235

Preface

Writing about a man who was devoted to preserving his privacy is a difficult task. This first full-length biography of Hall of Fame third baseman Jimmy Collins almost never came to fruition because Collins was so intensely private. The research items closest to being primary source material are a few snippets of information he reported, grudgingly, I suspect, to government and institutional data collectors that compiled the census and city directories. As for secondary source material, Collins rarely spoke to newspaper writers about himself during his playing days or, more helpful to a biographer, during his post-baseball life. Only in the months before his death in 1943, when he granted an interview with sportswriters at the *Buffalo Evening News*, did Collins open up. His wide network of acquaintances didn't have much to say to writers about him either. Other than the obligatory baseball-related aspects of his life, there is very little secondary source research material regarding Collins.

My pilgrimage to Cooperstown in March 2011 to view the Collins file at the National Baseball Hall of Fame was a metaphor for the research portion of this biography project: so much effort to yield so little result. I had hoped my trip would reveal some yet undiscovered details about Collins tucked away in a voluminous file. Alas, his player file was only a half-inch thick, scrawny for a Hall of Fame ballplayer. Beyond copies of the standard secondary source material on Collins and a sheaf of early drafts of a 1946 article by Ernie Lanigan about Collins' first professional ballgame in the minor leagues, I found only a few insignificant nuggets of new information. Since I was the only researcher at the A. Bartlett Giamatti Research Center on that snowy morning, the center's director of research, Tim Wiles, was able to spend some time with me doing computer searches into the online records of the center's various collections, all of which turned up nothing. When Tim checked the standard bibliographical volumes, he expressed surprise that so little material existed on Collins. The meager amount of written information is also reflected in the

Hall of Fame's few photographs of Collins. Pat Kelly, the photo archivist at the Hall, sheepishly replied to my inquiry that she could locate only three photos of Collins as an individual (and just three others where he was part of a group photo).

What I did acquire in my several hours at the cathedral of baseball information, while donning the historian's white gloves to examine the few papers existing in the Collins file, was the knowledge that over the decades even the most ardent of baseball researchers — the various archivists at the Hall of Fame, such as Lanigan — couldn't accumulate much about Collins' life. This gave me the confidence that my biography, once completed, would shed new light on Jimmy Collins, going well beyond the content in the handful of short chronicles that exist about Collins' life, each about 5,000 words in length, none which truly elucidates the man.

Due to the slim amount of available research material, potential biographers of Collins in the past surely abandoned the task early in the research process. The dearth of research material definitely tested my mettle to complete a manuscript that moved beyond the one-dimensional aspects of his baseball life. After beginning this project in 2005, I encountered two long hiatuses when it seemed impossible to craft a book-length biography of Collins. The epiphany for me came in 2010 when I was teaching a new college course on writing biography. As a sub-genre within creative non-fiction, biography resides on the cusp of the division between fiction and non-fiction as a combination of the historian's skill in solid research and the novelist's craft of storytelling and character development. As I encouraged my graduate-level creative-writing students to combine the best aspects of the two broad worlds of writing, I was struck by how well they could discern from the available research material some of the psyche of their chosen biographical subject and identify a conflict in that person's life. My students took to heart the advice of author Nigel Hamilton in his book *How to Do Biography: A Primer* that biographers need to use research material "as stepping stones into the mind, memory, manipulations, and personality of their subjects" and develop their character by reading "certain psychological signs that enable us to understand what people are really saying behind the faces they put on."[1] My students inspired me to jump back into the Collins project to try to formulate the less public conflicts in his life and understand his internal motivations from the available, albeit meager, research. Rather than once again try to extrapolate his baseball life to comprehend his personal life, I did the opposite. By mapping the lesser-known aspects of his personal life onto his baseball life, I was able to more easily detect conflicts and motivations. Finally, the scaffolding emerged for a biography that captures Jimmy Collins the person, not simply Jimmy Collins the ballplayer.

To move beyond the contours of his baseball life, I relied heavily on electronically searchable newspaper databases for the *Boston Globe, Buffalo Express,* and *Sporting Life* to mine minor details in contemporary reports that could amplify Collins' attitude or perspective on his life. These three sources were supplemented with contemporary coverage in the *Chicago Tribune, Philadelphia Inquirer, Washington Post,* and *New York Times* that often filled in gaps not covered by the Boston press. To augment these newspaper sources, I used archival material such as census records, city directories, cemetery records, and birth, death and marriage records (although I could not locate a record, civil or religious, to authenticate the very secretive marriage of Collins and his wife).

For unrestricted Internet access to electronic databases, I thank the Regina Library at Rivier College for access to the *Boston Globe*, Old Fulton NY Post Cards for access to the *Buffalo Express*, and the LA84 Foundation for access to the *Sporting Life*. My thanks also go to the Boston Public Library for its extensive collection of microfilm of defunct Boston newspapers, the Widener Library at Harvard University for its accessible collection of microfilm of newspapers from cities across the nation, and the interlibrary loan department at the University of Massachusetts–Lowell for help in obtaining numerous books and microfilm (especially the obscure, short-lived publication *Illustrated Sporting News*).

All these sources enabled me to conclude that Jimmy Collins was a very interesting person, a man who used, and sometimes abused, baseball to achieve other things in life through his entrepreneurial real estate investments.

CHAPTER 1

Businessman in a Baseball Uniform

After more than a half century of anonymity following his 1945 enshrinement in the Baseball Hall of Fame, Jimmy Collins once again made newspaper headlines in 1999 when his will was discovered stolen from its repository deep in the bowels of a Buffalo, New York, government building. "Jimmy Collins never had a problem fielding hard grounders to third base, but the Hall of Famer from Buffalo was defenseless when a thief stole his will from the Erie County Surrogate's Court," the *Buffalo News* reported. "Collins' will was offered for sale to a baseball autograph collector, who told investigators it was so expensive that he couldn't afford it."[1] Up in heaven, Collins must have smiled. People were breaking the law to make money from his *signature*.

His name regained more popularity a year later in 2000 with the publication of *Red Sox Century: One Hundred Years of Red Sox Baseball*, a book written by Glenn Stout and Richard Johnson to commemorate the 100th anniversary of the establishment of the Boston Red Sox ballclub in 1901. In a sidebar focused on Collins entitled "The First Third Baseman," Stout and Johnson summarized his impact on the new Boston team: "As player-manager he led the club to five straight winning seasons, two pennants, one world championship while still playing the best third base in all baseball.... Collins was [then] considered, without question, the best third baseman in the history of the game."[2] Collins must have chuckled from his perch among the angels. Authors Stout and Johnson were making money off Collins' blatant effort to cash-in on his baseball fame by jumping from the Boston team in the National League to the Boston team in the new American League.

Then in 2003, no fewer than four books were published to celebrate the 100th anniversary of the first modern World Series in 1903. The books portrayed Collins as not only a successful player-manager who led the Boston

Americans to victory over the Pittsburgh Pirates in the very first World Series, but also as a person who deeply inspired the people of Boston. "The story of the first World Series is the story of the birth of baseball as a modern game, as an American ritual," Louis Masur wrote in *Autumn Glory: Baseball's First World Series*. "Politics and culture divided Boston; the success of Collins' team in 1903 was that it helped to unify the populace and restore the city to national relevance."[3] Other authors extrapolated Collins' victory into a national impact. "The story of the 1903 World Series represents a microcosm of American life at the turn of the twentieth century," Roger Abrams wrote in *The First World Series*. "It is the story of American immigrants, the Yankees, and Brahmins, the Irish and the Jews. It is the story of Boston and of Pittsburgh. It is, of course, the story of America."[4]

Collins must have howled in laughter, backslapping St. Peter at the gates to heaven. Publishers and authors were making money to remember a series of exhibition games in which Collins had deftly negotiated a shakedown of Boston owner Henry Killilea to have three-fourths of the Boston ballclub's net proceeds from the games go to the ballplayers, with just one-quarter going to ownership. At the time, Collins never imagined that such a postseason series would ever attain the prominence that it did. Collins was not especially interested in the perceived glory of the upstart American League's victory in the World Series over the established National League; to him that World Series was simply a business venture that culminated in his receiving a $1,182 check that he could use to further pursue his non-baseball business ventures.

The game on the baseball field meant less to Collins than the paycheck that he received for playing in those games. In the one in-depth interview with Collins that was ever published after his playing days were over, conducted just a few weeks before his death in 1943, *Buffalo Evening News* writer Cy Kritzer observed that "while Jimmy narrated many incidents on and off the field, he couldn't recall once during the interview the size of his batting average in any one season." Yet, as Kritzer related in detail from that interview, Collins had an encyclopedic recall of the amounts of his salary as a ballplayer.[5]

Professional baseball to Jimmy Collins was all about the money. When Collins jumped to the new American League in 1901, *The Sporting News* paraphrased his motivation as "it was business and not sentiment that held him in the sport of base ball and that he was out for the dough."[6] Collins didn't just settle for the typical one-year deal in which he could be released on ten days notice without further payment; he negotiated what we call today a guaranteed contract for a three-year length, which he renegotiated several times over the course of his eight-year tenure in the American League. The

1. Businessman in a Baseball Uniform

Jimmy Collins raises the World's Champions flag on Opening Day in 1904 at Boston's Huntington Avenue Grounds, as men prepare to hoist the American League pennant next. By leading Boston to victory in the first modern-day World Series in 1903, Collins not only collected a check for $1,182 but was also able to negotiate a very lucrative three-year contract that he used to fund his real estate development activities in Buffalo (Boston Public Library, Print Department).

victory in the 1903 World Series allowed him to really cash-in on his baseball success.

In that 1943 interview with the *Buffalo Evening News*, Collins practically gloated about once earning $18,000 in one year, through a combination of a $10,000 salary and a profit-sharing arrangement that yielded $8,000.[7] While Collins never named the exact year that he received this compensation level, 1904 is the only reasonable year for that high of a payment to have occurred. Collins did name his 1901 salary in that 1943 interview and certainly would have connected that to the profit-sharing provision had it been part of his initial three-year contract. The lower salary level in his 1906–1908 contract was fairly well publicized; given the plight of the Boston team in 1905, the profit-sharing provision wouldn't have generated as sizeable a payment as the 1904 season would have.

When Collins played major league baseball for 14 years sandwiched around the turn of the twentieth century, the average annual wage for an American worker was roughly $500. In comparison, Collins was compensated quite well as a ballplayer, receiving more than ten times that amount during more than half of his major league career. While the exact compensation figures paid to Collins for playing baseball are lost to history, the following reconstruction from various newspaper accounts illustrates both the magnitude and the upward progression:

- 1895 — $1,200 in salary initially, increased to $1,650 upon his release to Louisville, plus a $500 bonus (about $2,000 combined).[8]
- 1896 — $1,800 in salary plus $45 from a postseason local barnstorming tour ($1,845 combined).[9]
- 1897 — $2,100 in salary plus $258 from the Temple Cup series and $442 from the postseason tour of the All-America Baseball Team ($2,800 combined).[10]
- 1898 — $2,400 in salary plus a $235 bonus for the team's first-place finish ($2,635 combined).[11]
- 1899 — $2,400 in salary.[12]
- 1900 — $2,400 in salary.
- 1901 — $3,500 in salary, the first year of a three-year contract, plus $110 from a postseason local barnstorming tour ($3,610 combined).[13]
- 1902 — $5,000 in salary, a renegotiation of the last two years of the three-year contract.[14]
- 1903 — $6,500 in salary, a renegotiation of the final year of the three-year contract, plus $1,182 from the World Series ($7,682 combined).[15]
- 1904 — $10,000 in salary, the first year of a new three-year contract, plus $8,000 from a profit-sharing arrangement with the ballclub ($18,000 combined).[16]
- 1905 — $10,000 in salary, plus $107 from the postseason city series with the Boston Nationals, plus an unknown amount from the profit-sharing arrangement (at least $10,107 combined).[17]
- 1906 — $8,500 in salary, a renegotiation of the final year of the three-year contract, as part of a new three-year contract.[18]
- 1907 — $8,500 in salary.
- 1908 — $8,500 in salary.

While Collins played professional baseball to accumulate wealth, it wasn't just about acquiring money but rather what he could do with it. Beginning in 1900, Collins used his baseball income to develop a real estate business by building multi-family rental housing in his hometown of Buffalo, New York, to capitalize on the movement of Irish-American workers from inner-city Buffalo to the burgeoning South Buffalo neighborhood. By 1908 he had accumulated an estimated $40,000 worth of real estate property.[19]

Collins also attempted to invest in baseball, by owning minor league ballclubs. In 1906 he made a small investment in the Worcester ballclub of the New England League.[20] However, when Collins tried to buy into ballclubs in the premier minor leagues at the time, the Eastern League and the American

Association, the market for minor league ballclubs was near its all-time high, so inflated prices thwarted Collins' efforts to be a true minor league magnate. He sold his interest in the Worcester ballclub in 1912.[21]

While Collins loved the money he made from baseball, he wasn't a mercenary; baseball's "greatest third baseman" did enjoy the game itself. In his later years he was the longtime president of the Buffalo Municipal Baseball Association, where he became an ambassador for baseball in the Buffalo area. "Despite the fact that he grew feebler each year, he never lost his love for baseball or his desire to talk to baseball fans about the game," Mike Quinlan wrote in the *Niagara Falls Gazette* a few days before Collins died. "Jimmy never passed up a chance to attend a baseball gathering and he seemed to take much delight in talking to the younger players."[22] While Collins was closely associated with his hometown of Buffalo, he always made it a point to attend baseball banquets held just north of the city in his birthplace of Niagara Falls.

CHAPTER 2

Policeman's Son

James Joseph Collins was born on January 16, 1870, in Niagara Falls, New York, where his Irish immigrant parents, Anthony and Alice Collins, lived in the village of Suspension Bridge, about two miles down the Niagara River from the famous waterfall, 15 miles north of Buffalo, and just a few hundred yards east of the Canadian border.[1]

Anthony Collins had arrived in the United States from Ireland in 1862 when he was 18 years old and came to Buffalo, New York, where some relatives had already settled.[2] Starting out as a laborer on the Buffalo docks, Anthony soon worked for the New York Central Railroad, getting the job through an uncle who worked in the railroad's freight house.[3] After Anthony married Alice O'Hara in 1867, they moved to Niagara Falls where Anthony worked as a detective for the New York Central Railroad, investigating criminal activity at the border crossing, where the tracks of three railroads merged into one to cross the railway bridge into Canada. Steady work as a policeman in the new Buffalo Police Department drew Anthony Collins and his family back to Buffalo in 1872, where his railroad crime-fighting background gave him an edge over other newly appointed patrolmen. Buffalo was home over the next several decades for all three of the Collins brothers: Jimmy, his older brother Henry, and younger brother Anthony, Jr.

Anthony Collins was one of the many immigrants in the nineteenth century who took advantage of the employment opportunities in Buffalo. By 1872 the city had grown immensely since its original settlement in 1804 by traders. Taking advantage of its location on the eastern end of Lake Erie at the mouth of the Niagara River, Buffalo quickly became a center of commerce for goods moving from the Midwest to the East Coast. The completion of the Erie Canal in 1825 fueled Buffalo's growth, as the inland waterway enabled goods to be efficiently transported to major cities in New York state. "From the moment that the Erie Canal was completed in 1825, Buffalo was seen as a way station, a conduit whose primary function was the movement of goods and people from east to west and vice versa," Mark Goldman observed in his book *High Hopes: The Rise and Decline of Buffalo, New York*.[4] Grain grown in Ohio, Indiana, and Illinois could now be shipped via the Great Lakes and the Erie Canal all the way to New York City.

The Erie Canal also brought the first wave of Irish immigrants to Buffalo. The Irish dug the canal and stayed in the Buffalo area since it was the terminus of the canal. They found new work on the docks, unloading grain from the barges on the lake onto smaller vessels that could transport the grain along the canal to interior New York. The arrival of the railroad in the 1840s spurred further growth in Buffalo. Rather than merely serve as a middleman in the transport of goods, Buffalo became a haven for the manufacture of raw material into finished goods. Breweries, leatherworks and furniture makers developed; iron foundries were established in response to the rail connections to nearby coal fields in Pennsylvania.

The Irish immigrants congregated in Buffalo's First Ward, a densely packed area south of the central business district near the city's waterfront, which teemed with grain elevators, mills, and warehouses. The Irish immigrants developed strong connections among themselves to establish an urban network of contacts to secure jobs and provide for their everyday needs. In his essay "The Remaking of Irish America," David Doyle writes how first-generation Irish-Americans accomplished this: "The urban and laboring Irish population salved its trauma and poverty and maintained its self-esteem and cohesion by constructing a peculiar subculture around the familiarities of the neighborhood, the saloon, and the [church] parish. Within these, Irishmen met, talked, and organized for the protection of their livelihood, the improvement of their social position, and the maintenance of their religious faith."[5] Despite the benefits of the social network of the neighborhood, there were many downsides to living in the First Ward, such as crime, alcoholism, poverty, disease, and foul air quality. Once an Irish-American family saved enough money, they generally fled the First Ward for a more hospitable section of the city.

Anthony Collins was one Irish immigrant who was highly motivated to escape from the First Ward. He immediately tapped into the social network existing in the First Ward when he arrived in Buffalo in 1862. His uncle Mathew had come to Buffalo in the 1840s, at the time of the infamous potato famine, from County Waterford in Ireland.[6] Mathew lived in the First Ward on Mississippi Street, right near the docks, and paid his dues as a laborer.[7] Mathew used the Irish-American network to secure a job with a railroad company, which financially allowed him to move up the social ladder and live in a house on Elk Street in the city's 13th Ward, just east of the First Ward.[8]

After Anthony Collins and his family came back to in Buffalo in 1872, they also returned to the Irish-American subculture of the First Ward, by living in various rental flats on Carroll Street. Although nominally located in the Second Ward, Carroll Street was just two blocks from the northern edge of the First Ward. The Collins family lived for a few years at 130 Carroll Street, before moving in 1883 to 184 Carroll Street, which was directly across from the main terminal of the New York, West Shore & Buffalo Railroad.[9] There was no shortage of saloons in the area to serve as social gathering places for the Irish-Americans. The 1884 *Buffalo City Directory* listed five saloons just on Carroll Street (including one run by Dennis Kenneally at 166 Carroll Street) and dozens more within the Second Ward.

Irish-Americans were the distinct minority in Buffalo as three ethnic groups tussled for economic and political control in the city during the middle decades of the nineteenth century. When Anthony Collins arrived in the city in 1862, German-Americans represented one-half of the population, native-born Americans one-quarter, and Irish-Americans one-fifth.[10] Putting the Irish-Americans at a further disadvantage, they held largely unskilled jobs while the German-Americans and native-born Americans had mostly white-collar and skilled positions. There were distinct patterns to where the ethnic groups predominately lived within Buffalo. The German-Americans lived on the East Side, the native-born Americans on the West Side, and the Irish-Americans were concentrated in the southern section of the city.

Despite the city's growth and influx of immigrant workers, the citizens of Buffalo were protected only by a small force of watchmen until 1866, when the state legislature established the Niagara Frontier Police District that covered both Buffalo and its neighboring towns. The Buffalo Police Department was created in 1871, initially divided into five precincts.[11]

In the fall of 1872 when the Collins family moved back to Buffalo, Anthony secured a job as a patrolman with the newly established Buffalo Police Department.[12] He was assigned to work in the first precinct, which included not only the central business district but also parts of the crime-ridden First Ward. Patrolmen were paid $800 a year, which was double what the average industrial worker earned at the time.[13] While police work was relatively steady and paid well, it was often dangerous. "Buffalo was one of the roughest and most dangerous cities in America," one historian wrote, noting its numerous saloons, brothels, and gambling joints. "There were streets where the police walked at midday only in pairs, for an officer who came alone might shortly be found floating face-down in the canal."[14] Policemen really earned their $800 annual salary when they were required to patrol the First Ward.

Irish-Americans played an important role in the development of the modern police system, which was one of the few opportunities that Irish-

Americans had in the urban environment to earn a steady income and become upwardly mobile economically. "The late nineteenth century policeman had a difficult job," James Richardson wrote in his book *Urban Police in the United States*. "He had to maintain order, cope with vice and crime, provide service to people in trouble, and keep his nose clean politically."[15] Anthony Collins learned to be very adept at the political aspects.

As a public employee before civil service laws reformed city government, Anthony Collins needed to be especially savvy to negotiate city politics to retain his position on the police force. The police board or the superintendent could fire, transfer, or demote police officers at will. Frequent reorganizations of the police department were common, especially after a new mayor was elected. The old adage that government employees "serve at the pleasure of" particular high-ranking government officials really meant something in the late nineteenth century. Anthony Collins established numerous connections and used them effectively to maneuver through the turbulent political waters to have a 30-year career on the Buffalo police force.

As his father rose within the ranks of the Buffalo Police Department, Jimmy Collins had an excellent tutor to learn from in how to get things done within the three ethnic groups that controlled many aspects of life in Buffalo. While the Second Ward provided a wonderful support network within the Irish-American community, the ability to work effectively with the German-Americans and native-born Americans in Buffalo was the essential skill that enabled Jimmy Collins to rise in stature well beyond the average expectations for a second-generation Irish-American. During his days on Carroll Street, Jimmy Collins grew up in a tight-knit environment, frolicking with friends in the streets and nearby railroad yards as a youth and participating in activities of nearby social clubs and the Catholic church. It was not a lavish lifestyle, but nor was it poverty either. No record remains of his early schooling, which he likely attended at either the neighborhood public grammar school or the nearby parochial school at St. Bridget's Church.

After he had diligently patrolled the streets of the first precinct for several years, Anthony Collins was promoted to sergeant in 1879 in a politically motivated police department reorganization. In the administration of a newly elected Democratic mayor, the police board now had a Democratic majority and moved to discharge the captain of the second precinct, who supported the Republican party, with an Irish-American who had little police experience; in the first precinct, the police board demoted the existing sergeant, who was also a Republican supporter, and promoted Anthony Collins to take his place.[16] The promotion was short lived, however. When Republicans regained control of Buffalo politics in 1880, Anthony was demoted back to patrolman in a wholesale police reorganization.

When Grover Cleveland, a Democrat, was elected mayor of Buffalo in November 1881, Anthony Collins caught his big break in police politics. Cleveland soon rose fast in politics, as he was elected governor of New York in November 1882 and then president of the United States in November 1884. As mayor of Buffalo, Cleveland "distinguished himself principally by two great exploits," writes his biographer Allan Nevins, "by his successful contest against an unblushing attempt to rob the city of approximately $200,000 on a street-cleaning contract, and his equally successful struggle to obtain expert and efficient treatment of the sewage problem in Buffalo." Cleveland worked hard to eliminate graft in the city's operation and improve life for its citizens. "He would not wink at little devices for getting public work done without competitive bids," writes Nevins, "and he had a blunt way of calling attention to all sorts of abuses."[17] When reformist Cleveland resigned in November 1882 before his mayoral term expired to become the governor of New York, Thomas Manning, a Democrat, was elected mayor in a special election to replace Cleveland. Manning was an avowed supporter of Cleveland's reform policies to reduce corruption and clean up Buffalo.

Anthony Collins was very well connected to Manning. On May 10, 1883, after Manning had made new appointments to the police board, the board ousted the existing police superintendent, replacing him with Thomas Curtin, who made sweeping personnel changes in the police force. "Three days after [Curtin's appointment], Mr. Collins, then a patrolman in the First Precinct, was made Captain of the Third," the *Buffalo Express* recounted in an article two years later.[18] Captain Anthony Collins of the third precinct was now one of the highest ranking police officials in the city's ten precinct houses, as captains headed just the first four precincts while lieutenants commanded the fifth through tenth precincts.

Captain Collins embraced the reform policies of mayors Cleveland and Manning, in part by enforcing the law against saloon openings on Sunday. One target was saloon-keeper William Durrenberger at 36 Broadway. In November 1883, the *Buffalo Express* reported that charges were brought against Durrenberger "for being open on Sunday in violation of the law," with "the charges against Durrenberger preferred by Captain Anthony Collins of the Third Police Precinct."[19]

However, it was not as easy for Anthony Collins to navigate the political waters as a police captain as it was as a patrolman. Police captains had enormous responsibility as well as extensive visibility. Mayor Manning was very unpopular and lasted just one year in office, returning to his malt-liquor business in January 1884. Under the new mayor, Curtin lasted just six months as police superintendent, being ousted in July 1884.

With Manning and Curtin both removed from office as a result of a change in the political winds, Anthony Collins lasted only two years as a police captain. On July 10, 1885, the police board ousted the top-ranking police officials in four precincts. While the heads of the fifth, seventh, and ninth precincts were all fired, "Captain Anthony Collins of the Third Precinct was reduced to the rank of a Lieutenant and assigned to the command of the Fifth Precinct."[20] Anthony Collins survived the political purge, no doubt based on his other connections within the city's political infrastructure. A writer for the *Buffalo Express* provided an in-depth analysis of the rationale for the removal of Collins as captain in the third precinct:

> Regarding the presumable causes for the removal of Capt. Collins from the command of the Third Precinct little need be said, although a long chapter might be written on the bad condition of the precinct. The territory on Elm and Oak streets, between Clinton Street and Broadway, is well known as the heart of a colony of houses of ill-repute. It is desirable that these places be kept under restraint, but this was not done.... The saloons of Patrick Lyons and William Carney on Eagle Street have been particularly obnoxious. It is well known that both have restaurants attached, and are practically open day and night, though other saloons are obliged to close. Disturbances at each have been frequent, and in several instances there have been cases of assault in the vicinity of Eagle and Washington streets which have nearly proved serious.... It is also stated on the most reliable authority that Capt. Collins was "too easy" and did not sufficiently exercise his authority over the men under him. The precinct, it was determined by the Board, needed more stringent government, and therefore the change was made.[21]

Although the demotion came with a reduction in salary — captains were paid $1,200 a year while lieutenants earned $1,000 a year — Anthony Collins continued to pay the tuition for his son Jimmy at St. Joseph's College, a Catholic educational institution run by the Christian Brothers at One Delaware Avenue in downtown Buffalo. Despite the use of "college" in its name, St. Joseph's was more like an advanced high school, more akin to a prep school today. As John Thelin notes in his book *A History of American Higher Education*, in the 1880s "the definition of the college experience, as a formal entity distinct from secondary education [high school], remained unclear."[22] Newspaper advertisements for St. Joseph's College noted that the school offered "studies in the classical, scientific, commercial and grammar departments," a smorgasbord of options.[23] The school granted three types of education credentials — certificate, diploma, and A.B. degree — so it basically operated as a middle school, high school, *and* college. Today, the successor to the school that Collins attended is known as St. Joseph's Collegiate Institute, a high school, which is located north of Buffalo in the town of Tonawanda.

Jimmy Collins graduated from St. Joseph's College in 1888, according to his plaque in the school's Sports Hall of Fame.[24] However, since the school no longer has any of the original records of students who attended prior to 1900, it is unclear exactly which credential Collins earned at his 1888 graduation. An article in the *Buffalo Express* about the graduation exercises in 1888 noted that the occasion was "private," and thus did not mention any names of graduates, probably because there were so few graduates as to be embarrassing to the school.[25] The number of students was dwindling at the time, which caused the school to eventually close down in 1891 when Manhattan College, whom the Christian Brothers were affiliated with, sold it to Bishop Ryan of the local Catholic diocese to be used as a parochial school.[26] St. Joseph's reopened two years later in 1893 at a new location.

It appears that Jimmy received a diploma in commercial studies at the 1888 graduation exercises, rather than an A.B. degree (which some chroniclers of his life have associated with his attendance at the school). St. Joseph's appears to have stopped granting A.B. degrees in 1886; by 1890 the school was only conferring diplomas and certificates.[27] Jimmy did receive a certificate in commercial studies in 1884, according to a newspaper report of the graduation exercises.[28] A business education for Jimmy was in line with the vocational training that the Christian Brothers were known for among the various other Catholic teaching sects. The graduates in 1888 were subject to "an exhaustive test by a special board of examiners" to test their knowledge before graduation; the board found that students of the commercial department were "thoroughly posted on all the essential branches and proved their ability to be placed in positions requiring a knowledge of intricate business operations."[29] The exact education credential that Jimmy received is inconsequential; what is important is that he did acquire a business education at St. Joseph's that he effectively put to good use in the coming years.

For Jimmy's father, the assignment to the fifth police precinct in North Buffalo turned out to be fortuitous beyond no longer having to deal with the crime-ravaged areas of the inner-city first and third precincts, his earlier tours of duty. By 1889 Anthony Collins purchased a house at 1278 Niagara Street, just a few blocks south of the fifth precinct station house at the intersection of Niagara Street and Clinton Avenue.[30] Anthony Collins seemed to use his connections to purchase this house, because the previous owner, Frank Case, operated an "oils and oil barrels" business at 39 Carroll Street, just a few doors down the street from the Collins' flat at 184 Carroll. Jimmy and his two brothers, along with his little sister Margaret (born in 1885), now experienced more comfortable living conditions in the residential North Buffalo section of the city than they did living in the flat in the congested Second Ward.

The new Collins homestead at 1278 Niagara Street was situated at the corner of Auburn Street on a lot that backed onto Mason Street. Directly behind the houses on Mason Street were the tracks of the New York Central

Railroad. The Frontier Canada Malt House (owned by former mayor Manning) stood between the railroad tracks and the Black Rock Canal, with three mills on a breakwater within the Niagara River. The ferry to Fort Erie, Ontario, was a few blocks south of the Collins' house, with the international railway bridge several blocks north.[31] Since the home was located on Buffalo's West Side, most of the neighbors were native-born Americans, with a few Irish-Americans like the Collins and an occasional German-American family.

Owning a home in America was a real cause for celebration for Irish-Americans like Anthony Collins. As Jay Dolan explains in *The Irish Americans: A History*, "In Ireland, owning one's own home was but a dream for most Irish ... driven from the land by famine and hard-hearted [English] landlords."[32] Such a purchase was not all that easy to accomplish in America in the late nineteenth century either. Anthony had to be thrifty in order to save enough for the down payment on the house, since banks at that time required at least a 50 percent down payment to issue a mortgage loan for the remainder of the purchase price. Anthony probably got his mortgage from the Irish-American Savings and Loan Association, which catered to its Irish-American customers following its establishment in Buffalo in 1884, although he eventually refinanced the mortgage with other local banking institutions controlled by German-American or native-born American owners, such as the Erie County Savings Bank.

Although Anthony Collins did rise above being "shanty" Irish through his escape from the First Ward into a comfortable middle-class life in North Buffalo, he never was considered to be "lace curtain" Irish. After he regained his police captain title in 1891, he settled for professional mediocrity, however, not taking any risks and not seeking further promotion or income growth, until he was able to negotiate a retirement pension in 1905.[33] At his death in 1910, a newspaper article described his police career lukewarmly as "though he made no remarkable records, he was always attentive to his duties."[34]

Jimmy's father passed down to his three sons a set of traditional Irish-American values, which included job security, and he used his connections to help them establish a foothold with the local railroads. After graduating from St. Joseph's in 1888, Jimmy worked as a clerk for the Delaware, Lackawanna and Western Railroad. "My dad had got me the job from his old friend, Bob Mason," Collins later recalled about the connection that led to his working at the railroad's Black Rock station, just a few blocks north of his parents' house on Niagara Street.[35] At that time, Jimmy's father also used his connections to get jobs for Jimmy's older brother Henry as a telegraph operator for the Buffalo, Rochester & Pittsburg Railroad and for Jimmy's younger brother Anthony as a clerk at the East Buffalo station of the New York Central Railroad.[36]

Ensconced in a secure job with the railroad, Jimmy Collins was set to live the conventional life of a second-generation Irish-American in Buffalo. However, the move from the Second Ward to North Buffalo — and baseball — changed Jimmy's perspective on life.

Chapter 3

Ballplayer in Buffalo

As a youngster, Jimmy Collins played baseball on the vacant lots and in the railroad yards of inner-city Buffalo, mostly in the Second Ward where he lived but also in the 13th Ward where a number of his relatives resided. Collins played on any open space where boys could assemble an impromptu "sandlot" ballgame. William Ferris, a boyhood friend from the Second Ward, remarked years later that Collins was a natural athlete who was good at "every boy's sport from shooting marbles to playing ball," and that the only coaching he ever received was an occasional tip from Tom Dolan, a former major league ballplayer who was a neighbor in the Second Ward.[1]

The teenaged Collins honed his baseball skills by playing for teams organized by the social clubs in the city. He participated in both informal games as well as competition among the "junior" versions of the teams that the social clubs sponsored in the organized amateur leagues in Buffalo. There were few formal baseball diamonds available within the city limits of Buffalo in the 1880s, so playing baseball for a social club team (with access to a decent ball field) was considered to be the height of amateur baseball.

Some chroniclers of Collins' life have asserted that he played baseball for St. Joseph's College. It is unlikely that such a baseball team was a school-sponsored one, however, given the small number of students at the school (200 or so) and the formative state of interscholastic athletics at the time. More likely is that several students at St. Joseph's organized a social club, which could include graduates as well as others loosely affiliated with the school, to play the social club teams associated with other schools. For example, as the *Buffalo Express* reported in 1889, "The Emerald Baseball Club of St. Joseph's College defeated the LeComeulx Club of St. Mary's Institute yesterday at the Parade, by a score of 28 to 8."[2] No box score accompanied the article.

More enlightening to how Collins developed the skill to play professional baseball, and its connection to St. Joseph's College, is an 1897 biographical sketch in *The Sporting News* that reported he "received his education in St. Joseph's College" and "it was while a student there that he became interested in the national pastime."[3] The sketch doesn't say he "played" baseball there — the often blunt Collins would have told the writer that he had played at the school if he had done so — but rather than he "became interested" in baseball there. Watching baseball, not just playing it, was the genesis of Collins' professional baseball career.

As a schoolboy, Collins had the good fortune to grow up in a city with a major league baseball team, as Buffalo fielded a team in the National League for seven years from 1879 through 1885. Collins likely viewed many National League ballgames in 1884 and 1885 when the Buffalo ballclub played its ballgames at Olympic Park, which was constructed in 1884 at the corner of Richmond Avenue and Summer Street in the northeastern section of the West Side. Olympic Park was an easy journey from St. Joseph's College in downtown Buffalo via the city's horse-drawn trolley system to get to the 4:00 P.M. ballgames. While Collins was less likely to have seen National League ballgames played before 1884 when they were staged at Riverside Park, which was located deeper into the West Side, he could easily read about the team in the several local newspapers.

The number of Irish-American ballplayers on the Buffalo team may have been a factor in attracting Collins to professional baseball. During the four years 1881 to 1884, Irish-American player-manager James O'Rourke led the Buffalo ballclub to three third-place finishes in the eight-team National League. Buffalo had another Irish-American as its prime pitcher, future Hall of Famer Jim "Pud" Galvin, who won 46 games in each of the 1883 and 1884 seasons. The "Big Four" supported Galvin: first baseman Dan Brouthers, second baseman Hardy Richardson, third baseman Jim "Deacon" White, and catcher Jack Rowe. There was even a Collins namesake on the 1884 club, Charles "Chub" Collins, who played a few dozen games at second base.[4]

Collins got to see not only fellow Irish-Americans O'Rourke, Galvin, and Brouthers who played for Buffalo but also flamboyant Mike "King" Kelly when the Chicago ballclub came to town. Kelly, "a hard-drinking, fun-loving [outfielder] who spoke in a heavy Irish brogue," became one of the first larger-than-life baseball heroes, "who dressed in silk suits with expensive patent leather shoes and an ever-present top hat and cane."[5] These men were in the upper tier of ballplayers during an era that writer Jerrold Casway calls the "Emerald Age of Baseball," when Irish-Americans comprised 40 percent of all major league ballplayers.[6] According to Casway, the large percentage of Irish-Americans then in professional baseball had an "allure to second-generation Irish-American youths" with its "acculturating flavor and non-elitist pretensions, a kind of sporting crucible" that led to social mobility and "a shortcut to the American dream."[7]

While the time that teenager Collins sat in the bleachers at Olympic Park helped to stoke a love for baseball, the experience likely fueled his ambition to finish his education more so than to become a professional baseball player. As boyhood friend Ferris later told Tim Murnane of the *Boston Globe*, Collins "would play ball and seemingly have a fine time. But when it came time for the examinations he was always the first in every study."[8] The teenaged Collins seemed to have already formed an attitude that education, not playing baseball, was the key to true "social mobility" for Irish-Americans.

Buffalo was expelled from the National League after the 1885 season, after the ballclub was sold to the owners of the competing Detroit ballclub in mid–September, who then gutted the team by moving the best players to Detroit. Jack Chapman managed the remnants of the Buffalo ballclub for the rest of the 1885 season. He stayed for three more years to manage Buffalo's minor league club in the International League, through the 1888 season when the five-year lease expired on the land underneath Olympic Park. When former Buffalo National Leaguers Rowe and White took over ownership of the ballclub for the 1889 season, they moved the ballpark to a new location on the East Side at the corner of Michigan Avenue and East Ferry Street. The new Olympic Park was about three miles due east from Collins' new home in North Buffalo. Rowe and White briefly brought major league baseball back to Buffalo again in 1890 when they secured a franchise in the new Players League. Despite having an energetic catcher named Connie Mack, the Buffalo team in the Players League was not very good, as it finished in last place in a league that lasted only one season.[9]

There were no Sunday games played by these professional ballclubs at Olympic Park, since New York state law then prohibited professional sports on the Lord's Day. During the 1880s, Sunday baseball was reserved for amateur ballclubs. What the New York state law actually prohibited was "public sport" on Sunday, as well as "all noise disturbing the peace of the day." Because of this vague definition, local judges had their own interpretations of what constituted "public sport," which often hinged on whether there was "disturbing the peace."[10] Therefore, the legality of Sunday baseball in New York in the 1880s and 1890s varied by each city and town. In Buffalo at the time when Collins was an amateur ballplayer, the dividing line was whether the ballplayers involved played in a professional or amateur league.

Sunday ballgames in Buffalo in the 1880s were the province of amateur ballclubs that were extensions of the local social clubs, many of which were organized along ethnic background. The Travelers Base Ball and Sporting Club, organized in 1883 by Dennis Ryan in the predominantly Irish-American

First Ward, was one of the oldest of the top amateur baseball clubs in Buffalo. In 1888, the Travelers played in the East Side League along with the Clippers, Lehighs, and Socials. They played their games at the East Side Grounds, located at the corner of Genesee and Barthol Streets. There was a separate West Side League, comprised of the West Ends, North Buffalos, Globes, Niagaras, and Queen Citys. The two leagues symbolized the societal division in Buffalo in the 1880s, where Main Street marked a tacit boundary between the East Side and the West Side. For the more well-heeled of Buffalo's citizenry who lived on the West Side, "it was possible and in the case of the more aristocratic segment of the population probable, for one to live one's whole life in the city without ever crossing Main Street to the East Side" due to its unsavory reputation.[11]

Collins played for the Socials in 1889, a ballclub comprised of Irish-Americans, which helped maintain ties to his old neighborhood in the Second Ward.[12] For the 1889 season the two leagues tried to merge together to form the Buffalo Baseball League. As a member of the Socials, Collins received an education in ethnic politics in Buffalo when John Floss, owner of the East Side Grounds, had a disagreement with the organizers of the proposed Buffalo Baseball League. "Mr. Floss objects to allowing certain clubs in the league to play on his East-Side grounds and refuses to enter his club [the Clippers]," the *Buffalo Express* reported during the winter of 1889. It seems that Floss didn't want clubs from the First Ward in the league, probably for competitive reasons, but the *Express* observed that "the league cannot live without a First Ward club as nearly all of the patronage at the East Side Grounds comes from that ward."[13] Floss' Clippers and several other clubs stayed out of the proposed league, and formed the Champion League to compete with the Buffalo Baseball League.

During the 1889 season Collins played left field for the Socials in the Buffalo Baseball League. He was particularly instrumental in two victories late in the season, when he went 2-for-5 in a September 29 game against the North Buffalos (of the competing Champion League) and 2-for-3 in an October 20 win over the Travelers. For the 1890 season, Collins again played left field for the Socials, but by midseason the Socials were losing consistently to their more talented competition. For instance, on June 29, the Travelers lambasted the Socials, 15–6, while only yielding one hit. Collins, frustrated at being humiliated by a rival Irish-American ballclub, was ejected from this game after he complained about a called third strike.[14] After a poor showing in the league standings for the 1890 season, the Socials, not surprisingly, left the Buffalo Baseball League to play in a less competitive league.

To remain at the highest level of amateur play in Buffalo during the 1891 season, Collins joined the North Buffalo ballclub, which played in the rival

Champion League. Since the ballclub was based in the Black Rock section of Buffalo where he worked and was near his parents' home, Collins made the difficult decision to forsake his Irish-American ties with the Socials from his old neighborhood to forge new relationships with the guys from his new neighborhood in North Buffalo. For the North Buffalos during the 1891 season, Collins played third base rather than the outfield. The 21-year-old Collins seemed to hit his stride with the North Buffalos, having numerous multiple-hit games. On May 10, Collins went 3-for-5 batting leadoff for the North Buffalos in their 9–5 victory over the East Buffalos. Collins, however, was not a natural fielder at third base, as he made three errors in seven chances. When the North Buffalos defeated the West Ends on July 19, Collins again had a 3-for-5 day at the plate. Collins started to generate some mention in the newspaper accounts of the games, as the *Buffalo Express* noted that "Collins did his best work at bat and pounded out hits just when they were most needed."[15] On September 27, Collins again went 3-for-5, but in this game he showed some improved fielding prowess, as "Collins made the best play of the day in his running catch of Tiedeman's foul fly, back of third base."[16] However, he still committed three errors during the day at third base.

It was during the 1891 season that Collins began to see baseball more as a money-making venture than simply as some Sunday afternoon exercise with the boys. Since the newspapers occasionally referred to the semi-pro nature of these amateur ballclubs — "the North Buffalo and West Ends, two of the best semi-professional clubs in the city"— there was obviously some money changing hands into the wallets of the ballplayers.[17] There was also money to be made through gambling on the outcome of these amateur games. Prior to the July 5, 1891, game, the *Buffalo Express* noted that "the North Buffalos are giving odds that they will defeat the Casinos."[18] That turned out to be a poor proposition as pitcher Bill Schellerman, a former minor leaguer, shut down the North Buffalos by striking out 17 batters and giving up just four hits in a 9–2 victory. Later in September, in what the *Express* called "a very shady ball game," several ballplayers seemed to be involved in throwing the game by making obvious errors. In the third inning after North Buffalo scored three runs against East Buffalo on "several errors and a few hits," the *Express* reported that "a bet of $25 to $20 on North Buffalo was heard." However, East Buffalo scored five runs in the seventh inning to win due to "the frequent errors of their opponents" combined with just only one hit and three walks. Collins made three of the eight errors committed by North Buffalo.[19] Besides the gambling income potential, by 1893 there was also an explicit gate-sharing policy at the East Side Grounds that divided admission fees for the amateur-league games among the winner (35 percent), loser (30 percent), and groundskeeper (35 percent).[20]

There was some warming of the rivalry between the Buffalo Baseball League and the Champion League by the end of the 1891 season when the respective league champions met in a three-game series for the city title. The two leagues finally consolidated for the 1892 season, operating as a unified, multi-ethnic, Buffalo City League. Collins, still playing third base, once again hit superbly for the North Buffalos. In a doubleheader on August 7 at the East Side Grounds, Collins batted leadoff and went 3-for-4 in the first game and 3-for-3 in the second game, although his team lost both games to the West Ends. By the end of the 1892 season, newspaper reports were singing the praises of third baseman Collins:

> Collins, the North Buffalos' third baseman, is a second Keeler, and yesterday made no exception to his regular game. He accepted every chance that came his way and fielded them with that precision that makes a game worth watching. He threw perfectly to first, caught Smith dawdling at third, after he had stolen second and third, and touched him so quickly that the latter was almost inclined to kick about it. He nipped Jerry Morrissey in the same position after the latter had made a brilliant attempt at a run, and in the second game he made a phenomenal back-handed catch, stopped and fielded a man out on an almost impossible light-bounding grounder and nipped another man off third by his old tactics. The consensus of opinion after yesterday's games was that Collins is worthy of better things than playing once a week in an amateur league.[21]

Collins experienced a change in his perspective on life before the beginning of the 1893 baseball season, which led him to consider leaving his secure job with the railroad and take a chance at playing professional baseball. His first few years living at his family's new home at 1278 Niagara Street in North Buffalo did more to shape Collins' values as an adult than did the previous dozens years when they lived on Carroll Street in the Second Ward. After four years of living and working in the former West Side stronghold of the native-born Americans, Collins was ready to abandon some of the Irish-American ideals that his father had passed down to him.

It wasn't just the traditional Irish-American goals that Jimmy Collins wanted to move beyond, though. He later seemed to make a concerted effort to avoid being labeled even as an Irish-American. Little information has survived about Jimmy's days in the Second Ward, as early biographical sketches of him are silent about his youth and move quickly from his birth to his days at St. Joseph's College and in North Buffalo. Collins used the skills of the Irish-American subculture that his father had taught him — to leverage connections and personal relationships — to achieve far loftier goals as simply an American, not an Irish-American.

While working for the Delaware, Lackawanna and Western Railroad,

Collins had met many businessmen, including a number of self-made men, and had hopped the train to travel to other places beyond Buffalo. He wanted a life beyond family, a steady job, and a few beers with friends at the local saloon — his father's Irish-American life. No matter how hard he worked for the railroad, he would never own it. After interacting with so many independent businessmen, he decided he wanted to build a business and not have to rely on others to earn an income.

He thought baseball offered him a decent possibility to attain that goal. A ballplayer's earnings were dependent on his ability to produce on the baseball field, not his connections to the boss. Since Collins was one of the better ballplayers in the Buffalo City League, he could turn professional with the Buffalo ballclub in the Eastern League and then advance to become a field manager and eventually perhaps become an owner. The biggest wrench in Collins' plan was that he didn't fully comprehend the reserve clause that bound a ballplayer to his ballclub until, and if, the ballclub consented to let him leave to join another ballclub.

The time to make the leap to professional baseball with the local minor league ballclub was 1893, since it appeared the City League would lose its monopoly on Sunday baseball in Buffalo that year and Collins would not have as many opportunities to standout with the North Buffalo team as he had in 1891 and 1892. James Franklin, the Buffalo ballclub owner, had leased the East Side Grounds from Floss to use for Sunday games in the Eastern League during the 1893 season, which served to relegate the City League to second-class status. The City League would only have unfettered access to the East Side Grounds for half the season, with the other half shared with Franklin's team or played on a diamond to be constructed on Grand Island in the Niagara River, which would be difficult for spectators to get to.[22] As for the sharing of the East Side Grounds, Franklin had negotiated for the prime 3:00 o'clock starting time, so the City League games would have to start earlier and be shortened seven-inning contests.

Sunday baseball was a big key to making money in the Eastern League, as it was in nearly all professional baseball leagues. Large crowds filled ballparks on Sunday, the only day of the week that working people — who then labored six days each week — could normally attend a game, which laws in all East Coast states then prohibited. Ballclubs in the East had to find out-of-the-way places to play Sunday games to evade the law. In New York, Albany had access to a ball grounds on Pleasure Island in the middle of the Hudson River, where legal authorities permitted Sunday games despite the New York law ostensibly prohibiting them. The Troy club also used Pleasure Island for Sunday games, where patrons had to use a boat to get there, which hardly characterized the games as "public" sport. Providence played Sunday games at

Rocky Point in contravention of Rhode Island law, since it was an isolated location ten miles down Narragansett Bay controlled by a politically connected resort owner. The Eastern League teams in Pennsylvania and Massachusetts didn't dare try to play Sunday baseball, since the laws in those two very conservative states then prohibited all baseball on Sunday, whether amateur or professional.[23]

The proposed Sunday games of the Eastern League in Buffalo had questionable legality, since they involved professional athletes, which under the city's former interpretation of the New York law would have been illegal. Since the residents living near the East Side Grounds generally didn't consider the games to be "disturbing the peace," Franklin, also a city alderman, expected the Buffalo police to give him some leeway under the interpretation of the law.

Franklin had a new manager for the Buffalo ballclub in 1893, as Jack Chapman returned to the city where had managed teams a few years earlier. The 50-year-old Chapman, now a part-owner of the ballclub, had been associated with baseball for more than three decades. A ballplayer in the formative years of professional baseball in the late 1860s and early 1870s, he played a few games in the inaugural year of the National League in 1876 for Louisville before becoming its manager in 1877. Chapman managed several teams in the major leagues, but during the 1890s he settled into managing in the minor leagues. The bachelor Chapman was a perfect example of someone who had achieved Collins' new life goal.

Chapman must have liked what he saw of Collins when he played his first game of the 1893 City League season on April 30, when the North Buffalos defeated the Elks, 5–1. Collins went 2-for-4 in the game, and fielded seven chances flawlessly in the field. Besides his baseball ability, Collins had one other quality that appealed to Franklin and Chapman. It didn't hurt to have the son of a police captain on the team, as the Buffalo ballclub prepared to play its first-ever Sunday games to test the state law.

When Chapman offered Collins the chance to play for the Buffalo minor league ballclub, he didn't immediately leap at the opportunity to sign a contract. Collins was a businessman right from the beginning of his professional baseball career. "I was tickled, but I thought, 'what if I failed? Could I get my job back?'" Collins later recounted about his signing, feigning concern over job security when he really used the issue as a negotiation ploy. "So I went to [Bob] Mason and put it to him in Chapman's presence. Mason said, 'Jimmy, you can have your job back any time you want to come back.' That gave me a lot of confidence."[24] Confidence to negotiate a baseball contract, that is. By having Mason make that statement in front of Chapman, Chapman knew that Collins wasn't bluffing when he contended that he had other options to make money besides playing baseball. In addition, Collins knew that he'd get a better deal if Chapman believed he was young, so Collins understated his age, telling Chapman he was only 20 years old rather than his actual age of 23 years. Many years later, baseball writers still often reported his birth year as 1873, not the correct 1870 year. When Collins signed his first professional baseball contract on May 23, the Buffalo newspapers heralded the occasion:

> COLLINS SIGNED
> North Buffalo's Third Baseman
> Becomes Professional

> Although the [Buffalo] club did not play yesterday, Manager Chapman was not idle, and his signing of Jimmy Collins, the North Buffalos clever third baseman, will meet with the approbation of every enthusiast in the town who has seen Collins play ball. If Collins does not get rattled in the company of his professional brethren he will teach many of the best of them points on batting, as well as the most approved tactics in handling the ball on the third bag.[25]

Collins played his first professional baseball game on May 25, 1893, when he played third base for Buffalo in its 8–7 victory over Erie at Olympic Park. Collins began the game on the bench, but when third baseman Jake Drauby was pressed into service as a relief pitcher in the third inning, "Collins took Drauby's place on the third bag for his first experience under fire."[26] Buffalo rallied with four runs in the ninth inning to tie the game, and then went on to win it with a run in the eleventh. Collins went 2-for-5 in his professional debut, and handled six of seven chances in the field.[27] Committing an error would, unfortunately, become a common occurrence for Collins during the 1893 season.

Buffalo's first-ever professional baseball game on a Sunday was played at the East Side Grounds on June 4, 1893, when 4,000 spectators crammed into the little ballpark to see a doubleheader. The opener was a City League game between the Casinos and the Travelers, with Buffalo taking on Albany in the main event. Buffalo slaughtered Albany, 30–11. "North Buffalo Collins' play during the massacre was a feature of the game, for he knocked out two singles, two doubles and a home run in the seven times he came to bat, and fielded like a veteran," the *Buffalo Express* reported of Collins' contribution to the slugfest.[28] Clearly, although the East Side Grounds attracted many patrons, the tiny ballpark made for laughable competition for the professional ballplayers.

After starting out at third base, Collins played mostly shortstop for Buffalo during the 1893 season, where he was extremely erratic in the field. "Collins is too heavy and somewhat unsteady," one writer explained the poor fielding of Collins. "One day he may put up a game that shines with brilliancy and the next day he may get tangled up with his feet, stand on his head and do everything but play ball."²⁹ Collins was simply an ambitious fielder, trying to reach everything he possibly could. "Collins is a hot favorite with the East Side crowds," another scribe wrote. "At the Sunday games the rest of the team are nowhere compared with Collins." He offered the comments of two (fictitious) German-American fans as evidence: "Holy Gee, wats Collins doing way ofer der?" to which the other replied, "Oh, he plays all ofer de field."³⁰

Because of the dubious nature of the competition at the Sunday games on the East Side Grounds, Franklin experimented with a Sunday game at Olympic Park on July 30. However, because of the proximity of a church to that ballpark, the police shut down the game. The following week he staged a Sunday game at the hard-to-get-to ball grounds on Grand Island, but poor attendance put an end to that experiment. While Franklin tried to iron out the Sunday game situation, Collins played a City League game for the North Buffalos on August 13.

With the East Side Grounds his only viable option, Franklin scheduled several Sunday games there as the 1893 season wound down. On September 3, the North Buffalos and Elks teams from the City League supplied the opening act of the doubleheader before the Eastern League game against Troy. "Every streetcar and Belt-line train running to the grounds was bursting with its overloaded cargo of human freight," the *Buffalo Express* reported of the 4,000 people that filled "every nook and corner of the grounds." Collins watched his old team the North Buffalos defeat the Elks before he went 2-for-5 in the main event, a 14–8 loss to Troy.³¹ On the next two Sundays, Buffalo played exhibition games with major league teams, losing to Cincinnati on September 10 (Collins going 3-for-5 with a home run) and to Cleveland on September 17 (Collins did not play).

Collins finished the 1893 season with a respectable .286 batting average, but his .863 fielding average with 65 errors was a serious deficiency. In addition to getting used to the higher caliber of play in professional competition than he was used to in the amateur City League, Collins also had to get accustomed to the harder-hit balls that resulted from the longer pitching distance implemented for the 1893 season.

Traveling by train to play games in the other Eastern League cities whetted Collins' appetite to see other parts of the country. After Buffalo's last game on September 15, Collins took a train trip to Chicago to see the World's Fair. "Jimmy has not been married, as reported," the *Buffalo Express* noted upon his return to Buffalo, "but he has been taking in the Chicago Fair for some weeks and looked to be in better condition now than ever."³² On October 8, Collins played one final game with the North Buffalos in the City League, picking up a few bucks while playing shortstop for his old team.

If Franklin and Chapman thought it was going to be easy to re-sign Collins to play for the 1894 season, they were mistaken. Playing in the October 8 game for the North Buffalos was more than just nostalgia for Collins; it allowed his name to be inserted on the roster of the North Buffalos for the 1894 season to use as a ploy to gain some leverage in his salary negotiation with Franklin.[33] It was widely publicized that Franklin had turned a significant profit in 1893, with the Sunday games at the East Side Grounds being a key contributor to that financial success.[34] Collins no doubt claimed some responsibility for having attracted those big Sunday audiences, based on his exploits in the City League the previous four years, which he felt should be reflected in a higher salary for the 1894 season. Given his miserable fielding statistics for the 1893 season, though, this approach was a risk for Collins.

Franklin, in discussing the composition of the Buffalo team with a writer in January 1894, was very coy about where Collins stood. Franklin did not consider Collins to be a returning regular player. Instead, Franklin thought a new player named Bradley would play shortstop and remarked that "Collins will probably be retained as a general utility man."[35] Franklin, like many nineteenth century capitalists, didn't seem to care that Collins had a viable employment alternative to return to his bookkeeping job with the railroad. In early February, Collins signed for the 1894 season, probably for the same salary level as the previous season.[36]

For the first game of the 1894 season, Collins was in right field for Buffalo. While Chapman put Collins to the outfield to minimize the negative impact of his fielding lapses, the move had the unexpected positive consequence of improving his batting average. Soon after the season opener on May 1 at Wilkes-Barre, where he was 1-for-4, Collins went on a hitting barrage and rattled off numerous multi-hit games: 2-for-5 on May 11, 2-for-5 on May 13, 2-for-4 on May 15, and 2-for-5 on May 27. "The clever game which Collins is putting up has surprised even his most sanguine admirers," the Buffalo correspondent to *Sporting Life* wrote about his performance. "Manager [Herman] Doescher [of Binghamton] thinks that he would make a success in the big League. It would certainly not be amiss to keep an eye on him."[37] With Collins now playing left field and among the league leaders in hitting, baseball writers took to calling him "Cuckoo" Collins, after the famed stunt runner of the time. Both were men who took too many chances in their respective professions.

One of his best games of the 1894 season occurred on August 20 against Springfield, when Collins had four hits at bat and made several good plays in the field. "Cuckoo smashed the ball every time he came to bat, making three singles, a home run and a long fly to center," the *Buffalo Express* reported. "Jimmy was also in good fielding form yesterday, and his catch of a foul fly in the fifth inning was by all odds the most brilliant feature of the game. The ball was descending against the fence about midway between the foul line and the clubhouse, but Collins, after a long run, snatched it with his back to the fence when it was about a foot from it."[38] Although Buffalo was then in second place in the Eastern League, the team trailed Providence in a battle for first place.

A week later Buffalo was out of pennant contention when the team lost three straight games to Providence, managed by Billy Murray who doubled at the team's right fielder. Collins was 4-for-12 in the three games played on August 24 to 26. On Sunday, August 26, the two teams played at Crescent Park, a short trolley ride from Providence, rather than at remote Rocky Point that required water transport.[39] It is possible that Frank Selee, the manager of the Boston ballclub in the National League, or another "scout" from Boston, took the train down to Providence to check out Collins, who had a very average day, going 1-for-4, in the 7–1 loss to Providence. Murray, who a week earlier saw Collins bang out four doubles against his team in a 13–10 victory, was later credited with recommending to Selee that he acquire Collins.[40]

Selee did see Collins play briefly on September 7 in an exhibition game between Boston and Buffalo, when Boston stopped in Buffalo on the team's trip west to Chicago. The game, however, lasted only seven innings due to rain, which held down the crowd to less than 1,000 fans who saw Boston defeat Buffalo, 11–3. "The visitors rubbed it into the crippled and demoralized Buffalo club in a manner that resembled a well-groomed college nine playing with a job lot of school boys," the *Boston Globe* described the soggy contest.[41] The *Buffalo Express* called the game "a farce" and "a bad comedy," as some of the Boston players didn't take the contest seriously, particularly pitcher Jack Stivetts, who joked with the fans while playing first base.[42] Collins played left field for Buffalo and went 1-for-4 at the plate. "I told Selee I would like him to take a look at Collins," Chapman recalled the game in an interview a few years later. "When I asked Selee what he thought of my find, he replied in his quiet way that he hadn't seen enough to judge by. But it seems that what he saw was sufficient, for later in the season he drafted him."[43]

Collins finished the 1894 season with a .352 batting average (among the top ten hitters behind leader Joe Knight at .371) and led the Eastern League with 198 hits to inspire Selee to acquire him for the Boston ballclub for the 1895 season.

CHAPTER 4

Sold to Boston, Loaned to Louisville

On November 14, 1894, manager Frank Selee of the Boston ballclub in the National League convinced owner Arthur Soden to part with $500 to obtain the services of an unproven outfielder named James Collins from the Buffalo ballclub. At the time, Selee said that he obtained the rights to Collins "simply because he thought he was a comer."[1] Since Selee had only witnessed Collins play a few innings in a rain-shortened exhibition game in Buffalo in September, there was a bit more involved in his decision to consider Collins for the Boston team beyond the recommendations from Eastern League managers Jack Chapman and Billy Murray.

Selee had a knack for transforming ballplayers with some raw talent into highly competent major leaguers by getting them to focus on the thinking aspects of baseball — execution, positioning, timing, and bat control — beyond the physical aspects of the game such as strength, speed, and endurance. Collins, with his private-school education, was a good candidate. It didn't hurt that Collins was also Irish-American, which at the time was the heritage of roughly one-quarter of all major league ballplayers.[2] Selee had watched Baltimore win the 1894 pennant with a roster packed with Irish-Americans, including the likes of John McGraw and Joe Kelley, and was willing to take a chance on Collins having the same Irish competitiveness that writers later attributed to "an expression of their survival instincts, a search for advantages and one-upmanship against society and its prevailing norms."[3] To Selee, Collins was a well-educated Irish-American "comer" with high potential to become a thinking ballplayer.

There didn't seem to be a natural place to insert Collins into the Boston lineup for the 1895 season, since there were few weaknesses in the Boston team that had finished in third place in 1894 after winning three consecutive pennants from 1891 to 1893. Six of the seven infielders and outfielders had played on the 1893 championship team: Tommy Tucker at first base, Bobby Lowe at second base, Herman Long at shortstop, captain Billy Nash at third base, Hugh Duffy in left field, and Tommy McCarthy in center field. If there was a weakness, it was in right field, where Jimmy Bannon had replaced Cliff Carroll in 1894. However, as the *Boston Globe* reported when Selee selected Collins, "The management are not altogether satisfied with the work of Jimmy Bannon, and the chances are that Collins will get a chance to play right field."[4] This is where Collins fit into the picture.

Although he was an unheralded player, Collins was not bashful about trying to negotiate a sizable salary to play for Boston. Soden, looking at Collins as merely a spare outfielder and insurance should Duffy or Bannon stage a lengthy holdout in their salary negotiations, looked to sign Collins for a very low salary, particularly given his lack of professional baseball experience, just two years in the minor leagues. Collins brazenly asked for a salary more commensurate with several years of major league experience. In mid–February 1895, Jake Morse reported in *Sporting Life* that "Collins has not accepted the terms offered him."[5] The following week, Morse wrote: "The Boston club is having a hard time with Collins, the young Buffalo player. The young man is not satisfied with a salary of $1000 for the season. He claims that when a player signs with a League club for a small salary he always finds it a difficult matter to get anything like a fair increase from year to year, no matter how clever he may turn out to be."[6] Collins obviously had received some coaching in salary negotiation, perhaps from Chapman. At the end of February, Selee announced that Collins had finally agreed to a salary figure, as he had received a letter from Collins in Buffalo indicating "he would accept the club's terms and sign a contract as soon as presented."[7] Later in life, Collins remembered the salary to be $200 a month, or $1,200 a year for the six-month baseball season.[8]

One week before the Boston players were slated to leave for their spring training trip to Charleston, South Carolina, Nash, Duffy, and Bannon all were still unsigned for the 1895 season. While Nash and Duffy signed before the March 16 departure for South Carolina, Bannon continued to hold out for more money. Collins seized the opportunity to take Bannon's place in right field. After hitting and fielding well in the team's several exhibition games down South, Collins was Boston's right fielder on Opening Day, April 20. In his major league debut, Collins went 2-for-5 with two doubles against Washington pitcher Otis Stocksdale in an 11–6 Boston victory at their home South End Grounds.

After ten games, though, it was clear that Collins was a less-than-adequate substitute for Bannon. Collins was hitting barely over .200 and had committed six errors in 18 chances offered in the outfield, for a very poor .667 fielding average. Bannon had called Soden's bluff and won. Soden quickly settled the salary question with Bannon, who returned to play right field in the May 6 game in St. Louis. A week and a half later when the Boston team arrived in Louisville, Bannon was hitting over .300 and had committed only three errors, to make Collins expendable.

After watching Boston drub the last-place Louisville team, Collins later recalled that he suggested to Selee that Boston transfer him to Louisville, where he'd get some playing time rather than sit on the Boston bench (or more likely be released or farmed out to the Fall River or New Bedford minor league teams in the New England League).[9] When Boston left Louisville after the May 18 game to travel to Cincinnati, Collins stayed behind as Soden worked out a deal with Dr. Thomas Hunt Stuckey, president of the Louisville ballclub. On May 20 the *Louisville Courier-Journal* announced that "the release of outfielder James Collins was purchased from Boston" at an undisclosed amount, but alleged "to have cost more than that of any player the club has secured in the past two years."[10] Collins made his Louisville debut on May 21. While he left the Boston club with few on-the-field accomplishments, he had acquired a sizable knowledge bank of techniques in how to deal with management to obtain a better baseball salary.

While the initial announcement indicated that it was a straight player sale from Boston to Louisville — "purchase the release" was a nineteenth century legalism meaning "sale" — the transaction involving Collins was a bit more complicated. It has often been stated that Boston "loaned" Collins to Louisville for $500, with a right of recall if Boston gave a week's notice and repaid the $500. This practice of "farming" a player to another team was a fairly common technique in the 1890s, but the receiving team was almost always a minor league team, not another National League team. This "loan" was in essence a sale with an option to repurchase, which was not covered by the standard player contract and thus required a series of extra-contractual side agreements, one signed by Stuckey (to agree to resell the player) and another signed by Collins (to agree to return).[11] While the combination of the three agreements effectively acted as a player loan, the precarious nature of the documentation created an enforcement problem down the road.

Collins played in the outfield during his first ten days with the Louisville team, when manager John McCloskey suddenly pressed him into service at third base in the sixth inning of the May 31 game at Baltimore after Walt Preston had committed four errors. The legend of Collins' first major league game at third base, like so many baseball legends, grew over time so that the more recent retellings, such as the following recasting in a 2006 biographical sketch, bear only a partial resemblance to the 1895 facts:

After the Orioles bunting caused Louisville's regular third baseman to commit four errors, Collins was summoned from his right field position to play third.... The Orioles [base coach], Hughey Jennings, patted Collins on the back and told him that the Orioles weren't going to bunt any more that day. Collins's immediate response to Jennings was "that's all right, Hughey, bunt 'em down to me and I'll show you something." ... As the game progressed, sure enough, the Orioles' John McGraw dropped a bunt down the line. Collins raced in and threw underhand to quickly catch McGraw at first. Willie Keeler tried the same and Collins likewise nailed him at first. Four bunters in a row were thrown out by Collins before the Orioles quit bunting for the afternoon.[12]

However, the legend has combined events from two separate dates to build a better story. The first half of this 2006 retelling is mostly accurate and occurred on May 31, 1895 (with the exception that Collins played center field that day, not right field), while the events in the second half of this retelling happened on a different day two months later.

The *Louisville Courier-Journal* article about the May 31 ballgame was very clear on the details in the first half of the legend: Third baseman Preston "fielded miserably, making four errors on batted balls, all of which resulted in runs" and in the sixth inning "Collins and Preston also changed places," in addition to Luby replacing Inks as the pitcher, by switching between center field and third base.[13] The *Baltimore Sun* account of the game added more detail about the bunts: "The number of bunts made by the Baltimores drove Inks to distraction. Seven times they tapped the ball down into the field and beat the throw to first. The poor work of Preston helped them in their task, while none of the other opposing infielders could do anything to stop the fun."[14]

No contemporary account can be located that verifies the second part of the legend that Collins successfully handled several Baltimore bunts on May 31. The fact that Collins had only one assist in the May 31 game indicates that he threw out one Baltimore player, who *may* have bunted, but not four and not even two. Certainly, the *Baltimore Sun* would have mentioned the Louisville player who finally stopped the famed Baltimore bunting attack, but instead reported that "none of the opposing infielders" could do so. Later in the 1895 season Collins did retire a few Baltimore bunters, but not in his virgin game at third base in the major leagues. On May 31, Collins played three uneventful innings at third base as Baltimore soundly defeated Louisville, 16–6. Further indicating that nothing eventful happened to Collins in those three innings, he didn't play third base again for another two weeks, until June 13.

The recollections of Hughey Jennings, published a quarter century later, provide the most plausible explanation about what really happened with Collins in the Louisville-Baltimore games during the 1895 season:

McCloskey yelled to Collins [in the outfield], "Come on in here and play third base." Collins wandered over to where McCloskey stood and told him, "I can't play third base. I'd just make a fool out of myself." Baltimore wanted to get the game over so we told Collins to play third. We promised him we would not pull any balls down the third base line and that we would not bunt on him. Finally he consented under those conditions. We kept our promise and Collins finished the game at third. The next glimpse we got of Collins was in Louisville. He was still playing third base. No longer bound to any promise we started bunting to third. Three men bunted in succession, and Collins threw out each man. He had learned to field bunts.[15]

According to Jennings' account, Collins' fielding exploits to shut down the Baltimore bunting attack occurred not on May 31 but rather in Baltimore's next series with Louisville, which began on July 25.

Collins later credited Dan Brouthers, a first baseman on the Louisville team, with suggesting to McCloskey that he put Collins at third base, based on seeing him play the infield for Buffalo in the Eastern League in 1893.[16] However, Brouthers was in the major leagues that year. Brouthers had some Buffalo connections, and may have talked with others who had seen Collins play third base there, but he had no direct observations. A more likely candidate for suggesting to put Collins at third base was Fred Clarke, who played left field for Louisville. Clarke later recalled that he told McCloskey: "That fellow playing center ought to be able to do it. He is quick as a cat and is a very fast thrower."[17]

Preston was back at third base for Louisville the next day, June 1, when he made two errors. McCloskey then replaced Preston, not with Collins, but with newcomer Bill Kemmer, who played third base unspectacularly for the next week as Louisville's road trip swung through Washington, New York, and Boston. Collins was back at third base when Louisville played its first game in Philadelphia on June 13. "Kemmer joined us at New York and did fairly, but at Boston he went to pieces," Collins said after the season was over. "When we reached Philadelphia, McCloskey was in despair and asked me to go in."[18] Collins impressed the writers with his play at third base that day. "Collins for an outfielder played third in brilliant style," the *Louisville Courier-Journal* reported, "making a number of pretty stops and throws."[19] Kemmer sealed his fate in the June 15 game in Brooklyn, where McCloskey gave him one more chance at third base. When a run scored in the second inning "on Kemmer's fumble of Corcoran's grounder," McCloskey had seen enough. In the next inning, as the *Brooklyn Eagle* reported, "a change was made in the Louisville makeup, McCreery going to right and Collins to third, Kemmer retiring."[20] At that point, Collins became the everyday third baseman for Louisville.

Collins flourished at third base under McCloskey's leadership, even though Louisville was the worst team in the National League. Collins had joined the team in the midst of a 15-game losing streak, and the team's 3–20 record during June cemented the team's cellar-dwelling position for the remainder of the 1895 season. With no pressure to win, Collins could concentrate on improving his game, which he seemed to do on his own. Collins never credited anyone with the improvement in his third base play at Louisville, and no one ever stepped forward to claim credit. "Honest John" McCloskey, the Louisville manager in 1895 who went on manage 47 teams and be an "organizer of more leagues than any other man," has been given credit for "discovering" Collins, but little more.[21]

The credit for Collins' development as a third baseman goes to the city of Louisville itself. Collins loved Louisville, saying of the city that "nothing could have been kinder" and commenting that "McCloskey treats his players like so many kings."[22] The city seemed like home to Collins, as its population resembled that of his native Buffalo. German-Americans were a large portion of the Louisville population, and there was a sizable Irish-American population as well, who worked in the breweries and other companies run by the German-Americans. While the German-American businessmen attended the weekday home games, Louisville played home games on Sunday, just like Collins had participated in back in Buffalo, where the Irish-American workers came out in sizable numbers to cheer him on. The treasurer of the Louisville ballclub, Barney Dreyfuss, was also German-American, and served as a mentor to Collins at this stage of his baseball career. The low stress of playing on a last-place team was an added bonus in Louisville, as Collins could only look good compared to the poor performance of his predecessors at third base, Preston and Kemmer. When Boston visited Louisville in mid–July, Boston manager Selee saw a vastly different Collins than he had observed back in late April and early May. The error-prone outfielder was now a steady third baseman, as in one game he kept Boston from getting men on base six times. As the *Louisville Courier-Journal* colorfully put it, "Collins, at third, dug them out of the dust, climbed the atmosphere, and pulled them down; fell side ways and scooped them up with his hands; went at them like a lightning bolt and stopped them."[23] The Boston baseball writers soon bemoaned management's errant decision to ship Collins off to Louisville, and clamored for the ballclub to exercise its option to bring him back. Even Selee got religion. "That boy put up the greatest game of ball I ever saw against our team at Louisville. He accepted more than 15 chances in the four games without an error, and some of his work was marvelous," Selee told the *Boston Globe*. "You will find him in Boston next season all right, as I can get him by giving the Louisville club one week's notice and the $500 they paid Boston for his release. I had Collins sign an agreement to come with Boston at any time we should want him, and therefore feel pretty sure of having a good man for the future."²⁴

When Baltimore came to Louisville in late July, Collins impressed McGraw and his fellow Orioles with his fielding of their bunts. This series helped to create the second part of the Collins legend, likely the Sunday game on July 28, when Louisville defeated Baltimore in a close game, 4–3, as Baltimore tried in vain to mount a winning rally. Collins had three assists and two putouts in the July 28 game, whereas he had only two assists in each of the preceding two games. However, neither the *Louisville Courier-Journal* nor the *Baltimore Sun* explicitly mentioned Collins fielding consecutive bunts in that game. The *Baltimore Sun* did provide a clue, though, in describing the first inning for Baltimore. Joe Kelley, the leadoff hitter, was hit by a pitch and "on Keeler's bunt to Collins went all the way to third."²⁵ Collins threw out Keeler at first base, but could not scramble back to third base in time as Kelley rounded second and kept going to the uncovered base. Baltimore did bunt on Collins in the July 28 game, and in a later inning, very likely could have tried several in a row.

"I came to the conclusion there was only one solution to this bunting game. A third baseman had to give himself a chance to get those fast guys," Collins later talked about his strategy to defuse the bunt. "Once around the circuit, you knew who would bunt and who wouldn't. You knew McGraw and Keeler were bunters. So I played them on the edge of the grass. McGraw bunted and I came in as fast as I dared, picked up the ball one-handed and threw it underhanded to first base. He was out. Keeler tried it, and I nailed him by a step."²⁶

The Chicago correspondent for *Sporting Life* wrote effusively about Collins' play at third base when Louisville visited Chicago in mid–August: "Collins has been boomed as such a wonder that the mob was wild to see him. We were disappointed in one respect — there was not enough chances hit down his way. But how he did gobble those that came! He grabs them off without the slightest fuss or flurry, contrives to be in front of the ball as soon as it leaves the stick, and throws to first perfectly, yet with ease and without any rush or hurry."²⁷

When Louisville defeated Boston on August 20 at the South End Grounds, with Collins as the visiting team's star, going 2-for-4 with a home run, the verdict was sealed that Boston would exercise its option to recall Collins to play for Boston during the 1896 season. However, when second baseman Lowe injured his leg on August 26 and would be out of the lineup for an extended period, Boston decided to immediately exercise that recall option to have Collins fill in at shortstop while Long moved from there to cover the vacancy at second base.²⁸

Collins, however, balked at returning to Boston, even though he had signed an agreement with the Boston to do so in the event they decided to exercise their recall option. "No doubt, the young man is sour at the way he was treated in Boston, and for this he has quite recently developed an aversion to coming back to manager Selee," the *Boston Globe* explained the possible thinking of Collins.[29] The brash Collins, looking to leverage the situation and get a better deal from Boston, told the baseball writers that if he couldn't remain in Louisville, he'd retire from baseball and return to Buffalo and get a job. The issue was fairly simple — Collins was paid more in Louisville than he had been in Boston, making $275 a month in Louisville compared to his original deal in Boston for $200 a month.[30] Collins was also astute enough to see that he would be just a temporary fill-in for the injured Lowe. Since he wanted to play third base, not the outfield anymore, what position would he play for Boston the following year? He thought he'd have more opportunity playing in Louisville for the 1896 season.

After ignoring the recall notice for a few days and continuing to play for Louisville, Collins was finally ordered by National League president Nick Young to report to Boston. Dreyfuss, hoping to eventually work out a deal with Boston to keep Collins, convinced Soden and Selee to recall Collins for the 1896 season, since it was obvious that Collins wasn't going to report for the rest of the 1895 season. Boston agreed if Collins didn't play in any more games for Louisville. When Collins played his last game for Louisville on September 12, the fans gave him an ovation. "As it was his last game Collins gave another exhibition of how the game should be played," the *Louisville Courier-Journal* described the play of Collins, "picking up six red-hot ones and also, by a brilliant catch and turn, putting out Decker who had tried to get around from second on O'Brien's high throw."[31] After that, as Collins later recalled the final days of the 1895 season, "I took Barney's advice and a $500 bonus, plus my salary for the balance of the season, returned to Buffalo and sat out the last two weeks of the campaign."[32]

Besides being paid more by Louisville than Boston, Collins also batted much better for Louisville than he had for Boston. For Louisville, Collins finished with a .279 batting average, compared to his meager .211 average during his early-season stint with Boston. His composite average for the 1895 season was .273. In the field at third base, Collins compiled a .926 fielding average, with 25 errors in 337 chances handled.

Not many observers thought the loaning of ballplayers was a good idea. "This loaning of a player by one club to another should be discouraged by the League," Jake Morse wrote in a *Sporting Life* commentary. "The Louisville Club made an immense mistake to take Collins on any such terms as they did. Had it not been for Louisville the powers of Collins as a third baseman might have laid dormant for a long time. Who can blame Collins for not wanting to be a wall flower and desiring to be in the game?"[33]

Collins didn't have to wait long to find out where he fit into Boston's plans for 1896. Two months after the end of the 1895 season, Selee executed a trade that clarified where Collins would play in the 1896 season.

CHAPTER 5

Boston's Third Baseman

On the eve of the National League meeting in November 1895, president Stuckey of the Louisville ballclub spoke enthusiastically about Jimmy Collins: "He drew out at least one-third of the people who attended our home games last season, and while we would like to have the young man, we nevertheless fully appreciate the fact that he is the property of the Boston club.... He is now working at his home in Buffalo, and I understand refuses to answer any correspondence from the Boston club." Stuckey tried to give the headstrong Collins some tips on securing his future with Louisville, "to call on Pres. Soden and explain just how he felt about the matter," but said Collins refused the advice. "Collins is a stubborn fellow and would not listen. I don't think that Collins will play with Boston even if that city shows him that he must give up the game."[1]

Boston manager Frank Selee was so confident that Collins would sign with Boston to play the 1896 season that he convinced owner Arthur Soden to trade their existing third baseman (and captain), Billy Nash, to make room for Collins in the infield. On November 13, Nash was peddled to Philadelphia in exchange for outfielder Billy Hamilton. "With Collins on third and Hamilton in left field, the team is certainly stronger than last season," the *Boston Globe* opined.[2] With Hamilton in the fold, Tommy McCarthy was dispensable, so he was traded the next day to Brooklyn.

Soden and Selee greatly underestimated what it would take to get Collins to agree to play for Boston. In mid–December Selee was still confident that signing Collins wouldn't be a problem, as he made preparations for spring training in Charlottesville, Virginia. "I hear that Collins is playing indoor baseball at his home in Buffalo and in fine condition to go out and play ball at a moment's notice," said Selee.[3] After merely one year as a major league ballplayer who had a respectable performance for a last-place team, Collins showed tremendous chutzpah in his negotiation with Soden, the principal owner of the Boston ballclub. Trading Nash so soon was a mistake on Boston's part, since it gave Collins a considerable advantage in the negotiation, since without Nash Boston had a huge vacancy to fill at third base. Collins held out for a big salary increase for as long as possible. Given the strong-willed nature of Collins, he probably tried to gain greater advantage by reminding Soden that he could always return to his railroad job in Buffalo if he couldn't come to an agreement with the Boston ballclub.

Soden was president of the Boston ballclub, a position he had held since 1877. He was the number one "triumvir," as the Boston owners were known, who ran the ballclub along with James Billings as treasurer and William Conant as secretary. They were tough businessmen. "The famed triumvirs of ancient Rome, Caesar, Pompey, and Crassus, were minor leaguers compared to the Triumvirs of the Boston Nationals, Soden, Conant, and Billings," Harold Kaese wrote in his history of the Boston Braves franchise. "Boston's threesome wielded fully as much power in the National League as their predecessors wielded in the Roman league, and they survived to live considerably longer and happier lives."[4] Soden and the other triumvirs successfully operated the Boston ballclub as a money-making venture, as a sidelight to their main occupations. Soden was a wealthy construction magnate in the firm of Chapman and Soden. While the Boston triumvirs were often "cussed and abused for penny pinching" in salary negotiations and ballpark operations — they gave out few complimentary tickets and were not averse to manning the ticket booth at the ballpark to assure appropriate payment — they didn't cut corners on traveling expenses. Second baseman Bobby Lowe recalled that "the team stayed at the best hotels, and each player was given $3 per day meal money in trains," to ensure that the team was in good shape to win road games.[5]

The success that Collins had back home in Buffalo and in Louisville, where he used his Irish-American wits to gain favorable results in dealing with German-Americans and native-born Americans, didn't translate to Boston. Soden, the classic nineteenth century industrialist, took the position that he was management and Collins was labor. Worse was the fundamental difference in ethnic relations in Boston than Collins had experienced in Buffalo. For the three centuries since Boston's founding in 1630 by Puritan settlers from England, Anglo-Americans had exercised control of the city's destiny. Maritime trade built the city for two centuries and created fortunes for the Lowell, Russell, Cabot, Lawrence, and Appleton families. The Boston Brahmin aristocracy, named after the priestly class of ancient Hindus that set moral standards for their society, established "a modern caste system in which they were clearly and indisputably the superior force" in Boston.[6] The arrival of droves of famine-impoverished Irish Catholics in the 1840s and 1850s threatened the status quo in Boston, which had retained its entrenched Anglo-Saxon Protestant character long after major cities such as New York, Philadelphia, Chicago, and St. Louis began absorbing immigrants into their culture. As historian Thomas O'Connor writes, "The possibility that Irish Catholics, with their alien culture and their detested religion, would ever be welcomed or even admitted into the exclusive ranks of such a long-established and highly self-conscious social system [in Boston] was extremely unlikely."[7] In Boston, the Irish continuously clashed with the Brahmins over political, religious, and economic issues. By 1896 the native-born Brahmins, like Soden, still controlled virtually everything in Boston, and considered the Irish-Americans, like Collins, to be simply pawns in their world.

On January 12, 1896, Collins issued a statement from Buffalo, saying he had decided to sign a Boston contract and "would have done so before had there not been a difference on the question of salary." He added that "as soon as the document in proper form arrives," he would sign it. By proper form, Collins meant "sufficient salary." Although he might get a higher salary in the short run with Louisville, Collins concluded that Boston gave him better long-term potential over Louisville, "as it is a larger city and is therefore able to support a higher-priced team." Louisville couldn't finish higher than tenth place, he believed, and he had received positive comments from several baseball writers that he would "be given a warm welcome as Nash's successor."[8] All that remained was to agree upon a salary amount.

A week later Selee told baseball writers that Collins would receive "a deserved raise," as management "has great hopes of superior work" from him in the coming season.[9] However, there was an obvious disagreement between the two parties about not only what a "deserved" amount was, but also what constituted a "raise." Soden offered to pay Collins $1,800 for the 1896 season. To Collins, this wasn't a raise, since the amount was roughly what he had earned while playing at Louisville in 1895. From Soden's perspective, the offer was a 50 percent increase from Collins' original contract in Boston for the 1895 season, so it was a healthy raise. Collins held out for a higher salary for two and a half months, until Boston threatened to drop him from the team if he didn't sign by April 1. Since ownership almost always had the upper hand in baseball negotiations in the National League, Collins learned a hard lesson and finally agreed to the $1,800 salary for the 1896 season.[10]

In the opening game of the season on April 16 at Philadelphia, Collins appeared in his first game at third base for Boston. He fielded eight chances flawlessly, but went 0-for-5 at bat in Boston's 7–3 victory. There was an interesting juxtaposition of Nash at third base for Philadelphia while his replacement Collins was at that position for Boston. Collins even handled the final out of the game off Nash's bat, as "Nash made his last try with a screaming hot grounder between third and short, but young Collins took the ball on the run and put it to Lowe for a force out, and the game was over."¹¹

Collins made his Boston third-base debut at the South End Grounds on Monday, April 20, on the Patriots Day holiday (usually celebrated on April 19, which was a Sunday in 1896) when a huge crowd jammed the grounds. Many in the crowd were there to see the four new Boston ballplayers: Collins, Hamilton, Bergen, and Mains. "It is safe to say that third baseman Collins was perfectly satisfactory," the *Globe* noted. "He fielded in beautiful style and hit well," going 3-for-5 and making no errors in five chances. The *Boston Globe* reported a number of old standby fans in the crowd, including Arthur Dixwell and George Appleton, as well as James Russell, who was on hand to watch his 26th consecutive home opener at the South End Grounds. Russell "went home a happy man when assured that Jimmy Collins was the real thing at third," since he had doubts "about any man filling Nash's place until he saw the young man from Buffalo." Collins "won the hearts of all true-lovers of the game from the jump."¹²

What Soden and the triumvirs sought as "true-lovers of the game," i.e., spectators, was the gentlemanly crowd and the small-business owner who could attend as often as his business would permit. One of these Boston fans was Arthur Dixwell, a member of the idle rich; because his father was a rich banker, Arthur never had to work a day in his life, as he subsisted on earnings from his father's trust fund. He never married, lived at the Copley Plaza Hotel, and spent a good deal of his time following the Boston ballclub. "There may have been earlier baseball rooters, but there were not any firmer ones," the *Boston Globe* wrote at Dixwell's death in 1924. "Dixwell was a regular attendant at the baseball games back in the '80s and he accompanied the Boston team on some of its trips." Dixwell's mode of travel to the ball grounds was a carriage, not the trolley.¹³

Just seven games into the 1896 season, however, Collins was severely injured in the April 23 game in Baltimore. "While the boys were delighted over their victory they would have taken several defeats rather than have Jimmy Collins injured," the *Globe* reported. "In the second inning Collins went to steal second. Jennings took the throw on the run to the right of the base. Collins tried to avoid a collision, and in scrambling over the base caught his toe and wrenched his instep."¹⁴ He was carried off the field in the arms of his teammates into the clubhouse under the stands, where the *Baltimore Sun* reported that "Dr. Standish McCleary bound up the ankle" before putting him in a carriage for the team's hotel.¹⁵

Fortunately, Boston's own medical person had made the trip, Prof. Walsh, who was there ostensibly to look out for sore arms from overwork following spring training. "They have a room at the grounds there for the express purpose of taking care of just such cases as Collins," Walsh praised the facility at the Baltimore grounds. "In the room was a lounge and a physician's complete outfit in the way of splints, sponges, bandages and everything necessary. No ground should be without just such a room as they have at Baltimore, with so many men in danger during the games."[16] After Walsh pronounced Collins to be out for a month, Tim Murnane of the *Globe* bemoaned that Collins did "marvelous work" at third base and "was fast developing into a fine batsman, and always carried a cool head on his shoulders."[17] Collins returned to the Boston lineup in the May 29 game with Cleveland.

Selee had a formidable lineup to challenge the two-time champion Baltimore team for the 1896 pennant. Collins and Hamilton were the only new faces in the infield and outfield positions from the 1894 team. The team was playing its second season at the rebuilt South End Grounds, after a fire in 1894 had destroyed its earlier incarnation. The playing field was roughly the same size as before the fire, but seating in the grandstand was reduced because the new covered pavilion lacked the second story of the old double-decked grandstand with its elegant twin spires atop the roof. Underneath the grandstand were clubhouses for both the home and visiting teams, as well as toilets for the spectators. Bleachers lined the foul territory beyond first and third bases.[18]

The layout of the playing field at the South End Grounds was constrained by the existence of Columbus Avenue (behind the first-base line), Walpole Street (behind the third-base line), and the New York, New Haven, and Hartford Railroad (behind the left-field fence). The limited amount of real estate between Columbus Avenue and the railroad tracks created one distinguishing feature of the South End Grounds — the short distance between home plate and the six-foot-high left-field fence, 250 feet down the third-base line, which made it an inviting target for home runs. Right field had similar dimensions, but there a 14-foot wall thwarted home runs. Center field was spacious, with the fence 416 feet away from home plate, while left-center was 430 feet distant and right-center 392 feet away.[19] Beyond the railroad tracks abutting left field was a large undeveloped parcel open all the way to Huntington Avenue, which was used for circus and fireworks shows. In 1896 a "Shooting the Chutes" entertainment venue leased the land, creating a man-made lagoon as a landing area for a toboggan ride, similar to a ride at today's water parks.[20] Five years later, the Chutes parcel would be retrofitted to serve as the home for Collins' new employer.

Unlike many National League ballparks, the South End Grounds was not located directly on a trolley line, since the grounds originally were built to draw spectators that would travel to the ballgames via horse-drawn carriages, not public transportation via a horse-drawn trolley. The Tremont Street

Railway was close by, with electrified trolley cars providing access to the South End Grounds in 1896 if patrons walked up Walpole Street from Tremont.

During the 1896 season, John Haggerty, the groundskeeper and general handyman/fixer-upper-man at the South End Grounds, would sound the gong for play to begin at 3:30 in the afternoon. "Every player in the leagues knew him. He was always ready to help them," the *Boston Globe* remarked years later about Haggerty. "Lumps were removed from the field at the players' requests, bats were arranged and oiled, uniforms were always made ready and hundreds of other odd jobs were done to please the athletes."[21]

However, Boston finished in fourth place in 1896, a distant 17 games behind first-place Baltimore. Collins played most of the rest of the season, getting into 84 games and hitting nearly at a .300 average. His renown was starting to spread, as the New York correspondent to *Sporting Life* wrote that September: "Jimmy Collins is certainly the most graceful player in the League. He makes stops and throws with apparently no effort whatsoever."[22]

Collins experienced his first postseason play in 1896, when he joined his Boston teammates to play in a series of games with the Providence team, champions of the Eastern League. Selee arranged the match, with the net proceeds to go to the ballplayers. The first two games were played in Providence, the next two at the South End Grounds, with the next four staged at neutral sites in Massachusetts and New Hampshire. One of the best attended games was in Haverhill, Massachusetts, on October 7, when 3,000 people paid 25 cents apiece to watch the exhibition game. Boston won six of the eight games in the series, which "put in the pockets of each player some $45."[23]

After the first three games, Collins turned down a chance to tour England with the National League champion Baltimore team, which would commence immediately following the completion of the Temple Cup series, the league's official postseason play between the first- and second-place teams. He even received a telegram from Joe Kelley trying to convince him to join the Orioles tour.[24] It was a wise decision by Collins, since the England tour was a bust, due to the cold English autumn and the lack of interest by the Englishmen for a sport they did not understand.[25]

When it came time to negotiate salary for the

After Jimmy Collins became the regular third baseman for the Boston Nationals in 1896, this line-drawing portrait of a youthful Collins appeared in numerous newspapers and baseball publications in 1897 and 1898 when his popularity soared as Boston captured the National League pennant each year.

1897 season, Soden offered Collins a salary increase to $2,100 a year ($350 a month).[26] Collins felt he should be paid the unofficial salary maximum of $2,400. "I didn't think $350 was enough," Collins later recalled. "Twice I returned [the contract] unsigned, and Billings (secretary of the club) wrote me to report March 17 and take the boat for Savannah."[27] The *Boston Globe* reported that Collins and Hamilton were aboard the *Nacoochee* sailing their way south with the team to spring training in Georgia "with unsigned contracts in their pockets."[28] As he had the year before, Collins eventually relented and agreed to the $2,100 annual salary for 1897.

After the team's slow start in the 1897 season, Selee made a change in the lineup that created the makings of a championship squad, when he moved Fred Tenney from right field to first base, replacing Tucker, and put rookie Chick Stahl in right field. Stahl, whom Selee had drafted the prior fall from the Buffalo ballclub, became fast friends with Collins. With some younger ballplayers now in the lineup, Collins must have felt more comfortable during the 1897 season than he had the prior season when he was the newcomer to an older lineup. Collins' maturity as a ballplayer, both as a fielder and a hitter, stood out as Boston put together a 17-game winning streak from May 31 to June 21 that propelled the team into first place in the National League standings.

Out of a number of sensational fielding plays that Collins made during that winning streak, several generated newspaper headlines, and two stood out. On June 5 with the bases loaded and two outs in the ninth inning, Collins made a diving grab to save the game for Boston: "Collins seemed to go nearly as fast as the ball, and, to the utter surprise of all, came up out of the dirt with it, still going toward second, where he tossed the ball to Lowe for a force out" to preserve the Boston victory. "There was no bound to the ball, so that Collins was forced to go clean to the floor for it, throwing him almost on his head."[29] Three days later on June 8 in the eighth inning, Collins chased a foul ball back of third base: "He hit the low fence in front of the bleachers and for a second balanced like a pole across it, his legs and hands extended. When the ball hit his hands it carried him down a shade on the other side, but he was soon on his feet and tossed the ball into the field. When the spectators realized that Collins had caught the ball the cheers were like the noise made by coupling freight cars."[30] Loud cheering by the spectators accompanied both fielding maneuvers by Collins.

In the first victory of the winning streak, Collins went 4-for-6 in a 25–5 rout of St. Louis, and followed that up the next day with a 4-for-10 day in a doubleheader, banging out two doubles and a triple. Over the course of the 17-game winning streak, Collins improved his batting average from .314 to .333. As Collins found his groove as a line-drive hitter who could find the outfield gaps, to contribute significantly to Boston's pennant possibilities in 1897, he became a fan favorite among the changing nature of the people who attended ballgames at the South End Grounds, dubbed the Royal Rooters.

By the mid–1890s, the mix of spectators at the South End Grounds had become more diverse than the largely gentlemanly crowds of the 1880s. For example, at Opening Day in 1897 at the South End Grounds, the *Boston Globe* noted: "Most of the old standbys were on hand to see the opening. Congressman Moody of Haverhill stopped off on his way to Washington ... Tom Lovell, John Morrill, George Appleton, Jimmie Connelly, Tom Pettitt, Dr. Merrill, Michael Moore, Toney Marsh and a score of other regular attendants were out." Arthur Dixwell sat in the bleachers, to get some sun, rather than in his usual seat in the grandstand.[31] Later that season, when 125 Rooters departed Boston on a train to Baltimore to see the Boston team play a crucial series in Baltimore, the traveling party included "many businessmen, a clergyman, physicians, seven women, and several others who daily occupy seats on the bleachers back of third base."[32] The key phrase is "bleachers" instead of "grandstand," in which the *Globe* tacitly recognized a changing mix of spectators from the "old standbys" at Opening Day.

The Royal Rooters group was closely identified with Mike "Nuf Ced" McGreevey, who owned the Third Base Saloon located near the South End Grounds and was listed as one of the 125 travelers to Baltimore. McGreevey was one of the new breed of small-business owners who wasn't quite of the same ilk as wealthy long-time Boston fans like Dixwell. McGreevey has been given far too much credit for his exploits with the Rooters. While he was an inveterate promoter of his tavern, he was a far better promoter of himself in later years, which is why chroniclers of Boston baseball history mention McGreevey so prominently. Charlie Lavis, who owned a bowling alley, was a less publicized, but more important cog in the Royal Rooters. Other, more middle class, members of the Rooters included Charley Young, who was an accountant; C.W. Smith, who was a druggist; and Charles Green, who owned a wholesale grocer.[33]

Boston held onto first place all summer through Labor Day, in a neck-and-neck battle with the despised Baltimore team, led by John McGraw, who did whatever it took to win ballgames, no matter how cutthroat or ungentlemanly. Baltimore "schemed, cussed, and maneuvered more frequently, more aggressively, and better" than other teams, especially when it came to attempting to browbeat umpires.[34] The Boston and Baltimore teams were personifications of their respective cities; Baltimore was hardscrabble, while Boston was Brahmin. "The Orioles' openly roughhouse tactics played right into the Bostonian stereotype of the immigrant shanty Irish Catholic forcing unwanted change on a stable nation," Bill Felder summarized the situation in his book about the 1897 pennant race.[35] Boston and Baltimore met in a crucial three-game series on September 24–27, with the two teams beginning the series in a virtual deadlock for first place, with Baltimore a mere one percentage point ahead since it had played three fewer games than Boston.

Boston won the first game on September 24, a 6–4 victory, in which Collins played third base with a swollen eye. In pre-game warm-ups, he took a bad-hop grounder above the left eye, which then swelled shut; Selee sent for some leeches from a nearby drugstore to help relieve the swelling.[36] While Collins was 0-for-4 at the plate, he helped stop the fearsome Baltimore offense by fielding five batted balls without error, even with his ailing eye. Collins made front-page headlines in the September 25 game, but for the wrong reason. His error in the second inning gave Baltimore two runs and an early lead that they never relinquished, as they won the game, 6–3. With runners on second and third, McGraw bunted along the base line toward Collins. While it might have rolled foul, Collins tried to field it and get the runner at home plate but the usually sure-footed Collins accidentally kicked the ball into foul ground to allow two runners to score. On September 27, on the strength of a nine-run inning, Boston took the rubber game of the series, 19–10, as Collins had five hits in six at-bats, including three doubles. Two days later on September 29, Boston clinched the pennant.

Collins was a member of his first championship team. He had a stellar season as a batter, finishing with a .346 average on a Boston team that had an overall .319 average. Every Boston starting infielder and outfielder batted over .300 for the season, ranging from Stahl at .359 to Lowe at .314.[37] The real value of Collins to the Boston team was his ability to produce runs. Although the RBI statistic wasn't yet invented in 1897, a retrospective determination indicates that Collins would have had 132 RBIs in 1897, second most among all National League batters.

With the regular season over, Collins moved on to the supplemental income opportunities of the postseason, in not only the anticlimactic rematch with the Baltimore team in the Temple Cup series but more importantly with the All-America Baseball Team in a cross-country tour with the Baltimore team.

CHAPTER 6

Temple Cup Series and All-America Tour

William Temple, the ardent Pittsburgh sportsman who donated the Temple Cup to be awarded to the winner of a postseason series between the top two finishers in the National League pennant race, was decades ahead of the time when such a playoff scheme appealed to owners, players, and fans. In 1897, the team that finished in first place during the regular season was considered to be the league champion.

The Temple Cup had never been accepted by the players as an authentic series of games since its founding in 1894, and the 1897 installment between Boston and Baltimore was no exception. "We didn't have any interest in the series in 1897, after winning the pennant as we did, in the last week," Boston first baseman Fred Tenney later said. "We had beaten Baltimore in the competition that counted, and this was just something extra."[1] Not only was the Temple Cup series anti-climatic after the hectic pennant chase between the two teams, but most of the Baltimore team and three members of the Boston team were focused on a bigger prize: a two-month cross-country tour that was expected to net the players more money than they'd receive from the best-of-seven-games Temple Cup series.

Jimmy Collins and his buddy Chick Stahl had already signed up to play for the All-America Baseball Team, a collection of National League players to be managed by Frank Selee, which would barnstorm the country for several months to play exhibition games against the Baltimore team, to be managed by Billy Barnie, the current Brooklyn manager and former Baltimore manager in its American Association days.[2] The first game of the All-America tour was booked for October 14, which gave the impacted players barely enough time to complete the Temple Cup series if it went the full seven games.

Although the Temple Cup rules called for the ballplayers to receive 100 percent of the net receipts — split 60 percent to the winning team and 40 percent to the losers — it was an open secret that the players usually conspired to split the proceeds 50/50, which further diluted the integrity of the Temple Cup games. Again, 1897 was no exception. Tim Murnane of the *Boston Globe* routinely reported that "each club would take 50 percent after all expenses are taken out."[3] From their actions on the field, there seems to be little doubt that the Boston and Baltimore players conspired to evenly divide the net proceeds rather than adhere to the stipulated 60/40 split.

Collins was certainly a disinterested participant. He had returned home to Buffalo after playing in the September 30 game at Brooklyn, when Selee excused him and the rest of the infield from playing in the team's final game. Collins spent Saturday and Sunday afternoon with his family and "in the evening he was around town among his friends," the *Buffalo Express* reported. "Naturally Jimmy was happy over the outcome of the pennant fight, but he was as undemonstrative as ever, except that his smile was perhaps a little broader and a little more continuous than usual."[4] Since Collins didn't leave Buffalo until Sunday night, and consequently didn't arrive in Boston until Monday morning, he was not fresh for the first game. He actually arrived late for the game, as the crowd was "decidedly impatient" over the missing third baseman, but "he got a fine reception when he finally appeared shortly after 3 o'clock."[5] He had no hits in his team's 12-hit barrage in that first game, and committed an error in the field in five chances.

He minimized his physical exertion on the field throughout the Temple Cup series, hitting just 5-for-22 to produce a .227 batting average, the lowest among the Boston regulars. To Collins, the Temple Cup clearly was simply a meaningless series of exhibition games, something not to be taken seriously from a competitive standpoint. His mind seemed to be squarely focused on the upcoming All-America cross-country tour. The experience with the Temple Cup series, along with his participation in the subsequent All-America tour, definitely shaped Collins' future attitude towards postseason games.

Baltimore was not exactly taking the Temple Cup seriously, either, as the team played an exhibition game in Hoboken, New Jersey, on Sunday, October 3, and didn't hop a train to Boston until midnight. Baltimore also arrived in Boston on Monday morning a bit groggy from little or no sleep for the first game. Although Boston won the first game, 13–12, the team's star pitcher, Charley Nichols, pitched only the first five innings, in the first indication that Boston was not taking the Temple Cup seriously. Nichols never pitched another inning in what turned out to be a five-game series, as Baltimore proceeded to rattle off four consecutive wins to cop the Cup.

About 10,000 spectators paid to see the series opener at the South End Grounds on Monday, October 4, but most were there more to honor the

Boston ballplayers for winning the National League pennant rather than to celebrate the first game of the Temple Cup series. Some of the spectators then proceeded to join the Boston ballplayers at the main event on October 4, the presentation of a pennant that evening during intermission of the play *The Swell Miss Fitzwell* at the Tremont Theater.[6]

Drowsy from the aftereffects of the Monday evening celebration, the Boston ballplayers lost the second game the next day, 13–11, before 6,000 fans as pitcher Fred Klobedanz left the pitcher's box in the fifth inning after yielding six runs that inning. The ballplayers were on their own Tuesday night, before the big banquet to honor the Boston team on Wednesday evening at Faneuil Hall.

Tired from another night's celebration, the Boston players dragged themselves to the South End Grounds for the third game on Wednesday, October 6. Selee started Klobedanz again, but he lasted less than two innings as Baltimore scored four runs in each of the second and third innings to win, 8–3. The game was called after seven innings, allegedly due to darkness, but also due to player indifference.

About 250 fans attended the banquet at Faneuil Hall that evening, where Congressman John Fitzgerald was the toastmaster. "The congressman got a rousing reception and made an address of welcome and congratulations which aroused the wildest enthusiasm," the *Boston Globe* reported, before he then talked about each ballplayer. Mayor Josiah Quincy then presented each player with a diamond pin and a watch charm inscribed "Boston champions '98."[7]

Further making the Temple Cup series a joke were the two exhibition games played between the two teams as they traveled to Baltimore for the next games scheduled in the Temple Cup competition. On Thursday, October 7, the two teams played in Worcester, Massachusetts, where Baltimore defeated Boston in a non–Temple-Cup game, 11–10, before 3,500 spectators. On Friday, October 8, 3,000 people saw the two teams play in Springfield, Massachusetts, where Baltimore won, 8–6. The Boston and Baltimore players made more money from these two exhibition games (about $60 apiece) than they would clear from the final two Temple Cup games in Baltimore.

When the series resumed in Baltimore on Saturday, October 9, Selee put Jack Stivetts in the pitcher's box and George Yeager behind the plate, since catcher Marty Bergen hadn't bothered to go with the team to Baltimore. Stivetts lasted a mere two innings, as the Orioles feasted on his serves to build a huge lead and eventually win, 12–11, before a small crowd. Boston's play "was as variegated as the colors of the Berkshire hills," the *Boston Globe* reported, with some plays "that bordered on the phenomenal" and others "of the most stupid kind seen on a ball ground." In the latter category was a first-inning fly ball over second base, which Long and Lowe could have easily caught but they "saw Collins trotting down the field [who] went within ten feet of the ball and stood, the ball dropping at the feet of the three men."[8]

No game was slated for Sunday, since Sunday baseball was legally prohibited in Baltimore. However, rather than rest, Selee and several players took the train to New Jersey to play an exhibition game there with the All-America team, which was waiting in New York City for the tour to begin. In an article entitled "They Don't Care; Bostons Not Playing Very Hard for the Cup," the *Globe*'s Murnane wrote that Selee was disinterested in the Temple Cup and this excursion showed "that the Temple Cup was not keeping him awake at nights."[9] Collins, Stahl, Duffy, and Long joined Selee from the Boston team, while Jennings and McGraw went along from Baltimore, as the All-America team defeated Collins and the Picked Team, 5–3.

Back in Baltimore on Monday, October 11, Selee put a makeshift lineup on the field for the fifth, and final, game to make a further mockery of the Temple Cup series. Stivetts played center field and little-used Charlie Hickman started in the pitcher's box, who was eventually replaced by seldom-used Jim Sullivan. The players renegotiated the umpires' $100 per game fee down to $50, to cut expenses and avoid taking a loss and thus reduce their share of the net proceeds, since "only a handful" of spectators were present. In exchange for the lower fee, the players saved the umpires some time by rushing their way through the game in an hour and a quarter. Boston batters intentionally made outs to end the game faster. "As a burlesque, it was a great success," wrote Murnane, "and plainly proved that the Temple Cup games have very little interest for the players when the crowd is not paying."[10]

The official tabulation of the player shares of the net receipts of the Temple Cup series called for $310 to go to each Baltimore player and $207 to each Boston player, with *Sporting Life* adding in its account of the payments that the sum would be "$258 if even," to recognize the widely held belief that the players on the two teams had agreed to evenly split the proceeds.[11] When interviewed in the days following the end of the series, the players always spoke in regard to the check amounts, and avoided talking about what the amount they had actually received. The players circumvented the stipulated 60/40 split mandated by the rules of the Temple Cup series by agreeing in pairs, usually by position, for a winning-team player to pay to a losing-team player the difference between his check amount and the even-split amount. In this case, Collins would have received $51 from John McGraw, Baltimore's third baseman, in addition to his $207 check as a member of the losing team.

Temple himself was very dissatisfied with the outcome of the Temple Cup competition and wanted the National League to investigate "charges that the Baltimore and Boston players this year agreed to an equal division of the receipts," contrary to his stated 60/40 split of the proceeds.[12] While in Kansas

Jimmy Collins was the third baseman on the All-America Baseball Team during an 1897 postseason cross-country tour to play a series of exhibition games with the Baltimore ballclub. In this promotional broadside from the California segment of the tour, Collins is shown in a dark uniform in the second row from the bottom, third from the right (Library of Congress Prints and Photographs Division, LC-USZ62-97621).

City with the All-America tour, Selee lamely defended his Boston players: "All that talk about the Temple Cup games being hippodrome is bosh. The players on both teams played to win and the money was not divided. The strain on the Boston players for the pennant was too great and they did not keep up the pace during the Temple Cup games."[13]

For agreeing to play on the All-America Baseball Team, Collins received an all-expenses-paid trip across the country, a chance to earn some additional income as a ballplayer, and the opportunity to closely observe the business operation of a baseball tour. The idea of the tour was hatched by Selee and Barnie in August 1897, when Frank Eline, a Baltimore businessman, agreed to back the tour. Eline agreed to front $10,000, while Selee and Barnie agreed to front expenses to a lesser degree.[14] Expenses included not only railroad fares and hotel costs, but, as Eline explained, we "had Pullman palace cars, straight through, and used no busses, but tallyho coaches, drawn by six or eight horses, to carry the party from railroad depots to hotels and from hotels to grounds."

The only expense the players were responsible for was their laundry.[15] The financial arrangements called for the players to divide among themselves 50 percent of the net profits of the tour, while the three financial backers shared the other 50 percent.[16]

The opening Midwest portion of the tour was fairly grueling for Collins and the other players, as they usually played one game in a city and then hopped on a train to travel to the next destination for a game the next day. Starting in Frostburg, Maryland, on October 14, the tour snaked its way west through Pittsburgh, Columbus, Cincinnati, Dayton, Indianapolis, Peoria, Cedar Rapids, St. Joseph, and Topeka before arriving in Kansas City on October 24.

The demanding travel schedule was necessary because the tour's backers expected to, at best, break even on this leg of the journey, where gates were small due to the colder weather and the non-novelty of the games (these cities all had professional ballclubs in Organized Baseball). Crowds for the games in Columbus and Dayton were in the 600 to 800 range; for the Sunday game in Cincinnati, only 1,500 showed up. One of the larger attendances, 3,000, was at the game in Cedar Rapids, Iowa, the hometown of Baltimore pitcher Bill Hoffer, who made a guest appearance for the Baltimore team and attracted a big crowd to watch him defeat the All-America team.[17] The 7,000 paid admissions for the October 24 Sunday game in Kansas City were a good sign that larger crowds could be expected on the next leg of the tour. At the time, Kansas City was the westernmost city with a ballclub in Organized Baseball. As the tour traveled farther west to play in cities that didn't have professional baseball teams, and eventually to California where the weather was warmer, the tour was expected to be more lucrative.

After a week and a half of barnstorming, the two squads had settled into a consistent lineup, with some players dropping out of the tour since the original September announcement and other players signing on to it. For the All-America team, the infield consisted of Patsy Tebeau (Cleveland) at first base, Billy Nash (Philadelphia) at second base, Bill Dahlen (Chicago) at shortstop, and Collins (Boston) at third base. In the outfield were Jesse Burkett (Cleveland), Bill Lange (Chicago), and Stahl (Boston). The catcher was Tim Donahue (Chicago), and the pitchers were Jack Powell (Cleveland), Charlie Hastings (Pittsburgh), and Billy Rhines (Cincinnati). Alec Smith (Brooklyn) was the substitute catcher and utility man to play infield or outfield when needed.

For the Baltimore team, the infield consisted of three-quarters of its regular-season team, with Jack Doyle at first base, Henry Reitz at second base, and Hughey Jennings at shortstop. Joe Kelley, an outfielder during the regular season, played third base for the barnstorming team. In the outfield was Tom

O'Brien with two non–Baltimore players, Mike Griffin (Brooklyn) and Patsy Donovan (Pittsburgh). The catcher was Bill Clarke and the pitchers were Joe Corbett, Arlie Pond, and minor leaguer Elmer Horton. When an injury necessitated a substitute, the replacement came from the All-America squad and he switched teams.

Tebeau and Jennings were the captains of their respective teams, with Jennings often handling the manager's duties as well for the Baltimore team, since Barnie often went ahead of the tour with Eline to serve as the tour's advance men, advertising the upcoming ballgames and drumming up interest among the local residents. Jennings and Kelley were on their honeymoons, as they brought their newly married brides on the tour; Nash, Tebeau, and Clarke also brought along their wives.[18]

After the stop in Kansas City, the tour had been slated to travel through Texas on the way to the West Coast, but an outbreak of yellow fever in that state caused Barnie and Eline to book the tour on a more northern route through Colorado and Utah. While the detour provided Collins and the other ballplayers with a first-hand view of the scenic Rocky Mountains and a sampling of the area's natural wonders between ballgames, the colder weather in that region wreaked havoc with the playing schedule.

It began to snow on the tour's trip from Emporia, Kansas, to Pueblo, Colorado. While the teams managed to get in a game in Pueblo, they were not so fortunate at their next two stops. Since snow forced the cancellation of the game at Colorado Springs, the tour took a break and the ballplayers visited points of interest in the area. "We arose early on our arrival there, and part of the party on horseback, and the rest in carriages, visited Manitou Springs, Garden of the Gods and Pike's Peak," Selee wrote in a dispatch to *Sporting Life*.[19]

Heavy snow in Denver canceled the two games scheduled there, which Eline estimated cost the tour $3,000 since Patsy Tebeau's brother George lived there and had generated significant interest in the upcoming Sunday ballgame on October 31. "We arranged with 50 men to clear the grounds of snow, for there it can be winter one day and summer the next," Eline later explained about the sunny day in Denver that Sunday. "The workmen, however, took the snow to high ground and when it melted the water ran back on the field and made a mud pool of it."[20] After the few days of relaxation, the tour moved on to Glenwood Springs where baseball could once again be played.

The ball field in Glenwood Springs was not enclosed by a fence, though. Eline thought the lack of an enclosure would be a financial problem, but he concluded, "Strange to say, nobody attempts to steal in nor to stand around to see the game without paying."[21] Barnie had the reason for spectator compliance: "In Glenwood Springs they had what is known as a shotgun fence.

This was of course made up of men with shotguns."[22] These men were spaced out at various points of the ball field to create a deterrent to spectators not buying a ticket to the game.

Before the game, Selee and the players sampled one of the area's natural resources. "We enjoyed our visit at Glenwood Springs very much indeed," Selee later wrote. "We had a perfect day there. This place is celebrated for the hot salt sulphur pool, which is out in the open air. We all enjoyed a bath in the open air, with snow surrounding us on the hills."[23] The sightseeing continued at Aspen, Colorado, where the players and several wives visited a silver mine. Later, at Salt Lake City, Utah, they saw the Mormon Tabernacle and the Great Salt Lake.

In additional to experiencing the scenic sights of the Rocky Mountains that were vastly different from the landscape of his hometown of Buffalo, New York, Collins also experienced a different feeling on the ball fields due to the thin mountain air. As Baltimore pitcher Arlie Pond related, "Why, you hit a ball out there and it goes about a mile; but it nearly kills you to run the bases, the air is rarefied."[24]

The thin air didn't seem to harm Collins' fielding in the November 4 game at Beck's Hot Springs, Utah. "Doyle popped up a high fly over Collins' head which looked to be a safe hit," *The Sporting News* reported in an extensive account of the game at the then renowned resort that featured natural thermal waters. "The nimble Bostonian made the star play of the day and caught the ball after a hard run out into left field amid terrific applause from the crowd." Later in the same game, "Horton sniped a grass cutter at Collins that seemed impossible for him to capture but that most remarkable third baseman fairly dotes on impossibilities and he gathered this one in as he did so many times during the latter part of the league season and made his usual clean assist to first."[25] Despite the two great plays by Collins, the All-America team lost to Baltimore, 4–3.

Following a two-day excursion through the deserts of Nevada and over the Sierra Nevada Mountains, the tour arrived in San Francisco for a six-week stay in California. During their extended stay in San Francisco, Collins and the other ballplayers stayed at the Baldwin Hotel, where they were pampered and "quartered in suites, with baths and all convenience." Eline arranged for the two teams to dine in their own private dining room at the hotel and to have the cooks prepare a midnight snack for them in the grill room each evening.[26]

At the first game in San Francisco on November 7, 13,000 spectators crammed into Recreation Park to watch the All-America team trounce Baltimore. The four players with the tour who made their homes in California (Nash, Lange, Corbett, and Reitz) received a loud ovation from the crowd, which had spilled onto the field and thus necessitated a ground rule for balls hit into the crowd. The All-America team pounded Pond for 19 hits in its 16–7 victory, with three by Stahl — including a home run that "sent the fans crazy when he drove the horsehide sphere over the right-field fence to Ringgold Street — and two by Collins.[27] The entire team collected nine doubles to take advantage of the ground rule with so many fans on the field.

"Our first game in San Francisco was the signal for a great outpouring of the cranks, who were baseball hungry," Barnie remembered. "The ropes had not been put up and so great was the crowd that the police came to the box office and told me to stop selling tickets. I got the players to push the crowd back and so let in a few more, but we turned away at least 4,000."[28] According to Eline, "From this game we carried 180 pounds of silver in a ticket box, filled to the top, in addition to some gold and $6 in notes."[29]

Not long after the tour pulled into San Francisco, back East at the National League meeting on November 12 the ballclub owners voted unanimously to abolish the unpopular Temple Cup series.[30] There would be no formal postseason play in the National League for the 1898 season.

The All-America tour proceeded at a more leisurely pace in San Francisco, as a dozen games were played over the course of four weeks, to crowds that numbered 2,000 to 5,000. During early December, the tour played a few games in Los Angeles before winding down in San Bernadino on December 13. California was where the tour made most of its profits. In the end, total net receipts from the tour totaled around $19,000, with approximately $9,500 to be split up among the ballplayers. Collins and the other men each netted about $440, receiving $342 in San Francisco and a bit less than $100 in Los Angeles.[31]

By Selee's accounting, the All-America team won 19 of 37 games played with the Baltimore team on the tour. Collins played third base in every game for the All-America team, based on a review of extant box scores that were published in the weekly *Sporting Life* newspaper.

More important, though, was the impact the tour had in expanding interest in baseball in the West. "Before we came baseball was practically dead west of Kansas City," Barnie told a reporter in Brooklyn after he had returned from California. "Our coming has caused a big boom in the game; it is once established throughout that section and leagues are springing up like mushrooms, with plenty of backing. A league is already playing ball in San Francisco as a result of our visit and three more are under way."[32] By 1899 the California League had rejoined Organized Baseball, and would soon turn into the Pacific Coast League.

CHAPTER 7

Long-Ball Hitter

As he rested at his parents' home in Buffalo during January 1898 to recover from the cross-country baseball tour with the All-America Baseball Team during the fall of 1897, Jimmy Collins quietly negotiated a contract with Soden through the mail to be paid the $2,400 unofficial salary maximum for the 1898 season.[1] After three years as a National League ballplayer, the 28-year-old Collins had reached the pinnacle of his profession, a pace much faster than it had taken his immigrant father to work his way up the ranks of the Buffalo police force to become the city's top cop in the fifth precinct. Collins was often touted by the baseball writers as one of the top third basemen in the league, if not the best, and he had now reached the top compensation as well.

The Boston ballclub could certainly afford the salary increase for its star third baseman, as Soden and the triumvirs reportedly cleared a profit of $120,000 during the 1897 pennant-winning season.[2] Expenses were fairly light for the Boston ballclub, compared to the other ballclubs in the National League. The *Boston Globe* estimated the club's expenses to be $70,000 with about half of that allocated to salaries for the ballplayers and the manager. "The Boston ballclub is by long odds the best managed piece of baseball property in this country," Tim Murnane wrote in the *Boston Globe*, "and has made more money for the owners than any two of the other clubs put together."[3]

However, the salary increase given to Collins was not largesse by Soden. When Collins began his salary discussions for 1898, the National League owners were plotting to lengthen the baseball season by 22 games, from 132 to 154, in order to recoup some of the financial losses incurred during the nation's economic depression from 1894 to 1897. The owners planned to begin the season a week earlier, with a mid–April start date, and add two weeks in October, to finish up in mid–October. On March 2, the owners announced the 154-game schedule for the 1898 season.[4] The ballclub owners didn't intend to offer the players any extra compensation for the additional 22 games.

Collins held out on signing his contract until mid-March, just before the Boston team left for spring training in Greensboro, North Carolina. Although the *Boston Globe* spun the situation management's way by reporting that "Jimmy is perfectly satisfied with his salary," Collins was unhappy.[5] He felt duped by Soden. Accounting for the 17 percent increase in the number of games to be played during the 1898 season, Collins actually received just a minimal pay increase.

Although the Boston team went on to capture a second consecutive National League pennant in 1898, this season was an important crossroads for the future economic success for Soden and the triumvirs that owned the Boston ballclub. Unfortunately, the owners chose the wrong road. The elongation of the playing season was only feasible if more Sunday dates could be used in those western cities where Sunday baseball was legally permissible. The decision by the New York and Pittsburgh ballclubs to play Sunday road games in 1898 was a key to the extended season. With Cleveland planning to host Sunday games based on a favorable 1897 court decision, the league could now count on five Sunday dates whenever the eastern teams were traveling within the west. Boston and Philadelphia were now the only National League ballclubs that did not play road games on Sunday, which put these teams at a severe disadvantage economically. The triumvirs also failed to anticipate the changes in the nature of spectators at their South End Grounds ballpark, which by 1898 was a more than gradual shift from the well-heeled to the common man. The Royal Rooters trip to Baltimore in September 1897 should have been a warning sign that structural changes were impending in the nature of baseball fandom in Boston.

With the Boston ballclub's pious never-on-Sunday policy, Collins had every Sunday to himself during the baseball season. While he subscribed to the Catholic faith, it is unclear how devout he was in attending church on Sunday, which at the time often entailed both morning and evening services. There weren't many entertainment options in Boston because of the strict Sunday laws of Massachusetts. Permitted activities within the "day of rest" doctrine included reading the Sunday newspaper, riding a bicycle, taking a carriage ride, or visiting the shore. For more cerebral activity, the Boston Public Library was open on Sunday, where patrons could read books in the majestic Bates Reading Room of the new library building in Copley Square that had opened in 1895. Train service was available to take short day trips to destinations outside Boston.

One of the most-touted statistics of Collins' baseball career is that he led the National League in home runs in 1898 with 15 round-trippers. He never hit more than seven homers in any other season. His volume of home runs in 1898 was purely accidental, as he did not modify his swing to intentionally take advantage of the short distance to the left-field fence at the South End Grounds. Many of his long hits that had gone for triples in 1897 landed over the fence for a home run in 1898. During the 1897 season when he hit .346, Collins had 28 doubles, 13 triples, and 6 home runs; in comparison, in 1898 he had 35 doubles, 5 triples, and 15 home runs. Compensating for the longer season in 1898 than in 1897, Collins had the same relative rate of long hits in both seasons but had far fewer triples and far more home runs in 1898.

There was no advantage for Collins to hit home runs, since the four-base hit was not nearly as valued in the 1890s as it is today. As *Sporting Life* noted in 1898, "Doubles and triples count for more than the home run hits, as a rule, as the latter are largely lucky by reason of going over fences. Doubles and triples are made on merit."[6] Nap Lajoie, who led the league in doubles, and John Anderson, who led the league in triples, received far more laud than Collins did for being the home run leader. In the above-mentioned 1898 article in *Sporting Life*, there was only one sentence about Collins' feat, while complete paragraphs were devoted to the achievements of Lajoie and Anderson.

To many at the time, the home run was a cheap hit, especially in Boston with the cozy distance to the left-field fence, 250 feet down the foul line. As one Philadelphia writer commented after the 1898 season, "Collins made 15 home runs and is the league's boss four-base puncher, but what wouldn't Delahanty or Lajoie do had they such a convenient left field fence to bat over at Philadelphia."[7] Harry Von der Horst, the treasurer of the Baltimore ballclub, complained about the friendly fence at the South End Grounds when he contended that "hits over that nearby fence should be nothing more than two-base hits."[8] Von der Horst proposed a rule change for the 1899 season, which would require outfield fences to be at least 285 feet from home plate, and if a fence was a shorter distance, then any hit over the fence would be a double, not a homer.[9] Since Boston obviously opposed such a rule, and Soden held a lot of sway with the other owners, the proposed rule was voted down at the league meeting that winter.[10]

Collins, a 5'7" 160-pound right-handed hitter, didn't have the physical presence of a power hitter.[11] That was because he was a gap hitter, not an over-the-fence hitter, preferring to use his speed to rack up doubles and triples. During the 1898 season, he belted 12 of his 15 home runs at the South End Grounds. Some were "cheap" homers, while others were legitimate long shots. After two home runs on the road at Washington on April 30 and New York on May 4, Collins hit three homers within a span of four days at the South End Grounds from May 10 to May 13. His fifth home run, against

Brooklyn on May 13, helped to propel Boston into third place in the standings.

The 1898 season was a good example of how Frank Selee deployed his quiet, mild-mannered approach to produce results, as he delivered a fifth pennant for Boston within a span of eight years as the manager of the Boston team. The son of a Methodist minister, Selee wasn't a loud-mouthed authoritarian manager as were many nineteenth century baseball leaders. "If I make things pleasant for the players, they reciprocate," Selee once explained his managerial style. Selee could use the gentlemanly approach because he excelled at being able to assess player talent, both physical as well as mental. This way he could simply put the players on the diamond without the need for heavy-handed motivational tactics. "He was a good judge of players," Lowe characterized Selee. "He didn't bother with a lot of signals, but let his players figure out their own plays. He didn't blame them if they took a chance that failed." As Harold Kaese wrote in his book *Boston Braves*, Selee's teams "outthought the opposition, besides outplaying it."[12] Collins, who didn't take kindly to having a boss, not only responded superbly to Selee's approach to leaving the ballplayers alone to play the game, but also took careful mental notes of his observations of Selee's managerial style for future use.

Jimmy Collins led the National League in home runs in 1898, an underpublicized hitting achievement at the time since doubles and triples were then more valued than home runs. Many of Collins' home runs were stroked over the hitter-friendly left-field fence at Boston's South End Grounds, where the handsome third baseman was a fan favorite (National Baseball Hall of Fame Library, Cooperstown, New York).

Boston slowly moved up in the standings over the course of the summer in 1898, moving into second place on June 13, where the team hung close to first-place Cincinnati for the next eight weeks. Collins hit his sixth and seventh homers on July 6 at Brooklyn and on July 16 in Boston against Brooklyn. Because hitting home runs was not necessarily viewed as being a meritorious skill, newspapers described most of Collins' homers in 1898 in lackluster terms. For example, the *Boston Globe* reported his homer on July 16 as simply: "Collins put the ball over the left fence for a home run."[13]

On August 16 Boston took over first place for several days, as Collins hit home runs number eight and nine at this time, the former against Cleveland on August 15 and the latter against Chicago on August 17. In a Labor Day holiday twin bill on September 5 against Washington, Collins hit a home run in each game, to up his total to 11 at this juncture of the season. In the morning game, "Collins broke the tie by driving the ball on to the railroad tracks," beyond the left-field fence.[14] This description indicates that the hit was more legitimate than cheap. The Boston newspapers generally went beyond generality only when it was a particularly well-hit homer, such as describing one as reaching the "car shops" on the other side of the right-field fence.

Collins added his twelfth homer on September 16 against St. Louis and his thirteenth on September 26 against Brooklyn. He capped his seasonal home run tally on September 29, with two homers off Al Orth in the eighth and ninth innings of the game with Philadelphia. His fifteen homer of the season was a grand slam in the ninth inning, which propelled Boston to an 11–10 victory. Here's how the *Boston Globe* described the clutch grand slam: "A home run would now tie the game. Collins at the rubber. The first ball sent in was an outcurve and was fouled off. Then came one to Collins' liking, and his stick went out like a flash. All eyes were turned toward the west, where they saw the ball sailing high over the fence well down the field for one of the most timely home runs of the season."[15] In a review of home runs at the South End Grounds after the season was over, Murnane of the *Globe* defended this Collins blast as a legitimate four-base hit: "Collins put the ball over the fence fully 300 feet from home plate, showing that it was not the punk hit that the quakers tried to make their friends believe."[16] On the following day, when Collins went to bat in the second inning, a fan jumped from the stands onto the field and gave Collins an envelope with a $50 bill in it, "as a present from the 'royal rooters' for Collins' winning home run of Thursday."[17] The grand slam must have secured the fans a healthy payoff on a gambling wager.

Due to the extra 22 games in the 1898 season, with its many doubleheaders during the last six weeks that crippled most pitching staffs, Boston decimated the competition during the final stages of the season. In its 37 games from September 1 on, Boston compiled a 31–6 record. The team moved into first place for good on September 7, and rolled to a 102–47 final mark, a comfortable six games over second-place Baltimore and 11 games over Cincinnati, which had faded to third place. Collins finished the season with a .337 batting average, sixth highest in the league behind Willie Keeler of Baltimore with his .381 average.[18]

After the final game in Baltimore on October 15, the Boston team stopped in Connecticut on the way back to Boston to play an exhibition game with Jim O'Rourke's Bridgeport ballclub of the Connecticut League. Bridgeport defeated Boston, 6–5, before a small audience of 600 fans. What was more interesting to Collins, though, was O'Rourke, whom he had watched as a youngster play for the Buffalo team of the National League. O'Rourke was an Irish-American success story to Collins, since O'Rourke had prospered enough to own not only his own ballclub in a minor league, but also the ballpark where the team played its games.[19]

Back in Boston, the players attended a testimonial in their honor at the Music Hall on October 20. After the musical portion of the program, the ballplayers, dressed in their uniforms, were introduced to the audience and received a hearty ovation. Selee was presented with a check for $2,500 from the ballclub's ownership. "We trust this gratuity will be accepted as evidence of our high appreciation of the united and successful efforts of the Boston team in again winning the championship," the accompanying letter from Soden read. "Great praise is due the team for its correct deportment and clean, manly ball playing. Skill, intelligence, and harmony have won a well-deserved victory."[20] Each ballplayer received $235 from the "gratuity" provided by Soden.

The use of the term "gratuity" was carefully chosen by Soden to disconnect the payment from the players' normal remuneration. It must have galled Collins to receive a "tip" as if he were a Pullman car porter, being paid for his service in keeping the ballpark spectators happy (by his "correct deportment"), not for hitting and fielding well. It was one more signal to Collins that his income potential was very limited by working for the Boston ballclub. Collins began to contemplate how he could more easily supplement his baseball salary with other income, in a more comfortable manner than an arduous two-month journey across the country as an itinerant ballplayer (as he had with the All-America team in 1897) or more exciting manner than shuffling paper at a desk job with the city.

Collins knew a number of ballplayers who had invested in saloons, including the bowling alley and saloon operated by Tommy McCarthy on Washington Street in Boston and the Diamond Café in Baltimore that John McGraw and Wilbert Robinson owned. However, his visits to those establishments indicated that running a saloon was not just challenging but also fraught with risks. Owning a baseball ballclub like O'Rourke was intriguing. So was a lifestyle of Arthur Dixwell, the Boston baseball rooter who lived off the income from investments and never had to work at all. During the off-season, as Collins pursued his "nice winter job in the City Treasurer's office at Buffalo," he thought long and hard about how to earn income outside of baseball.[21]

CHAPTER 8

Fielding Wizard

By the end of the 1899 season, after five years in the National League, Jimmy Collins had developed a stellar reputation as one of the league's best fielding third basemen. In the opinion of many contemporary observers, Collins was *the* best third baseman in the league. *Sporting Life* was already calling him "the greatest third baseman the game ever produced."[1] This was all high praise, for in the late nineteenth century, third base was a very difficult position to play, after having gone through periods of ease and challenge during the previous quarter century.

Prior to 1877, third base had been difficult to play because the third baseman had to guard the foul line (i.e., stay close to the actual third base) in order to field a possible fair-foul hit. Under the rules of the time, any ball was considered a fair hit if it initially hit in fair territory, even if there was enough rotation on the ball to cause it to travel into foul territory. Many batters were adept at bunting the ball initially into fair territory and have it roll into foul territory. Essentially, the third baseman needed to cover an equal amount of the field in both fair and foul territories.

When the rule was changed for the 1877 season (a fair hit now needed to stay in fair territory until it passed by the third base bag), third basemen strayed farther from the base and bunts declined in popularity as a hitting technique. In 1886, though, the bunt returned as an offensive tactic when the flattened bat was legalized. This rule change greatly altered the nature of playing third base, since batters could now much easier execute a bunt for a base hit with the flattened bat than they could with a rounded bat. Exacerbating the nature of third base play was the change in pitching style since the last heyday of the bunt in 1876. With the overhand delivery now legal in 1886, a right-handed batter could really slam the ball when he made contact with the pitch; now "playing far enough in to defend against the bunt put the third baseman in great peril from a hot line drive." This is how the term "hot corner" evolved to describe third base. In 1893 with the movement of the pitcher to a plate 60 feet, 6 inches, from home plate, from the back line of the pitcher's box 55 feet away, third base became an even tougher position to play since a right-handed batter could now hit with more power and pull the ball more often. Bunts increased in the mid–1890s, even with the outlawing of the flattened bat in 1893 and the rule change in 1894 that resulted in a foul bunt being called a strike.[2]

Collins was often called the first third baseman to play away from the base. This is patently untrue, since many third basemen in the 1880s did so when the bunt was not a popular hitting technique. What is more precisely true is that Collins was the first third baseman in the 1890s to regularly play in toward the batter, thus risking injury in order to field bunts. This positioning gave him the opportunity to field more chances than other third basemen in the league.

In the late 1890s, the "deliberate foul" was still a legal batting tactic, despite attempts to legislate it out of existence. Although a fouled bunt was a called strike beginning in 1894, any other foul ball was simply a non-event, neither ball nor strike, unless the umpire determined that the batter deliberately attempted to foul it away. Because an umpire could not reasonably determine the batter's intention, the "deliberate foul" remained a viable strategy for some batters. This also enabled Collins to field more chances, as he was adept at catching some of these deliberate foul attempts. The foul-ball rule was not changed until 1901 in the National League and 1903 in the American League, when any foul with less than two strikes became a called strike.[3]

Collins was judged by contemporary observers to be a superior third baseman in the National League because he had a quick eye, good hand dexterity, extensive range, and a strong right arm.

With great reaction time to balls hit his way, Collins had a natural advantage at third base. "It's remarkable how he gets away," Buck Ewing, manager of the Cincinnati ballclub, said about Collins' reaction to the crack of the bat. "He makes hard plays easy, simply by getting a quick start and playing the ball in front instead of on the reach."[4] William Phelon, a Chicago sportswriter, observed that "Collins and Clingman get a bushel of those sharp, short grounders that dart by the other fellows, and get them so quietly, so effectively and so regularly that the crowds get used to it and don't give them the praise they so well deserve."[5]

Initial reaction is one thing, but then deftly executing the play is another. "It is in his work on ground balls that Collins makes the strongest impression upon the spectators," a Boston correspondent (under the pseudonym "Bunker Hill") wrote in *The Sporting News*. "He plays a ball with wonderful judgment. The most hard-hit balls find their way into his hands as if by magic. Whether the bound is long or short, high or low, on one side or the other or if it comes on the most difficult pick-up imaginable, it can not escape him and is never so quick to evade him."[6] Collins fielded balls with a "graceful ease," one baseball writer noted, not clumsily or awkwardly as did many other third basemen.[7]

Collins covered a lot of territory at third base, including not just hits to third (bunts and hard hits) but also foul balls and pops to short left field. Jake Morse of the *Boston Herald*, writing in *Sporting Life*, wrote this extensive description of Collins' abilities:

> He fields balls in the most scientific and cleanest manner possible. There is no guess work about his play. It is all the real thing. He has a wonderful eye and gauges his ball as can no fielder in the country.... He is a perfect whirlwind in looking out for bunts. I never saw a man handle balls it seemed impossible to get to first in time — balls that he would gather but a few feet from the rubber, wheel and get to first in time, and on runners of no mean speed at that. Such one-handed stops as he has made well back of his position and at times going into foul territory after handling the ball and without pausing a second, making a wonderfully swift and accurate throw to first. He rarely missed his man on this kind of a throw.... Then the third baseman is called upon to do a great deal of work in securing foul balls, and in the Boston Club at least there was never a player that would begin to compare with Collins in covering ground on foul balls.[8]

What set Collins apart from other third basemen was his ability to reach pop flys to short left field. Coordinating with left-fielder Hugh Duffy, especially at the South End Grounds with its short distance to the left-field fence, Collins snagged many a fly ball that otherwise would be a base hit.

Lastly, Collins had a strong right arm to make accurate throws to first base. "His plays back of the bag are wonderful and his throws are so strong that he can catch the fastest runner," the "Bunker Hill" correspondent added to his description of Collins' abilities.[9] His aptitude for bowling — "one of the best bowlers" in Buffalo — may have helped Collins throw out runners on bunts through the comfort level of having used a body-bending motion to throw the bowling ball down an alley to knock over pins.[10]

Collins played in more ballgames than any other third baseman each season from 1897 to 1899. He missed only one game in 1897 — October 3, the last game of the season, after the pennant had been clinched — when George Yeager replaced him at third base and proceeded to commit five errors in eight chances offered. In 1898, Collins played every game at third base for Boston, although not every inning — Duffy had to substitute for him on July 2 in Cleveland when Collins was ejected from the game for uncharacteristically arguing with the umpire. Collins took a few days off in 1899, as Charlie Kuhns

Because of his acrobatic fielding exploits during six seasons in the National League, baseball writers acclaimed Jimmy Collins to be the "greatest third baseman" of the time. In this photograph of the four Boston infielders in 1900, Collins is shown sitting on the floor; clockwise from Collins are Bobby Lowe, Fred Tenney, and Herman Long (Boston Public Library, Print Department).

spelled him for three games, including the season finale on October 14 in Philadelphia where Collins watched from the stands in street clothes as Kuhns flubbed three balls for errors in a meaningless ballgame, since Boston had clinched second place the day before.

The combination of playing in so many ballgames and reaching more batted balls than other third basemen enabled Collins to establish in 1899 a new National League record for chances accepted in a season by a third basemen.[11] Because of the rule changes discussed earlier in this chapter that have reduced the number of fielding chances for third basemen, Collins' chances-accepted record for a single season still stands more than one hundred years later. Contemporary accounts indicate that Collins finished the 1899 season with 225 putouts and 376 assists, for a total of 601 chances accepted.[12] Collins edged out Pittsburgh third baseman Jimmy Williams, who compiled 249 putouts and 351 assists for a total of 600 chances accepted. In recent retabulations of game statistics, though, eight putouts have been subtracted from Collins's original total, so that his chances-accepted record is now recognized as 593. Williams is now considered to have two additional putouts and four additional assists during that season, for a total of 606 chances accepted. For some reason, perhaps simply inertia, Collins is still considered to hold the National League chances-accepted record for third basemen, not Williams.[13]

Collins compiled a .952 fielding average in 1899, based on the contemporary statistics noted above, to finish just behind Lave Cross, the leading third baseman with a .957 average. His .952 fielding average in 1899 was the highest ever during Collins' major league career. Despite the graceful play and spectacular catches and throws during his career, Collins never was a league leader in fielding average for third basemen. The same two factors that led to his large volume of chances accepted — his iron-man playing habits and aggressiveness to reach batted balls — also conspired to lower his fielding average, since over the course of a season he would inevitably commit errors on batted balls that other third basemen would never reach.

However, Collins didn't need to have a league-leading fielding average to become a renowned fielder at third base, since he was a legendary bunt buster based on his exploits in 1895 against the vaunted Baltimore bunting attack. The making of the legend started two years later in 1897 when *The Sporting News* published a short biographical sketch of Collins, which included one sentence simply indicating that on May 31, 1895, "Collins was sent to third base" after Preston committed four errors.[14] During the 1898 season, the Boston correspondent for *The Sporting News* wrote about Collins' fielding ability and added this detail to the previous basic description: "The Baltimore champions found to their dismay that Boston had a third baseman who could handle a bunt as easily as the ordinary ball, and that it was almost certain death to try his territory."[15] A few weeks later a biographical sketch in the *Sporting Life* noted that Collins was "the only third baseman who ever made the Baltimores stop bunting."[16]

Collins, in getting some experience manipulating the press, was no doubt the source of the facts in these two biographical sketches, as well as the additional detail about his initial game at third base in 1895 that found its way into print in 1898. At the time, his intent was to present some meaningful evidence of his fielding ability to enhance his ability to negotiate a higher salary with the Boston ballclub. The actual details of what occurred in 1895 were superfluous — shutting down the infamous Baltimore bunters was enough to serve his intended purpose. There was no mention of multiple consecutive bunts stopped by Collins in these early accounts, which eventually were incorporated into the legend; those were added later as the legend, as with all legends, began to bend from fact into fiction.

Once Collins had cashed in on his fame by jumping to the American League in 1901, there was ample contemporary evidence that he could more than adequately field bunts, so the tale of his fending off the Baltimore bunters in 1895 was no longer needed. While it was occasionally mentioned over the next decades, it wasn't a prominent part of the Collins story anymore. Two decades after Collins retired from baseball, the legend was resurrected in 1933 when *The Sporting News* published the first lengthy biographical sketch of Collins. This sketch added the interchange between Hughey Jennings and Collins that transpired at the 1895 event: "McCloskey called Collins in from center to exchange places with Preston and when Jim went to third, Hugh Jennings patted him on [the] back and told him [the] Orioles weren't going to bunt any more. Collins' response was: 'That's all right, bunt 'em down to me and I'll show you something.' He did. No more errors charged against third base that day."[17] Again, there was no mention of multiple consecutive bunts stopped by Collins; actually, the 1933 account doesn't even specify that Collins fielded a bunt on May 31. The text implies that Collins fielded bunts in his first game at third base, but the exact text only says that there weren't anymore errors at third base that day.

The legend gained some momentum in 1936 when Collins talked to an Associated Press writer about his first game at third base. The AP account added the actual fielding of one bunt in 1895, saying, "The first bunt the batter laid down his way Jimmy fielded perfectly. He came in fast, snared the slow roller and whipped it to first four feet in front of the runner."[18] Once again, there was no mention of multiple consecutive bunts stopped by Collins. This aspect of the legend apparently developed sometime between 1936 and Bob Stedler's campaign in 1943 to elect Collins to the Baseball Hall of Fame, when it was mentioned in numerous newspaper accounts.

While Collins established several fielding standards during the 1899 season, his hitting proficiency declined markedly from the prior two seasons, as his batting average dropped to .275. The Boston team's winning proficiency also declined, as Brooklyn captured the National League pennant in 1899. Boston finished in a distant second place, eight games behind Brooklyn and just one game ahead of third-place Philadelphia.

By 1899 Collins was firmly established as a fan favorite in Boston. As a serious, all-business ballplayer who could hit and field well, he was an on-the-field favorite. As an educated person with common-man roots, he was also an off-the-field favorite because he could socialize with people from all walks of life. Collins was cultured enough to mingle with high society while attending the theater, yet he was equally comfortable drinking a beer and smoking a cigar with manual laborers in a saloon. With the middle-ground Royal Rooter, Collins could chat about and offer opinions on a variety of topics, not just baseball; given his business education, he probably asked interesting questions about the businesses operated by these men. He loved to travel, thinking nothing of an eight-hour train ride to go home to Buffalo to spend a day there before returning to Boston for a ballgame the next day. One writer summarized the reasons for Collins' popularity:

> He is a credit to baseball. He made the most of an excellent education received in his home in Buffalo, is a good conversationalist and there are few people outside of baseball who can write as fine a hand. He is quiet in his manners and is a favorite everywhere. He plays the game, attends to his business, never kicks, never scowls if he is getting what he thinks is the small end, but does the best he can, and, if he does not succeed, takes the result like a man. Collins is a model all players would do well to follow.... Collins has shown that one does not need to be a rowdy or a kicker to achieve success on the diamond.[19]

Collins' deep hold in the hearts of Boston baseball fans was summed up by his father after he visited Boston during the summer of 1898 to watch his son play baseball, when Anthony Collins told a Buffalo reporter, "He's next to the mayor there" in popularity.[20] The quiet leadership qualities of independent-minded Jimmy Collins went completely unnoticed by the management of the Boston ballclub.

CHAPTER 9

Players Union Representative

During the 1899 and 1900 baseball seasons, money began to sour Collins' relationship with the Boston ballclub, which led to his highly publicized departure from the ballclub before the start of the 1901 season. After producing a lofty batting average and brilliant fielding in 1898, Collins had no success in convincing Soden to increase his salary for the 1899 season. Soden's position was quite simple. Collins was already one of six players at the $2,400 salary limit, along with his fellow infielders Fred Tenney, Bobby Lowe, and Herman Long, as well as catcher Marty Bergen and outfielder Billy Hamilton. Soden also couldn't pay Collins more than the two players already topping the maximum, team captain Hugh Duffy and star pitcher Charley Nichols.[1] The same stalemate occurred in his salary negotiation for the 1900 season, as Collins had little leverage to counteract Soden's position.

When Collins turned 30 years old on January 16, 1900, he was working the winter months at the city water department in Buffalo.[2] Unlike the run-of-the-mill ballplayer, Collins began actively planning for his life beyond baseball. He had earned a sizeable salary as a major league ballplayer the previous five summers — although less than he thought his value was — and augmented that with an offseason job easily obtained through his father's connections as a captain on the Buffalo police force. But Collins realized that such economic largesse was not going to last much longer, since he would slow down on the ball field in a few years and his father planned to retire soon.

Three days after his 30th birthday, Collins received a telegram that reinforced his growing concerns about the uncertainties of post-baseball life. His teammate Bergen had committed murder-suicide at his family's home in rural North Brookfield, Massachusetts. Bergen killed his wife and two young children on January 19 before taking his own life. It was a particularly grisly act, as Bergen crushed the heads of all three members of his family with the butt end of an ax, before cutting his own throat with a razor. Collins did not attend the burial service on January 20; the only baseball presence was teammate Hamilton, who lived in nearby Clinton, and Connie Mack, who lived in neighboring East Brookfield.[3]

Collins was a 30-year-old bachelor, one of the historically high percent of unmarried men across the country who were then changing the demographics of American society. As historian Howard Chudacoff writes in this seminal work *The Age of the Bachelor*, "American cities contained consistently large numbers and proportions of unmarried men" during the decades of the late nineteenth and early twentieth centuries, with the 1890 federal census recording the highest proportion of unmarried males over age 15 until the late twentieth century. Chudacoff cites data that 67 percent of men in 1890 between the ages of 15 and 34 — which included Collins — were unmarried and that of men born between 1865 and 1874 — again including Collins — nearly 40 percent were still single in the early 1900s when "according to the averages and to the norms of virtually every ethnic, religious, and racial group, they should have been married."[4] Collins was the norm, not the exception, for being 30, male, and unmarried in 1900.

The percentage of bachelors in 1890 was particularly startling for males born in the United States to foreign-born parents — which included Collins whose parents were both born in Ireland — "an extraordinary propensity to stay unmarried through their early and mid-twenties," according to Chudacoff. "For example, in Boston in 1890, while 46 percent of all males aged fifteen and over were unmarried, 70 percent of native-born men of foreign parents were single."[5] The rationale for so high a rate of unmarried men in the work force, as Chudacoff explains, was not for demographic (too few women) or economic (low earnings potential) reasons, but rather for cultural ones. In the late nineteenth century there were numerous leisure-time diversions to tempt bachelors with money in their pockets, such as dance halls, amusement parks, vaudeville theaters, saloons, pool halls, cafes and cabarets, and red-light districts. Men no longer needed to be married to have a fulfilling adult life outside of work, either socially or sexually.[6]

Collins had influences in his own life to cause him to embark on an extended bachelorhood. He observed older bachelors who never married, such as Jack Chapman, his manager in Buffalo, and Arthur Dixwell, the rabid baseball fan in Boston, who were well off and led happy lives. On the opposite side, his brother Henry had married in 1892 and struggled to support a wife and three children on his police patrolman's salary.

While in Boston during the baseball season, Collins lived in a lodging house like many unmarried men did at the time. Collins lived at the Hotel Langham, located on Washington Street about half a mile from the South End Grounds, along with several other Boston ballplayers including Chick Stahl, Vic Willis, Buck Freeman, and Bill Dinneen.[7] The residents at the Langham, which included single women (usually actresses) as well as men, were a sort of surrogate family to Collins during the baseball season. Stahl, in particular, was a constant companion of Collins, which exemplified the "intense and affectionate ties to male friends" that developed in a non-sexual, sibling-oriented manner among the vast number of bachelors in this era.[8]

At the Hotel Langham, Collins had access to meals in the dining room, and with no shortage of available male companions could patronize the many all-male retreats in the neighborhood, such as cigar stores, barber shops, bowling alleys, billiard parlors, and saloons. More high-end entertainment options, such as the theater, were available only a short distance away in the central business district, while vaudeville and other more sordid activities, e.g., prostitutes, were available slightly farther away in the Scollay Square district.

While his baseball income was more than enough to fuel a comfortable bachelor lifestyle, particularly during the offseason when he lived at his parents' house, Collins did have designs on eventually marrying and raising a family. He had also saved a portion of his earnings, which he could use to support his post-baseball, married future. During the snowy Buffalo winter of 1900, Collins decided to make an investment to take advantage of the explosive future growth he saw in the South Buffalo neighborhood. South Buffalo was growing because many Irish-Americans were leaving the inner city to move to the new neighborhood being developed south of Buffalo Creek.

Collins had kept his eye on this part of South Buffalo since the mid–1890s, when he visited his many relatives that lived on Elk Street and Perry Street, which were close to the Seneca Street bridge over Buffalo Creek that separated the heavily populated 13th Ward from thinly inhabited South Buffalo. After the city extended the Seneca Street streetcar line into South Buffalo to help create a "streetcar suburb," Collins closely observed the progression of development. His level of intelligence about the potential for the area increased when his brother Henry and family moved into the house of his mother-in-law Dorothy Arndt at 1173 Seneca Street, near the police station where Henry now worked.[9] Henry lived just a few houses down from William Fitzpatrick at 1266 Seneca Street. Fitzpatrick was a housing contractor that actively developed South Buffalo on the southern stretch of Seneca Street. It was Fitzpatrick and other Irish-American builders who established South Buffalo's Irish-American contours by buying the land from German-Americans and subdividing it into building lots. After his death in 1932, Fitzpatrick became known as the "builder of South Buffalo."[10]

Sometime before he left Buffalo in late March for spring training in North Carolina, Collins purchased a house lot in South Buffalo and made plans to build a rental unit on it. No longer would Collins work for someone else in the offseason; he was going to be self-employed as the landlord of his own real estate. If everything worked out well, he could also pursue this occupation in his post-baseball years.

Collins had his suspicions about the future of the aging Boston team, since six of the eight position players on Opening Day were age 30 or older: third baseman Collins (30), catcher Clarke (31), left fielder Duffy (33), center fielder Hamilton (34), second baseman Lowe (34), and shortstop Long (34). The two youngest players were Stahl (27) and first baseman Fred Tenney (28). This aging group of players was not about to repeat the team's first-place heroics of the past decade, when Boston had won five pennants. The Boston team careened to a fourth-place finish in the 1900 season.

With a slim chance of additional income from a first-place finish and little leverage to negotiate a higher salary than the implicit salary maximum that he was already being paid, Collins had no upside to staying with the Boston ballclub. Given the penurious ways of the Boston owners, he was likely to face a decrease in salary in the future years as age took its inevitable toll on his playing skills. This possibility was compounded by the increased leverage that ownership had now that the National League had contracted to eight ballclubs for the 1900 season from the dozen in the prior eight years. There were plenty of potential player replacements waiting in the wings, biding their time now with minor league ballclubs at lower salaries.

Collins' only chance for a pay increase was to become the team captain once Duffy no longer served in that capacity. Duffy got an extra $600 a year to serve as captain of the Boston team.[11] This income potential was quickly expunged, however, in the spring of 1900 when Tenney was named captain to replace Duffy, who had stepped down as an everyday ballplayer to scout minor leaguers to find new blood for the aging Boston team.

One ray of hope for Collins to get an increased salary was the formation of the Players Protective Association in June 1900. Showing some concern for his fellow ballplayers, Collins volunteered to be one of Boston's player representatives in the fledgling baseball players union, but he was also looking out for his own interests to improve overall salary prospects. The idea of banding together the ballplayers as a union surfaced in early April 1900, as an outgrowth of Chicago pitcher Clark Griffith's earlier agitations in 1897 and his conversations in 1899 with Samuel Gompers, the president of the American Federation of Labor, one of the country's largest labor unions.[12]

Chicago was a two-team city in 1900 for the first time since 1890 (when the Players League operated in addition to the National League team). The

9. Players Union Representative

Jimmy Collins, in the bottom row at the far right of this 1900 team photo, poses characteristically with his arms crossed. Disenchanted with Boston ownership because they wouldn't increase his pay above the unofficial salary maximum, Collins became a players union representative in 1900 to lobby for a change in compensation practices. Others in this team photo, from left to right, are: Top row: Bobby Lowe, Shad Barry, Chick Stahl, Hugh Duffy, and Bill Clarke. Middle row: Nig Cuppy, Buck Freeman, Billy Sullivan, Bill Dinneen, Vic Willis, and Ted Lewis. Bottom row: Jack Clements, Billy Hamilton, Charley "Kid" Nichols, Frank Selee (manager, holding mascot dog), Herman Long, Fred Tenney, and Collins (National Baseball Hall of Fame Library, Cooperstown, New York).

minor league Western League, headed by president Ban Johnson, had transferred its St. Paul franchise to Chicago and renamed itself the American League. This was the first stage of the transformation of the Western League into a second major league to compete with the National League. Charlie Comiskey ran the American League club in Chicago out of the city's South Side, part of the deal struck by Johnson to not encroach upon the National League club's turf, then on the city's West Side. By June 1900 Griffith, the union agitator, already had had some preliminary conversations with both Comiskey and Johnson about playing in their league for the 1901 season, when

Johnson expected to execute stage two of his plan to upgrade the circuit to major league status. The rise of the Players Protective Association helped to expedite Johnson's plan for the 1901 season, because the disgruntled National League ballplayers created a ready supply of talent for the new league (presuming, of course, that they could circumvent the reserve clause in their contracts that bound them to their National League teams).

The first meeting of the Players Protective Association was scheduled for Sunday, June 10, 1900, in New York City. The meeting was held on this date because it was one of the few times during the entire playing season that representatives from all eight teams could conceivably meet together. All four western teams — St. Louis, Chicago, Cincinnati, and Pittsburgh — were scheduled for Saturday and Monday games with the teams in the eastern cities — Philadelphia, Boston, New York, and Brooklyn — and all eight teams were idle on Sunday, since laws in Pennsylvania, Massachusetts, and New York prohibited the playing of baseball games on Sunday.

On Saturday, June 9, Chicago played Boston at the South End Grounds, where Griffith scattered ten hits (Collins was 1-for-4 at bat) to pitch Chicago to a 6–2 victory over Boston. Immediately after the game, Collins and Griffith left Boston to travel overnight to New York City to attend the Players Protective Association meeting, along with Duffy of Boston and Jimmy Callahan of Chicago. After taking a hack to Back Bay Station, they took a train to Providence that connected with a steamer that landed them at New York Pier at seven o'clock on Sunday morning. Upon landing in New York, Collins and the other players made their way to the Sturtevant Hotel, at Broadway and 29th Street in Manhattan, where the meeting was held.

During the six-hour meeting of the formative union, Collins listened to Gompers of the AFL talk about the benefits of unionization and the ballplayers discuss injustices meted out to them by the ballclub owners, such as being farmed out to a minor league rather than being released to cut their own deal with any team. There was no discussion of salaries. The twenty-three players in attendance agreed to form an association, although not to affiliate with the American Federation of Labor, and set the next meeting for July 29.[13] When Collins returned to the Sturtevant House eight weeks later for the second meeting, again there was no discussion of salaries, although the ballplayers did pick Chief Zimmer to be president of the union, adopted a constitution written by Harry Taylor, the union's new lawyer, and looked to make changes to the standard player contract.[14] Collins skipped the September 9 meeting, where the players targeted an upcoming National League meeting for Taylor to present the union's proposals.[15]

When the National League season mercifully ended for the Boston team on October 13, with an 8–3 loss in Philadelphia, the team finished in fourth place in the standing with a sub-.500 record of 66–72. Collins played the entire game — his last ever in the National League — going 1-for-4 at the plate and handling four chances at third base without error. His two putouts that day enabled Collins to establish a still-standing National League record for putouts by a third baseman in a single season. Collins finished the season with 252 putouts, topping the mark set by Williams of Pittsburgh the year before with 251 putouts.[16] In recent retabulations of game statistics, however, one putout has been dropped from Collins' original total; consequently, the putout record is now recognized as belonging to Collins with 251 putouts. As with the chances-accepted record he set in 1899, Collins continues to be recognized as the record holder for putouts, even though it appears that Williams should share the record with him.[17]

Before embarking on his new offseason occupation as a real estate mogul, Collins took a train from Philadelphia to get some rest and relaxation at a famous mineral-bath resort in Michigan. "Collins and Stahl started for Mt. Clemens, where they intend to hibernate for two or three weeks before turning up at home," Tim Murnane wrote in the *Boston Globe*, adding, "Collins has a new house to build, and will be very busy until spring."[18] Another business venture in the coming months would also occupy a large amount of time in the businessman-ballplayer's life.

CHAPTER 10

Jump to the American League

In October 1900 Jimmy Collins was not one of the original confederate ballplayers looking to secede from the National League to join the upwardly mobile American League for the 1901 season. While Ban Johnson focused on constructing the optimal combination of eastern and western cities to build a national footprint for the enhanced American League, he was also lining up several soon-to-be ex-patriots of the National League to be managers, such as Clark Griffith, Hugh Duffy, and John McGraw. The city of Boston was not even in the American League's plans at the time, as Johnson's upstart organization was barely starting to make inroads on the East Coast.

At the American League meeting in October, Johnson decided to add ballclubs in Baltimore and Washington, two territories that had been abandoned by the National League after the 1899 season, and possibly add another in a third eastern city. By early November, Johnson decided that the third city would be Philadelphia, which created a second ballclub in addition to Chicago that would directly compete with the National League. By Thanksgiving, the proposed major-league American League consisted of the four existing western ballclubs in Chicago, Cleveland, Detroit, and Milwaukee balanced with the three new eastern ones in Baltimore, Washington, and Philadelphia that complemented the existing Buffalo franchise.

With Buffalo still in the mix in the fall of 1900, it is conceivable that Collins had some preliminary discussions with Buffalo owner James Franklin, who had signed Collins to his first minor league contract in 1893, about joining the soon-to-be-major-league Buffalo ballclub. Any such conversation likely didn't get very far, though, given Collins' strong-willed personality and Franklin's autocratic style (e.g., he switched managers three times in 1900). It's tempting to conjecture what might have been had Collins joined his hometown Buffalo team for the inaugural American League season; however, like Milwaukee, any such Buffalo team probably would have had only a brief one-year tenure in the new major league. Both the Players Protective Association and the American League hoped to peacefully coexist with the National League ballclub owners. However, in December, representatives of both organizations were rebuffed by the National League magnates at their meeting in New York, when the owners discarded the Association's proposals and refused to talk to Johnson. United in their rejection by the National League, the two organizations joined forces to try to achieve their individual objectives. The Players Protective Association took the stance that its members shouldn't agree to terms with their National League employers until the owners acceded to the Association's demands.[1] Johnson basically declared war on the National League and began an active raid on its ballplayers (who were also members of the Players Protective Association) to sign contracts to play in the American League. The combination of actions gave the ballplayers new options for their baseball services, with an opportunity to achieve higher salaries than they were currently being paid. For Collins, Soden most likely sought his services for the 1901 season at the same rate as the prior season, $2,400 annually. The Association's position on signing contracts gave Collins ammunition to stall Soden, not that Collins was ever in a rush to agree to terms with the Boston ballclub.

After Johnson was snubbed by the National League owners at their meeting on December 12, he decided to exact revenge on the National League by locating a ballclub in Boston, and therefore drop Buffalo from the American League lineup. "They sent back word that I could stay there until hell froze over," Johnson later recalled about the snub, which precipitated the Great Baseball War, as the writers called it, and brought Boston into the American League picture. "I meant to put them on the defensive," Johnson remembered, "I did so by securing locations for baseball fields not only in Washington and Baltimore, the abandoned cities, but also in Philadelphia and Boston, where the Nationals were the sole occupants."[2] Charles Somers, a Cleveland coal magnate who was also American League vice president and owner of the Cleveland ballclub, helped initially support the Philadelphia and Boston ballclubs while Johnson searched for permanent owners. When a ballpark location was secured in Boston in mid–January, Buffalo was officially ousted at the league meeting in Chicago on January 28.

Exactly when and how Collins decided to leave the Boston Nationals and become the manager of the Boston Americans has never been completely explained. After he signed his contract to join the Boston Americans, Collins told the *Boston Post* that he first considered jumping when Duffy stopped by Buffalo in January on his way to the Players Protective Association meeting in Cleveland.[3] This seems far too late in the process.

After Johnson's snubbing at the National League meeting in mid–December, the generally accepted timeline of events progressed as follows: (1) the Huntington Avenue ballpark location was selected on January 17, (2) the Boston franchise was established under Somers' support on January 28, (3) rumors swirled in February that Collins would jump leagues, (4) Collins was announced as the manager on March 2, and (5) the Boston baseball fans (including the Royal Rooters) switched their allegiance from the Boston Nationals by the time of the Boston Americans' first game on April 26. However, Collins and the Boston baseball fans more likely entered the picture at the beginning of the accepted timeline, before the ballpark location was secured.

Lining up the support of the Boston baseball fans first would have created a better business case for Somers to put up the capital to operate the new Boston ballclub, since the implicit "build it and they will come" strategy was a huge risk for both Somers and Johnson — especially with the in-your-face decision to locate the new ballpark adjacent to the Boston Nationals' South End Grounds. Given the entrenched nature of Soden and the National League ballclub in the Boston community, Somers would have wanted some assurance that enough baseball fans would be in the stands to produce a reasonable level of revenue. Somers was too good of a businessman to take a huge financial risk in an unproven Boston ballclub without *some* underlying factors in his favor.

Three weeks before Johnson sent Connie Mack to Boston to scout out new locations for a ballpark, which led to the leasing of the Huntington Avenue Grounds location on January 17, Somers had journeyed to Boston in late December to talk with Arthur Irwin about leasing the existing ball grounds at Charles River Park.[4] Because Johnson had earlier that fall spurned Irwin's overtures to establish a Boston ballclub in Johnson's new league, Somers' talk with Irwin went nowhere. In fact, Irwin was working to establish another major league — the National Association — and was in competition with Johnson to see who could develop the best organization to rival the National League.

Somers was back in Boston on January 3, however, with a vague agenda "to show the men back of Irwin how strong is the American League and what a winner they could make of Boston."[5] Since Irwin was in Philadelphia at the time, Somers' agenda had nothing to do with leasing the ball grounds; more likely Somers was then in Boston to more fully assess the Boston baseball market. Since Hugh Duffy, one of the early confederates, was helping Johnson to establish a team in Boston (he helped Mack secure the Huntington Avenue ballpark location), Duffy easily could have set up Somers to talk with Arthur Dixwell, the long-time Boston baseball fan, to get a better understanding of the likely spectatorship situation for the new ballclub. Dixwell was a very key component to the establishment of the Boston ballclub in the American League, and thus Collins becoming its initial manager. Two significant pieces of evidence back this assertion: (1) Dixwell was the honored dignitary to shovel the first spade of dirt at the ground-breaking ceremony for the Huntington Avenue Grounds, and (2) Dixwell threw out the ceremonial first ball at the opening game at the Huntington Avenue Grounds.[6]

In January 1900 there were three distinct levels of baseball fans in Boston: the patrician Brahmins (like Dixwell), the middle-class Royal Rooters, and working-class Irish-Americans. All three groups would play a role in supporting the American League ballclub in Boston. Dixwell, part of the dwindling old guard of baseball patrons, was clearly disenchanted with the National League ballclub since he hadn't attended a ballgame the previous two years.[7] Dixwell, who had been part-owner of the Boston franchise in the ill-fated 1890 Players League, was certainly not averse to improving the status quo. Dixwell would have candidly told Somers that there was no love lost between Boston baseball fans and Soden and the other triumvirs that owned the Boston Nationals. If a popular player or two could be convinced to jump from the Nationals to the Americans, then most of the fans would very likely abandon Soden and support the new ballclub.

Somers banked on Dixwell's support for the new Boston ballclub to attract the allegiance of the Royal Rooters, which would then pull along the working-class Irish-Americans. Why didn't Somers just talk to John Fitzgerald or Charlie Lavis or another Royal Rooter? For one, that would be too low brow for Somers, and secondly, as a fellow social elite, Dixwell could be trusted to stay quiet. Any Royal Rooter would have been a risk as too talkative. One of the few overt newspaper accounts about Dixwell's role in the making of the new ballclub, before the ground-breaking ceremony in early March, was a *Chicago Tribune* note in late January that Dixwell had ordered 100 season books to the American League grounds in Boston "as evidence of his support of their cause."[8]

The discussion of a popular player to draw the allegiance of Boston baseball fans would have quickly led to Collins topping the list of spectator-favorite ballplayers among the Boston Nationals. It appears that soon after January 3, 1901, Collins was approached to consider switching leagues, probably by a telegram from either Dixwell or Duffy, and encouraged to talk with Somers. Both Dixwell and Duffy knew that Collins was motivated by money and very displeased with his recent salary negotiations with Soden, so he would be willing to take the risk of switching over to the Boston Americans. Duffy wasn't willing to take the Boston job, concerned about the reaction of Soden, and thus took the manager's position with the Milwaukee ballclub.

Somers might have even stopped in Buffalo to chat with Collins on his train ride back to Cleveland after his meetings in Boston on January 3.

Before Somers left Boston, he had concluded that Boston was good for the American League, as he told reporters, "We would like Boston to fill out an eastern half of the circuit," and thus drop Buffalo.[9] Back in Cleveland, Somers said that he had "looked over the baseball situation" in Boston and was pleased with the outlook.[10] Since Somers refused to talk about the ball grounds in Boston, his choice of the words "baseball situation" supports the assertion that he was investigating the broader aspects of baseball in Boston, such as the potential spectatorship, not really the ballpark aspect.

Duffy helped Mack secure the Huntington Avenue location for the new ballpark, and Mack signed the lease on January 17. Somers fronted the money for a lease on the former "Shooting the Chutes" attraction on the land located just west of the intersection of Massachusetts Avenue and Huntington Avenue. Only the tracks of the New York, New Haven, and Hartford Railroad separated the Huntington Avenue Grounds, as the ballpark would be called, from the neighbored South End Grounds. *The Sporting News* tipped Somers' hand a bit when it reported that "Roxbury sports can also get there quickly and without trouble," referring to the Royal Rooters who only had to travel a short distance from the South End Grounds on Columbus Avenue to watch the games of the Boston Americans.[11]

Collins seems to have made progress toward his decision to switch leagues before the new ballpark location was secured. On January 11, a "war strategy" committee of the Players Protective Association met in Buffalo, where Collins talked with Zimmer, Clarke, Jennings, and attorney Harry Taylor, according to a *Chicago Tribune* account of the meeting.[12] The big decision of the committee was to schedule an Association meeting in Cleveland on February 1. While not named in the newspaper article, Clark Griffith could have been there as well.

Decades later, Griffith took credit for convincing Collins to jump leagues: "That was the winter of 1900–01 when I was traipsing around the country helping to organize the American League and persuading good ball players to jump the National League. We wanted Collins, who was a star third baseman for the Boston Nationals, and to get him we promised to make him manager of the Boston American League club."[13] Griffith, though, didn't specify a time frame on his persuading of Collins. Griffith was the logical person to convey to Collins how the American League would be vastly different than the National League, as a foundation to discuss the merits of jumping to the new league. Johnson held in escrow 51 percent of each ballclub's stock as well as the ground leases on the ballparks; he also an option to buy each ballclub if the owner wanted to sell.[14] Not only could Collins be a manager, but former ballplayers could also be part-owners, as exemplified by Comiskey in Chicago and Mack in Philadelphia. The ownership opportunity intrigued Collins. The league was going to adopt the Players Protective Association proposals, which included stipulated contract lengths, so the open-ended reserve clause was not an issue. The clincher was that Collins could help topple the National League owners and inflict pain on tightwads like Soden.

Because people such as Mack and Griffith saw the leadership potential in Collins that escaped the attention of Soden and Selee, they convinced Johnson that Collins could handle the on-the-field duties of manager and quickly learn the other responsibilities. Player acquisition fell in the latter category, which wasn't an immediate concern in 1901 since Johnson and Somers were doing the bulk of the work to stock the Boston ballclub.

In late January Johnson shared his confidence publicly that the Boston ballclub would attract customers, saying, "I was very much surprised at the standing which the American League has with the baseball public of the East, particularly in Boston, which I was doubtful of our reception."[15] Johnson said, when asked about who would be the manager of the Boston team: "We have selected our manager, but cannot state at present who he is. Suffice it to say that he will be a man fully capable to fill the position."[16] Unless Johnson was completely bluffing, Collins had decided to seriously consider being the manager of the Boston Americans.

On January 28, Boston officially became a new franchise in the American League. At that league meeting Johnson also recognized the Players Protective Association and agreed to include the Association's proposals in the contracts of the American League ballplayers. These terms included abolishing player sales and farming systems, among other items, and more importantly a fixed-term reservation period (three to five years) rather than the National League's perpetual reserve clause.

After Collins attended the Players Protective Association meeting at the Hollenden Hotel in Cleveland on February 1, he met with Somers and verbally agreed to the broad outline of a deal to join the Boston ballclub. The exact initial terms have been lost to history, but they probably were for Somers to pay Collins $3,500 per year for three years to be the team's third baseman, captain, and manager, with the freedom to negotiate with other teams after that three-year period. This was nearly a 50 percent increase to his $2,400 salary for the 1900 season, and he would rise to be manager, not just a ballplayer. This $10,500 package was a key aspect of the deal for Collins, not just being the manager, so that he'd have sufficient capital to invest into his real estate business.

A week later, on February 9, a wire-service report was widely published across the country stating that Collins was "another man, who, it is claimed, has accepted the terms offered him" by the American League.[17] Collins responded to the rumor by carefully crafting his words. "There is absolutely nothing in the story," he told the Boston baseball writers, all the while knowing that he was referring to the report that he had *accepted* terms to join the new league, when he was still simply *negotiating* terms. "I think the wise players will stick to the men who have paid them good money till they see something better. They would have to show me a lot of money to make me throw manager Selee down. I have not signed yet, but I expect that this trouble will all be settled in a few days and then I will put my name to a contract in large letters."[18] This was a non-denial denial if there ever was one. Collins very coyly inferred that he'd be returning to the National League for the 1901 season, when he never said specifically on which ballclub's contract he would put his name in large letters.

The rumor about Collins jumping to the American League was coupled with the announcement that Napoleon Lajoie had signed with the Philadelphia Athletics. The National League owners complained vociferously, but didn't go to court immediately to enforce the reserve clause in their contracts, figuring that they had sprung a trap for Johnson. However, Johnson had ensnared the National League owners. It was a poker game and Johnson called the owners' bluff. It took six weeks before a court case was mounted by the National League owners. In the meantime, there was enough anger among the ballplayers that Lajoie's signing emboldened many to take the same step and others, like Collins, to hike the stakes. Throughout February the rumors persisted. In an article entitled "Somers May Get Collins," the *Washington Post* reported, "The denial of Jimmie Collins to the contrary, the impression prevails here that he will be seen with the American League when the season opens."[19] The *Chicago Tribune* wrote that "Collins is persistently rumored to be the new manager of the Boston club."[20] However, there was a different perspective in Boston, where "the officials of the Boston league club laugh at the idea of Collins playing elsewhere than [with] his old team."[21]

As rumors of his departure swirled, Collins told Tim Murnane of the *Boston Globe* that he "is with the league who gives him the most money, with a preference for the crowd who make it look the surest."[22] Collins demurely lay back in this negotiation, emulating the way he had observed the German-American businessmen in Buffalo do when they negotiated with his parents and other Irish-American customers. Be patient, maximize the customer's desire for your wares in order to be paid top dollar. He saw the German-Americans parlay that tactic into control of the political and economic establishment of Buffalo. The trick was not to alienate the other person, not make him beg, but still maintain the strong hand in the verbal arm wrestling. He had Somers convinced of his value to the American League ballclub.

Up until the final moment that he signed a contract with Somers, Collins was never upfront with Soden, initially indicating that he would re-sign with the Boston Nationals and then leading him on that he was considering offers from both ballclubs. While this was a low point on the integrity front for Collins, it was probably necessary for him to secure the best deal possible from Somers. It seems that Collins never bothered to negotiate with Soden, whose position was that the reserve clause in the current contract legally bound Collins to the National League ballclub for the 1901 season. Soden publicly said that he would pursue legal action against any ballplayer, e.g., Collins, if he signed with an American League ballclub. Collins used Soden's legal threat to get Somers to improve his offer to Collins, since he didn't want the risk of being a legal test case. Although Collins never divulged who his lawyer was in these contract negotiations, Harry Taylor would have been an obvious choice, given his expertise in player contracts from his work with the Players Protective Association (he developed the union's legal opinion that the existing reserve clause in player contracts had no legal value) and the location of his law office in downtown Buffalo. Somers agreed to add some personal guarantees concerning the payment of the salary amounts in the contract.

When it became obvious to Soden at the National League meeting in New York City on February 26 that Collins was seriously considering a jump to the American League, he dispatched his business partner Billings and manager Selee to meet with Collins in Buffalo to try to sign him for the 1901 season. The trip was a waste of time, since Collins was insulted that a smug Soden couldn't be bothered to make the trip to Buffalo to personally negotiate with him. At the February 28 meeting, Collins listened politely to Billings' pitch to increase his salary to $5,000, said he'd think about it, and then escorted Billings and Selee to the Buffalo train station.[23] Billings returned to Boston empty handed while Collins embarked for Cleveland to finalize his deal with Somers.

On March 2 in Cleveland, Collins signed a contract with Somers to be paid $3,500 a year for three years, with Somers's personal guarantee that the money would be paid. Collins' negotiation strategy had worked perfectly. Somers held a meeting with newspaper reporters to announce that Collins had signed to be manager of American League ballclub in Boston. "This is only the beginning. Similar announcements may be expected to follow shortly," Somers told the reporters who had congregated in his office. "We are not asking players to break any legal contracts with the National League. But we hold that the option clause in the National League contract is not valid, and therefore practically all players are free to sign American League contracts if they so desire."[24]

At the time, Collins wouldn't divulge his salary figure. "He declined to state the terms, but says the salary is far in advance of anything he has ever received," the *Buffalo Express* reported, adding, "with a block of stock in the new league thrown in."[25] Collins, indeed, was a nominal owner in the Boston ballclub, as confirmed by the ballclub's incorporation filing five months later.[26] The few shares of stock in the ballclub weren't worth much, perhaps $10, but symbolically the shares were priceless to Collins.

Peter Kelley of the *Boston Record*, writing under a nom de plume in *The Sporting News*, was the only Boston baseball writer to report a specific salary figure. "Collins accepted the chance from the Americans. It was the better offer by a good deal, and it is said that he will get $4,000 for the year's work as captain and manager. He has signed for three years and will get the same money each year. His salary is guaranteed by Somers, and should his services be conjoined he will be paid through a personal contract."[27] Jake Morse of the *Boston Herald* expanded on the guarantee aspect in his *Sporting Life* column: "Jimmy Collins says he has a cast-iron personal contract with Mr. Somers, at a fat salary, for three years. If the Boston League [club] succeeds in enjoining him from playing, he will, according to his contract, manage from the bench."[28] Because this $4,000 figure was the only specific salary figure published in contemporary sources, many later writers have cited it. However, later in life, Collins told the *Buffalo Evening News* that $3,500 was his annual salary in 1901.[29]

Somers agreement to a personal guarantee was a key point for Collins, since this provision made the venture virtually risk-free to him. Not only would the $10,500 in salary over three years go a long way toward expanding his real estate business, but it could also possibly allow him to retire as a ballplayer at the end of the three-year duration of his contract.

Before heading to Boston to begin his duties with his new employer, Collins returned to his home in Buffalo and sent the following telegram to every Boston daily newspaper:

> I have given the National League people my best efforts for several years past and often asked them for more money, knowing that I was worth it. But until now they have turned a deaf ear to all my requests, and so it is the same with many others. They tried now when it is too late with their liberal offers. I have not the least disparaging remark to make against Mr. Soden, he has always treated me nicely and paid every cent that his obligations called for, but I saw a chance to better myself and took it and I can name fifty others that will do the same thing.[30]

Just five days after the official announcement of Collins's signing, Dixwell was accorded the honor of shoveling the first scoop of dirt at the groundbreaking for the Huntington Avenue Grounds.[31] Collins was not at the groundbreaking ceremony. He was still in Buffalo, making deals with carpenters to erect a series of two-family houses on Seneca Street in South Buffalo. He didn't arrive in Boston until March 10, when he elaborated on his earlier statement about why he switched teams. "I've studied it over carefully and I do not think I have acted unwisely," was the standard line that Collins told baseball writers. "Of course we are all out to better our position in life and I saw what I believe a good chance for improvement and I took it."[32] Indeed, to ballplayer Collins, ever the businessman, the decision was a no-brainer.

Collins had no upside to staying with the Boston Nationals, with the lack of potential promotion to captain and the near certainty of never being named manager. He would always have been just a third baseman with that ballclub. A three-year guaranteed contract that would pay him his salary even if a court determined that he was required to stay with the Boston Nationals, combined with the opportunity to manage the Boston Americans, drove Collins to take a flyer with the new league. As a bonus, Collins received not only a few shares of stock in the Boston ballclub, but he also secured a long-lasting place in Ban Johnson's heart when he made the Boston venture a huge success.

Chapter 11

Rookie Manager

When Jimmy Collins arrived in Boston from Buffalo on March 10, 1901, to perform his first official acts as the manager of the Boston team in the upstart American League, he got off to a rocky start in his first foray into press relations in his new job.

When he was simply a ballplayer, Collins often made candid remarks to baseball writers that were routinely treated as background material and never printed in the newspaper. Therefore, in his first interview as the Boston manager, Collins didn't think twice about commenting about his friend Hugh Duffy that "we all know that Duffy's days a ball player are over" and he would have a tough time as manager of the Milwaukee team.[1] However, since Collins was now the manager and not just a ballplayer, writers could — and did — construe all of his comments to be public statements and thus fair game for publication. Collins was embarrassed when he read his comments in the newspaper the next day and tried to retract his words by sending messages to the writers he had talked with.

Collins was clearly a novice in his role as public face of the Boston team. "Jimmie Collins paid Boston a visit last week and made a very poor impression with the newspaper men," Tim Murnane wrote in the *Boston Globe*. "He seemed very new in the business and failed to keep several engagements made by himself without sending an explanation." Murnane also took Collins to task as being "not conscious that his remarks would appear in print" and then lamely trying to back away from those remarks "by sending a card to the papers saying he would follow Duffy's lead to the end of the earth."[2] Collins had to rapidly acclimate to being a press spokesman, since he obviously couldn't ask for pointers from Boston Nationals manager Frank Selee, whom he had just jilted to join the Boston Americans.

After his initial clumsiness in dealing with the press, Collins developed great rapport with five Boston writers: Tim Murnane of the *Globe*, Fred

O'Connell of the *Post*, Walter Barnes of the *Journal*, Jake Morse of the *Herald* (and correspondent for *Sporting Life*), and Peter Kelley of the *Record* (and correspondent for *The Sporting News*). The *Globe*, *Post*, and *Journal* covered baseball the most extensively in 1901 among the eight Boston dailies. The *Herald* and *Record* had basic coverage while the *Daily Advertiser*, *Transcript*, and *Traveler* had limited coverage. The Hearst publication, the *American*, didn't come onto the scene until 1904.

Fortunately, dealing with the press was one of the few management responsibilities that Collins actually had to perform in 1901, which allowed him to use the 1901 baseball season to ease into his twin roles as captain and manager though on-the-job training. Ban Johnson, the president of the American League, and Charles Somers, the owner of the Boston Americans, executed many of the manager's duties that Collins would otherwise have had to do, most importantly those involving ballplayer acquisition.

There wasn't a universally clear-cut delineation between the duties of captain and manager in 1901, as the two jobs often differed on each team. At the time, the captain of the team was a player who was responsible for many of the functions that today are solely performed by the manager or a coach. Typically, in 1901, the captain was responsible for informing the umpire of the team's lineup, batting order, and ground rules at the ballpark, dealing with the umpire regarding his calls on the field (the rules expressly prohibited the manager from doing this), and coaching baserunners within the designated "captain's lines" on the field. The manager in 1901 was typically in charge of player acquisition and dismissal; activities related to spring training; procurement of uniforms and equipment; and press relations. Determining the batting order and player lineup, especially the pitcher, could be performed by either role or shared; most often, the captain would decide the eight men to play the field positions and the manager would decide who would pitch.

Because the bulk of the Boston team needed to be put together before the announcement of the signing of Collins, Johnson and Somers did the vast majority of the player acquisition work for the 1901 season. Johnson made the league-wide decisions to allocate rights to various ballclubs to sign National League contract jumpers, based on his own preferences for competitive balance (or more accurately imbalance, as was the case), while Somers handled negotiations with individual ballplayers to stock the Boston team. Collins was no doubt involved with some of these early personnel decisions, particularly the signing of the two other Boston jumpers, outfielders Chick Stahl and Buck Freeman (who would play first base in 1901), and the initial decision by Boston pitcher Bill Dinneen to defect from the National League.[3]

With veterans Collins and Freeman at the corners of the infield, Somers completed the Boston infield with minor-leaguers Hobe Ferris and Fred Parent

Exemplifying his business attitude, Collins, in the bottom row, third from the right with his arms crossed, had this 1901 team photo of the Boston Americans taken with the ballplayers dressed in business attire rather than baseball uniforms. Others in this team photo, from left to right, are: Top row: Fred Mitchell, Ambrose Kane, and Tommy Dowd. Middle row: Charlie Hemphill, Fred Parent, Kit McKenna, Hobe Ferris, Win Kellum, Nig Cuppy, and Buck Freeman. Bottom Row: Ossee Schreckengost, Lou Criger, Larry McLean, Collins, Cy Young, and Chick Stahl (Boston Public Library, Print Department).

to play second base and shortstop, respectively. To flank center fielder Stahl in the outfield, Somers signed Charlie Hemphill and Cozy Dolan. At catcher, Somers secured veterans Lou Criger and Ossee Schreckengost to work with Dinneen and other pitchers to be acquired later.[4] After Collins officially joined the Boston Americans, Somers then brought in Tom Dowd to replace Dolan, who changed his mind about jumping to the new league, and pitchers Nig Cuppy and Win Kellum.[5] The pitching cornerstone for Boston was laid when Johnson decided that ace Cy Young should be allocated to the Boston team, possibly as a reward to Somers for his hard work to help develop the new league; Young signed to play with Boston in late March.[6] Three weeks later, Collins personally made his first major player acquisition when he coaxed former Boston Nationals pitcher Ted Lewis out of baseball retirement to temporarily forsake his college teaching position and pitch for the Boston

Americans.[7] Several other ballplayers were given tryouts at the team's spring training site in Charlottesville, Virginia.

Because Collins was both captain and manager, he made no attempt to distinguish between the two roles. Collins, though, preferred to be called "Captain Collins," not "Manager Collins," from the very first day of spring training and the Boston newspapers acceded to his preference. Perhaps it was more comfortable for Collins to first accept the mantle of the captaincy before bearing the weightier manager title. Or perhaps it was to honor his father, a police captain back in Buffalo. Whatever the reason, the decision established his leadership style as more "one of the men" than autocratic boss.

After leading his charges through three weeks of soggy spring practice in Charlottesville, Collins had to make his first big decision as manager — who to keep on the Boston roster for the opening game with Baltimore? With the eight regular position players fixed from the earliest days of the team's formation (Criger at catcher; Freeman, Ferris, Parent, and Collins in the infield; and Dowd, Stahl, and Hemphill in the outfield), Collins only needed to decide who to keep as pitchers and reserves. Collins decided to take six pitchers and two reserve players north with the team, to round out an initial 16-man squad. In addition to pitchers Young, Cuppy, and Kellum that Somers had signed, Collins added Fred Mitchell, Kit McKenna, and Ambrose Kane to the team (Lewis would join the team in Boston). The reserves were catcher Schreckengost and first baseman Larry McLean; Mitchell could also substitute in the infield if needed.[8]

Boston's first game in the American League was played in Baltimore on April 26, 1901, after two days of rain had postponed the opener originally slated for April 24. Boston lost, 10–6, as Collins put Kellum in the pitcher's box for Boston, rather than the veteran Young. Collins made Boston's first hit in the fourth inning, a double, and scored the team's first run a few moments later when Freeman singled him home. Collins had two hits in four at-bats in his first American League game. Interestingly, the umpire in this game was Joe Cantillon, who was an old friend of both Charlie Comiskey and Clark Griffith, the owner and manager, respectively, of the Chicago White Sox.[9] Cantillon would have a big impact on Collins' life in 1909. The now more press-savvy Collins said after the game, "Our boys will do better work after they get into their strides. You couldn't judge much by today's game."[10] Collins would quickly become the new media darling of the Boston newspaper corps.

Collins changed how baseball was reported in Boston newspapers. When the Boston Nationals had been the only team in town during the previous ten years, baseball writers for the several Boston dailies had to deal with aloof manager Frank Selee or condescending owner Arthur Soden. The quiet but friendly Collins was able to connect with the newspapermen, especially as a player-manager who could better explain the happenings on the baseball diamond. Collins also made it a point to talk to the reporters after the game had concluded, whereas Selee only infrequently offered commentary and Soden rarely attended the ballgames.

As Collins adjusted to his new role as the face of the ballclub — and he was *the* face, since Somers only twice came to Boston before the season-ending games in September — he soon exploited the newspapermen to further his own self-promotion. Collins, ever the businessman, knew the *Globe* and the *Post* catered to lower-income readers (like working-class Irish-Americans), unlike their morning competition the *Herald* and the *Journal* that had an upscale readership, so he especially sought out writers Murnane and O'Connell to feed them commentary. Workers who couldn't sacrifice 25 cents to see a ballgame could afford two cents to buy a newspaper to read about the ballgame. As the baseball reports helped to sell more newspapers, companies spent more money to advertise in the newspaper, which drove the newspaper profits up and created more demand for baseball material to print in order to sell even more newspapers. Soon Murnane and O'Connell, as well as the other Boston baseball writers, were pandering to Collins to capture his thoughts.

The timing of Collins' switch to the American League and coincident synergy with the newspapers was impeccable from a cultural perspective, as his move intersected with the rise of Irish-American politicians in Boston. John Fitzgerald, a rabid Boston baseball fan and member of the Royal Rooters, was a Congressman in Washington. Closer to home Patrick Collins became the second Irish-American mayor of Boston in the December 1901 election. During the four years from 1902 to 1905, there were two men named Collins who were the toast of Boston among the city's Irish-American citizens: the mayor and the baseball manager. Improvements in transportation at this time also enabled more spectators to travel longer distances from outside Boston to attend ballgames and want to buy a Boston newspaper to read about the ballgames. The advent of the interurban trolley connected outlying smaller cities among each other, which increased access to rail lines into the Boston center city. These new rail routes enabled a whole new segment of society — businessmen in outlying towns and burgs — to more easily come into Boston to see a ballgame. In June 1901 the Boston Elevated Railway opened, which was an aboveground trolley line that connected to the South Station railway terminal and more easily allowed these new suburban spectators to get to the ballpark. Automobile transportation also took hold among upper-income patrons, as a few "horseless carriages" transported spectators to the ballpark to supplement those arriving by horse-drawn carriages and the legions of fans who arrived via electric trolley cars.

The Huntington Avenue Grounds, the home of the Boston Americans, seated about as many spectators as the South End Grounds did for the games of the Boston Nationals. The Huntington Avenue Grounds had a grandstand for 2,400 fans and bleachers on the right- and left-field sides that each sat about 3,000, for a total seating capacity of 9,000 people. The field was much larger, especially down the foul lines. The distance to the right-field fence was 350 feet down the foul line (about 100 feet longer than at the South End Grounds), while the similar distance to the left-field fence was 320 feet. It was 530 feet to the center-field fence. Trolley cars ran directly to the Huntington Avenue Grounds, and crosstown streetcar lines unloaded passengers at the nearby corner of Huntington and Massachusetts Avenue.[11]

Besides its more spacious playing field, the Huntington Avenue Grounds cost less for people to enter to watch a ballgame than did the South End Grounds. Admission to the Boston Americans games was 25 cents, half the 50-cent price to see the Boston Nationals, as Somers banked on a pent-up demand among Bostonians to watch quality baseball at a cheaper price than Soden offered.[12] Murnane of the *Boston Globe* thought the strategy was sound: "I find here in conservative Boston a great number of well-wishers for the American League. The newcomer [ballclub] is sure to receive good support at the start."[13] Murnane's reasons included the lower admission price and "well-located grounds" directly on a trolley line.

The difference in admission charges between the Huntington Avenue Grounds (25 cents) and the South End Grounds (50 cents) reflected the different nature of the spectators that each ballclub attempted to attract to the ballpark. The difference in marketing can be readily seen in side-by-side advertisements in the May 10, 1901, edition of the *Boston Globe*. The Americans advertised the 25-cent price for admission, with an additional charge for a reserved seat in the grandstand; tickets could be purchased at Wright & Ditson's, a sporting goods store located downtown that was owned by former ballplayers George Wright and John Morrill. The Nationals didn't identify the price, either for admission or for a reserved seat; tickets could be purchased at Appleton & Bassett's, an upscale fishing tackle store. While the Americans presumed patrons would come to the ballpark by public trolley, the Nationals explicitly advertised "bicycles checked free."

The first American League game at the Huntington Avenue Grounds was played on May 8, 1901, when 11,500 people packed the grounds to watch Cy Young and the Boston Americans defeat Nap Lajoie and the Philadelphia Athletics, 12–4. Captains Collins and Lajoie received the loudest ovations from the crowd when they met with umpire Haskell to discuss ground rules just before the start of the game. At home plate, Collins was presented with flowers, a wreath of roses and a five-foot-high horseshoe of jonquils and mixed flowers. "The flowers slightly expressed the great regard the lovers of baseball both in the profession and out have for the lad from Buffalo," the *Boston Globe* described the ceremony, who is "the greatest third baseman of this or any other age, and as unassuming as the little sprig of maidenhair fern that trailed from the flowery horseshoe." Besides owner Somers and Arthur Dixwell, who threw out the first ball, Murnane noted that spectators included "clergymen, business men, professional people, ex-ballplayers, old-time fans, and an army of fresh recruits" who came from Bangor, Maine, to Newport, Rhode Island, and many cities in between.[14]

The huge crowd at the Huntington Avenue Grounds was the first of many in 1901 for the American League team. While Soden had the baseball world convinced that he had an unassailable monopoly in Boston, the Nationals were a sandcastle that collapsed upon the incoming tide of the Americans. Soden vastly underestimated his National League team's popularity with middle-class Boston baseball fans, and completely ignored the working-class ones. When the Nationals were the only game in Boston, baseball fans had to patronize the South End Grounds to see a major league ballgame. Given a competitive option when the Americans were formed, the middle-class baseball fans jumped and the working-class ones felt wanted. As it turns out, the middle-class fans were barely tolerant of the Nationals, with many actually despising Soden and his ballclub. On June 19 Soden abandoned the standard 50-cent admission charge and lowered the price to 25 cents to match that of the Americans, following another box-office drubbing in head-to-head competition on the Bunker Hill Day holiday on June 17. The Americans drew 10,210 fans to their afternoon game, while just 1,500 fans paid to see the Nationals.[15] "Boston baseball fans have a long score to settle with Soden," the *Chicago Tribune* commented on Soden's action. "It's even betting that they will not be tempted back from Jimmy Collins and his mates, to whom they have sworn allegiance."[16]

In addition to failing to anticipate the changing nature of baseball fans, Soden was also blinded by the inventor's obsessive belief in his creation, the reserve clause, which he had conceived in 1879, to protect his investment in the ballplayers, which formed part of what Soden believed was an indestructible monopoly. However, as seen in the Lajoie case, the reserve clause was not as airtight as the National League owners were led to believe. The April 1902 decision in the Lajoie case only restricted him from playing for any other ballclub in the state of Pennsylvania, the site of his 1900 contract with the Philadelphia Phillies. While the reserve clause precluded him from playing for the Athletics in the American League, it didn't stop him from playing with Cleveland in the state of Ohio. Lajoie just couldn't play in Cleveland's road games in Philadelphia. Soden did initially seek legal counsel to determine the efficacy of enforcing the clause against Collins, but after the 1901 season the damage was already done. Far more fans attended ballgames at the Huntington Avenue Grounds than went through the turnstiles at the South End Grounds. Soden turned his efforts instead to negotiating a peace treaty with the new league to resolve his problems.

Collins piloted the Boston Americans to a strong finish in the American League standings for the 1901 season. After winning 15 of 16 games in a June streak, the team bolted from fifth place into first place. Although Chicago recaptured first place in July, Boston remained in second place throughout August and September as Collins chased the White Sox, managed by Clark Griffith, who the previous winter had recruited Collins to jump leagues.[17] Collins enjoyed the relative freedom of running the team without an ever-present boss, as Somers stayed most of the season in Cleveland. Even when Somers was present, most often at a road game in Detroit or Chicago, he let Collins run the team without interference. One time, when a reporter asked Somers about the chances of Boston winning the game he was attending, Somers replied: "Really I don't know a thing about it. You will have to ask Collins about that. He told me the club was good, and what he doesn't know about ball players is not in Reach's guide or Spalding's manual."[18]

By August Somers was divesting himself from ownership in the Boston ballclub. On August 12, 1901, the Boston ballclub of the American League was incorporated under the laws of New Jersey with authorized capital of $100,000. There were only three named shareholders: James Collins, Joseph Pelletier, and Edward Hearn.[19] Somers was not named in the filing, since, it was later learned, coincident with the filing, he had sold the majority of his stock to Henry Killilea, one of the current owners of the Milwaukee ballclub that was managed by Hugh Duffy. Because Ban Johnson couldn't allow the actual investors to be publicly named in the summer of 1901, he arranged for two Bostonians (Pelletier and Hearn) to be the straw investors for the filing along with Collins who held just a few shares. For the last several weeks of the 1901 season, Collins secretly corresponded with Killilea by letter or telegraph about any baseball matters that required his attention.[20]

On September 19, there was an unanticipated day off in the baseball schedule. All major league baseball games were cancelled that day in respect for the funeral of President William McKinley, who had died on September 14 after being shot by an assassin on September 4 at the Pan-American Exposition in Buffalo. On September 15, McKinley's body was moved in a funeral procession to Buffalo City Hall, when he lay in state.[21] Collins' father, Captain Anthony Collins, was likely on duty along with all members of the Buffalo police force to help control the crowds that lined up to pay their respects to the former president.

Chicago had already clinched the American League pennant before the McKinley day of mourning. Boston finished in second place, four games behind first-place Chicago, as Chicago finished its season on the road in Boston. Somers was in Boston for the Chicago games, where he signed most of the Boston players to contracts for the 1902 season.[22] The Chicago team stayed in town to participate in a benefit game for the Boston players on September 30. Close to 3,000 spectators watched Boston defeat the American League champions, 7–5, as each Boston player received $60 from the net receipts of the game.[23]

Following the benefit game, Collins' team went on a short tour for four games north and west of Boston. The tour started out in nearby Lynn, where Boston defeated a local all-star team, proceeded to New Hampshire with a victory in Manchester and a loss in Nashua (where Stahl pitched in relief of Mitchell), and concluded with a win in Greenfield, Massachusetts, where the teams transposed their batteries with Cy Young pitching for Greenfield and Dillon hurling for Boston.[24] With attendance at the four games varying from 600 to 2,000, the players netted an additional $50 to go with the $60 from the benefit game in Boston.[25]

All the extra work as captain and manager didn't impact Collins' play on the field; as a matter of fact it seems to have enhanced it. Collins compiled a .332 batting average to be one of the top five hitters in the league. Collins was also among the leaders in hits (187), doubles (42), triples (16), and total bases (279). He also continued to draw rave reviews from the baseball writers about his fielding play at third base.

After the season Collins jettisoned outfielders Dowd and Hemphill, and planned to play Freeman in right field for the 1902 season. He acquired outfielder Pat Dougherty from Jim O'Rourke, who ran the Bridgeport ballclub of the Connecticut League, and with Somers' assistance (as one of the owners of the Cleveland ballclub) traded Schreckengost to Cleveland in exchange for Candy LaChance to take Freeman's spot at first base.[26]

In mid–November, after Somers essentially consummated the LaChance deal with himself in Cleveland, Collins left Buffalo to travel to Waterbury, Connecticut, to sign LaChance to a 1902 contract. After negotiating the deal with LaChance, Collins took the train to Boston to finalize the paperwork with the club's business manager. Unfortunately, Collins had to leave immediately upon his arrival in Boston to head back to Buffalo, since a telegram awaited him that his father, Anthony, was very sick. To remove some calloused skin on the heel of his right foot, Anthony Collins had used a penknife. Besides lifting the dried skin, he also drew some blood with the knife, which led to blood poisoning. There was a potential for losing the foot, but doctors lanced the foot to drain the fluid to avoid amputation.[27]

While Collins was traveling through upstate New York in mid–November, he stopped at Syracuse to visit with his former teammate, pitcher Bill Dinneen, who was disenchanted with the state of the Boston Nationals team, especially with the recent departure of manager Frank Selee. Collins had no problem convincing Dinneen to join the Boston Americans for the 1902 season.[28] After securing Dinneen's name on an American League contract, Collins had his lineup established for the Boston Americans to make a serious run at first place during the 1902 season and then capture pennants in 1903 and 1904.

CHAPTER 12

Soft-Spoken Leadership

The secret that Henry Killilea was the majority owner of the Boston Americans ballclub went public on January 28, 1902, with an announcement from his office in Milwaukee. Charles Somers remained the nominal president of the ballclub. Killilea could now go public with his secret ownership of the Boston ballclub, as he and his brother had recently sold their ownership of the new St. Louis ballclub in the American League that had been transferred there from Milwaukee. In early February, Jimmy Collins went to Chicago to meet with Killilea and American League president Ban Johnson to discuss matters related to the change in ballclub ownership. After the meeting, Killilea announced that Collins "will have full charge of the team, with authority to sign or release whatever players he desires."[1] Now that he had full responsibility as team manager, Collins took the opportunity to renegotiate the salary in his contract for the 1902 season up to $5,000 from the $3,500 amount stipulated in his original three-year contract with Somers.[2]

By now Collins was actively using his baseball income to fund his real estate development activities in Buffalo, which was then the nation's eighth largest city (Boston was the fifth largest). The $1,500 increase in his 1902 salary provided an ample amount for Collins to invest in the construction of another housing unit to add to his real estate holdings in the growing South Buffalo neighborhood. Based on housing prices at the time of $2,500 to $3,000 for an existing house in that area, Collins was probably building a new house from scratch at an outlay of $2,000 or so, with $500 for the lot of land and around $1,500 for material and labor. As a novice housing contractor, Collins likely fronted the cash to build a house, then secured a mortgage from a bank to take money out of the property to reinvest in another. At best Collins could get a mortgage for 50 percent of the value of the house, since a 50 percent downpayment was the minimum level in those days for a bank to issue a mortgage loan for the remainder of the house's value. Mortgages at the time also were only normally issued for a length of three to five years, with the principal due in a balloon payment at the end of the period (the homeowner only had to pay interest on the loan during that period).[3] With these types of restrictions, homeowners had to have confidence that they could either repay the principal amount at the end of the term, or still be creditworthy enough to be able to refinance the mortgage. If not, the bank would then institute foreclosure proceedings, in which case the property owner could lose some or all the money he had put into the house.

Collins initially was only able to secure short-term mortgages on his properties, as indicated by the published listings of deeds and mortgages recorded at the Erie County Court House that were often printed in the *Buffalo Express*. In September 1902, a published mortgage discharge of "James J. Collins to Buffalo Saving Bank" showed that the original mortgage had been granted just two years earlier.[4] For larger mortgage amounts, or longer terms, Collins used his mother as a co-signer, based on a September 1902 listing for a $3,500 mortgage by "Alice Collins and one to Buffalo Savings Bank, corner of Pomona Place near Seneca Street."[5] Since Collins did own a three-story, multi-family property at that location, the anonymous "and one" in the mortgage listing appears to be Collins.[6]

Collins was quite confident that his investments in South Buffalo real estate would not only provide a solid income stream from their rents but also increase in value. Collins and other developers were willing to take the risk of building houses in this isolated section of Buffalo because they believed there would be demand for additional housing, especially by Irish-Americans in the First Ward who saw Polish and other Eastern European immigrants arrive in the city and desire housing in low-cost areas such as the First Ward. In addition to streetcar transportation that encouraged people to move into the neighborhood, the Catholic Diocese of Buffalo established a new parish in the area, which culminated in the building of St. Theresa's Church in 1899 at 1974 Seneca Street. Mount Mercy Academy, a Catholic high school, was constructed in 1904, as well as a nearby Catholic hospital affiliated with the Sisters of Mercy. Work opportunity was provided by the Lackawanna Steel Company, which announced in 1899 that it was relocating to Buffalo from Scranton, Pennsylvania, and established a huge plant in 1902 on the western edge of South Buffalo in the town of West Seneca.

William Fitzpatrick and the other housing developers in South Buffalo, including Collins, predominately built houses that were known as a "Buffalo double," a utilitarian housing unit designed for working-class people that had two flats, one atop the other. The Buffalo double closely resembles a single-family home, except that there is often an upper porch on the second story of the building.

By 1900, Fitzpatrick had focused on building up South Buffalo on the southern end of Seneca Street, near Cazenovia Park, the Frederick Law Olmstead–designed public oasis on the city's border with the town of West Seneca. Meanwhile, the land on the northern portion of Seneca Street remained largely undeveloped. This area of South Buffalo was a neck of land surrounded on three sides by water (Buffalo Creek on the north and east, with Cazenovia Creek on the west), which was plagued by persistent flooding. Since housing lots in the flood plain were inexpensive, this is where Collins built his houses since he believed the land was undervalued. He considered the risk of continued flooding on this land to be slight, since the city of Buffalo was on the verge of allocating money to straighten the two creeks and rectify the flooding issue. Collins focused on developing properties near the junction of Seneca Street and Pomona Place, which was about midway between the Seneca Street bridge to the north and St. Theresa's Church to the south. His brother Henry, who lived in one of his houses at 1828 Seneca Street, became Collins' rent collector and property overseer.[7] As a policeman, Henry was an effective agent to deter potential deadbeat renters from reneging on their payments.

Collins was successful as a baseball manager because he extended his general contracting skills, where he had to depend on highly skilled, motivated workers to build well-constructed houses for him, to his responsibilities on the baseball diamond. In this fashion, Collins adopted the same general philosophy that his former manager, Frank Selee, had used during his five years playing for the Boston Nationals: find good ballplayers and let them do their jobs without interference.

Because Collins was viewed as a "quiet, unostentatious chap" who always wore a smile, many considered him ill-equipped to be either captain or manager of a team during an era when intimidation of both players and umpires was considered de rigueur for success on the baseball diamond.[8] His soft-spoken attitude, though, was exactly one of the reasons for his success.

Because he didn't often lose his temper and argue unnecessarily, umpires generally respected Collins, which likely gave his team more than its share of the close calls. But Collins was not bashful about disputing an umpire's call when he thought the call was clearly inaccurate, and had his share of ejections. For example, after he was thrown out of the game on June 24, 1902, for disagreeing with the umpire, Johnson later suspended him for three days for his outburst. As Jake Morse characterized the situation in his column in *Sporting Life*, "When Jimmy Collins enters a protest there is always good and sufficient reason."[9] Collins used his soft-spoken approach to elevate his team's play.

Rarely did Collins raise his voice with his players or even verbally criticize their play. "I overlook errors when I know the men are trying hard, for good

As a leader "among" men more than a leader "of" men, player-manager Jimmy Collins (left), the third baseman, poses with the other three members of the 1901 Boston Americans infield, from left to right, Fred Parent, Hobe Ferris, and Buck Freeman (Boston Public Library, Print Department).

players make mistakes," Collins once explained his approach to not highlighting player errors. "In fact, they will make more errors than the weak players for the simple reason that they will take longer chances, and often the game calls for longer chances."[10] Collins wanted his players to be as aggressive as he was in fielding balls, since he committed many errors on balls that other third basemen would not reach.

Because he was able to motivate his players through his on-the-field activities as a third baseman, he was more of a leader "among" men than a leader "of" men. As pitcher Cy Young once described the managing style of Collins, "He did not rule his men with a rod of iron."[11] Chick Stahl was less oblique in his description: "Collins has been loyal to his players, fought for them, and is simply one of us."[12] It was that "we're all in this together" attitude that enabled Collins to win two American League pennants as player-manager and lead his team to victory in the first modern-day World Series. "The success of the club has been largely due to Collins on account of the hold he has upon the players," Morse explained of those championship teams. "To a man they think the world of him and would go through fire and water for him."[13] Stahl called the magic "a system combined with open personality," in comments after the 1903 World Series victory. "The boys on the Boston team swear by Collins," Stahl said. "It is to this fact — the confidence which he enjoys of the entire team — which has made the teamwork of the Bostons a by-word in the baseball world during the past year."[14] The key to Collins' success in creating successful teamwork was his ability to simultaneously be "one of the boys" yet command respect as the boss, "to compel them to obey him implicitly without argument" as if his word was the law.[15]

Beyond his "everyman" approach to leadership, Collins was at the core a master strategist, which was the real catalyst to his winning of championships. "Collins, like all great leaders, whether in sports, business, or politics, is a thinker," baseball writer Fred O'Connell characterized Collins.[16] But Collins did not overthink a relatively simple sport. "I pass up the sign business, only working with just enough to make the plays. Too many signs are disastrous," Collins explained his hands-off approach. "There is nothing like hitting the ball and being alive to the other man's stick work. By working together a team becomes familiar with each other's play, and therein lies the strength of a ball team."[17] In those few instances when Collins decided to call for a hit-and-run or a double steal while on the coaching line, he used even fewer overt signs to communicate with his players. "It takes the closest kind of observation to detect a signal," O'Connell wrote about the casual nature of Collins' system. "A quick move of the arm, a turn of either foot, or a shake of the head tells the baserunner or batsman what he is expected to do."[18]

Offsetting these positive attributes as a manager, Collins had several flaws that didn't surface as a concern until the 1905 and 1906 seasons. These leadership deficiencies would have been observed much earlier in his tenure as manager had Collins not been given a built-in advantage by Ban Johnson to succeed as manager of the Boston Americans. Johnson arranged for better ballplayers to be acquired by the Boston, Chicago, and Philadelphia ballclubs than those he allocated to the other five clubs, to ensure that these three teams had the best chance to win the battle for spectators in the competition with their crosstown National League rivals.[19] Clark Griffith and Connie Mack enjoyed a similar advantage as managers of the Chicago and Philadelphia teams, respectively. It was no coincidence that Boston, Chicago, and Philadelphia were the only teams to capture an American League pennant during the first six years of the league's existence, with each team winning two titles in that time frame.

The biggest knock on Collins has been that he stayed too long with veteran players and failed to adequately mix in younger players to prepare the team for the future. The most critical observers say that Collins was resistant to change. This attitude surfaced in late 1901 when owner Somers was signing numerous minor-league players to give Collins enough bodies to sort through in the spring of 1902, and even try out a few in the waning days of the 1901 season. Collins was definitely resistant, saying, "I know that I have all I want of that style of player, and the only ones that I will favor are the tried men who know something about the game."[20] Reluctance is a Collins trait that can be seen in the few photographs of Collins that exist — he is most often shown with his arms crossed while other players have their arms in a more relaxed position (see photo in Chapter Eleven). This is a classic signal of body language that indicates defensiveness, impatience, or reluctance. As a mature businessman, Collins did not take a lot of chances unless he saw the potential reward for the risk taken. This was a personality trait that hindered not only his success as a baseball manager but also his future success as a business entrepreneur.

Collins' problem with handling aging ballplayers was compounded by his weakness in talent evaluation. When he couldn't identify a player prospect with a strong likelihood of success, Collins stayed with the veteran player rather than experiment with other possible players. Much of this weakness stemmed from his inability to build an effective network of contacts to acquire new talent. In the days before minor league teams were farm clubs for the major league teams, having scouts and relationships with minor league managers, along with a dose of luck, was essential to locating new ballplayers. Collins was not completely inept at finding new ballplayers, just inefficient and ineffective. He used contacts with his former teammates on the Boston Nationals to secure two ballplayers in the fall of 1902: outfielder John O'Brien who played for Hugh Duffy in Milwaukee and pitcher Norwood Gibson who played for Charley Nichols in Kansas City. Both turned out to be significant role players for Collins during the 1903 season.

Before Collins led his team through spring training in Augusta, Georgia, to get ready for the 1902 baseball season, the American League ballclub owners voted to increase prices for certain seats at the ballpark to capitalize on the popularity in 1901 for baseball "at popular prices," i.e., the low 25-cent admission fee. At a league meeting in early March, the ballclub owners approved a proposal to mandate three levels of seating at the ballpark. While the price for an uncovered bleacher seat remained the same at 25 cents, the price for a pavilion seat (bleachers under a roof) was set at 50 cents and a grandstand seat (chair seat under a roof) was increased to 75 cents. At the Huntington Avenue Grounds, the third-base bleachers were transformed into pavilion seats to collect an additional 25 cents from each customer, while the first-base bleachers remained in the sun and still priced at a quarter. Admission to the grandstand was now an additional 50 cents beyond the 25 cents admission price, up from an extra quarter in 1901.[21] The price increase didn't deter many customers from buying a ticket to the Huntington Avenue Grounds to watch Collins and the Boston Americans, as crowds packed the stands for most ballgames in 1902.

Collins had an improved team in 1902. He had six holdovers from the 1901 lineup, and had secured Dougherty and LaChance to fill in for the departed Dowd and Hemphill. Although Ted Lewis had left baseball to become a college professor, Cy Young was still the team's mainstay at pitcher and Collins had convinced Bill Dinneen to jump from the Boston Nationals to join him with the Americans. In July Collins acquired Tom Hughes from the Baltimore ballclub, in the wake of John McGraw's departure there as owner and manager, who became a third regular for Boston in the pitcher's box.

With Killilea an absentee owner ruling the ballclub remotely from his office in Milwaukee, and Somers a president in name only, Collins had an unfettered hand to direct the Boston Americans into pennant contention in 1902. The team stayed close to the top of the standings, being within five games of first place for most of the season and within three games for long stretches. As late as Labor Day, Boston was one game behind first-place Philadelphia, but just couldn't muster the gusto to take over first place. When Collins strained a tendon in his leg on August 20 and didn't play in the vast majority of games for the remainder of the season, the team stumbled to third-place finish, six and a half games behind the champion Philadelphia Athletics piloted by Connie Mack.

Although Killilea never attended a ballgame in Boston during the 1902 season, he did take in the team's games in Chicago during the summer. In mid-August Killilea traveled to Chicago to meet with Collins to sign all the Boston ballplayers to contracts for the 1903 season, to forestall attempts by National League teams to sign one or more of Collins' charges. "The players all seem anxious to play with Jimmy Collins in Boston," said Killilea. "It was an easy matter to come to terms with all the men."[22]

Two weeks earlier Collins had been personally solicited by his leadership mentor Frank Selee, who was then the manager of the Chicago team in the National League, to play for him again in 1903. While in Boston, Selee met Collins and Chick Stahl at their seasonal residence at the Hotel Langham to try to convince them to return to the National League. When Selee told them that money was no object, Collins reportedly smiled and replied that "he didn't think Selee had money enough to get him to Chicago." Collins told Tim Murnane of the *Boston Globe*: "Selee made me no offer and the chances are that he will not, after the talk we had. We are doing pretty well here, and there is nothing like being on the popular side."[23] The episode with his former manager at the South End Grounds convinced Collins to take defensive action with his other players and be even more aggressive in trying to poach more players from the National League.

After the 1902 season concluded, Collins met in Chicago with Henry Killilea, Ban Johnson, and Clark Griffith in mid–October as part of a group to map out the details of stocking a new team in New York to compete with the National League team there now run by American League ex-patriot John McGraw.[24] Griffith would become the manager of the New York Highlanders, as the new team would be called, for the 1903 season. At that October meeting, the group met with Willie Keeler, former star with the old Baltimore team who was now playing for Brooklyn. Collins was not only helpful in convincing Keeler to jump to the new American League team, but he was also instrumental in persuading old teammate Herman Long to jump to the New York team.

The 1902 season was the last spectacular year for Collins as a ballplayer, as he finished with a .327 batting average and was one of the leading third basemen with a .961 fielding average.[25] While he continued to perform as a third basemen in Boston for four more years, henceforth, Collins focused more on the leadership functions of his job and his activities to improve the stature of the American League, which secured him the everlasting thanks of Ban Johnson.

CHAPTER 13

Champions of the American League

Two developments in 1903 solidified the great admiration of American League president Ban Johnson for Jimmy Collins as the leader of the Boston Americans, to the extent that one baseball writer wrote that Johnson would "never forget the loyalty of Collins" for his efforts in joining the new league, resisting inducements to return to the old league, and helping to make the American League a huge success.[1]

The first development was the peace conference between the two leagues in January 1903, following the 1902 season when the American League ballclubs in Boston Chicago, Philadelphia, and St. Louis all successfully outdrew and outperformed their crosstown National League rivals. The two leagues forged the first National Agreement at a meeting in Cincinnati to respect each other's player contracts (including enforcement of the reserve clause, since the Players Protective Association had all but disbanded by then), provide for a governance structure to encompass both major leagues and the minor leagues, and recognize the entrance of a New York team into the American League for the 1903 season.[2] With peace established with the National League, Charles Somers sold his remaining holdings in the Boston ballclub to focus on running his Cleveland ballclub, as majority owner Henry Killilea became president of the Boston club.

The second development was the playing of the first modern-day World Series in October 1903 between the pennant-winners of both leagues. Such a postseason series was one item not covered by that first National Agreement. At the time, such a series made little economic sense to the ballclub owners, since attendance had been poor at the series in the 1880s between the winners of the National League and the American Association as well as at the Temple Cup games in the 1890s. The owners felt that more money could be made in arranging their own postseason games, especially in those cities with teams in each league where an intracity series could be played. Once the games between pennant-winners Boston and Pittsburgh in October 1903 proved to be such a lucrative venture, though, the two leagues soon established an official postseason series between the pennant-winners.

While both 1903 developments solidified Johnson's stature as an influential baseball executive, they also enabled Collins to enjoy several more years of financial prosperity — and indulgence by Johnson — as his reward for switching leagues two years earlier. Collins immediately cashed in on the peace-conference development when he traveled to Milwaukee in February to meet with Killilea to renegotiate his salary for the final year of his three-year contract that was due to expire at the end of the 1903 season.[3] Collins asked for a $7,500 salary, which represented a 50 percent increase over his $5,000 salary in 1902, but settled for $6,500.[4] Instead of staying in Buffalo for the three weeks before heading south for spring training, Collins took the train to Boston where he arrived on February 28 to deliver "some private information for business manager Gavin" to attend to, among other more mundane baseball matters.[5] A week later Killilea surprisingly arrived in Boston, where he publicly inspected the Huntington Avenue Grounds for possible improvements, which had ostensibly been the subject of his meeting in Milwaukee with Collins, but privately signed the paperwork to increase the salary in Collins' contract.[6]

Collins and his ballplayers were soon on a train headed to spring training, which was conducted that year in Macon, Georgia, for the first time. The second 1903 development of the first modern-day World Series was not very evident in March 1903, not even the Boston Americans winning the American League pennant. When Collins left Macon in early April for the team's barnstorming tour north through Indiana and Ohio, he simply said, "There is not a man on the team who is not in fine condition, and by the time we reach home they will be ready for the work I have cut out for them."[7] The team barely defeated Buffalo, 8–7, when Collins returned to his hometown for Boston's final exhibition tune-up before the start of the regular season.

On Opening Day, with both the Americans and Nationals slated to play twin bills in Boston on the Patriots Day holiday, there was no question that Collins' team was the favorite among Boston baseball fans. In the head-to-head competition for spectators on the holiday, the Americans attracted nearly five times as many people for the morning and afternoon games at the Huntington Avenue Grounds (27,658 total) than attended the two games that the Nationals played at the South End Grounds (5,694 total).[8] Two years after Collins had left the Boston Nationals, his Boston Americans were pummeling his old employer at the ticket office.

After the Americans split the two holiday games with Connie Mack's Philadelphia Athletics to begin the season at .500, the team hovered around that level for several weeks. On May 28, in fifth place in the American League standings, Boston proceeded to win 11 games in a row and jump into first place in early June. Defending-champion Philadelphia nipped at the heels of the Americans for the next two months until Boston won five of six games from the Athletics during a one-week stretch in August. Boston then surged into a commanding lead by Labor Day and eased its way to the 1903 pennant with a 91–47 record, 14 games ahead of second-place Philadelphia.

Killilea was an absentee owner who spent most of his time in Milwaukee. There are few indications that he ever visited Boston during the 1903 playing season, after inspecting the Huntington Avenue Grounds during his visit in early March. With Somers out of the picture and Killilea in Milwaukee, Collins was virtually in complete charge of all baseball matters, in his twin roles as manager and captain.

As manager, Collins didn't need to do much recruiting of new talent in 1903, since he had the same starting eight players in 1903 as he did for the 1902 season: LaChance, Ferris, Parent, and himself in the infield; Dougherty, Stahl, and Freeman in the outfield; and Criger at catcher. He only had to make a few targeted player acquisitions. Collins initially signed Charley Farrell to be the backup catcher, and after he was injured early in the season then signed Jake Stahl to give Criger a periodic rest. The most important addition for 1903 was the signing of John O'Brien as utility player, who had played for old friend Hugh Duffy in Milwaukee in 1902. When Chick Stahl was injured for a good portion of the season, O'Brien capably stepped in as the substitute center fielder. Since the Americans, with the exception of Stahl, seemed immune to injury, Collins had a fixed lineup, which combined with players drawing large salaries in long-term contracts was a recipe for excellent player performance. Collins continued to deploy the simple strategy used by his former manager Frank Selee to put talented ballplayers on the field and let them do their jobs with minimal intrusion. With Collins also in the field as third baseman, he could also lead by example.

Collins had four pitchers carryover from the 1902 season — Young, Dinneen, Hughes, and George Winter — which he augmented with Norwood Gibson, whom he signed in the fall of 1902 to be a fifth pitcher. With a steady pitching staff in 1903, every game but one was started by one of these five pitchers. Collins deftly managed this pitching staff, which was the key to Boston winning the pennant in 1903, but he took little credit. "When a team has pitching such as I have, it is bound to win a lot of games," Fred Lieb quoted the modest Collins in his 1947 history of the Boston Red Sox.[9]

Cy Young and Bill Dinneen comprised the core of the pitching staff.

Young, at age 36, was the ace of the staff. As biographer Reed Browning described him at the start of the 1903 season, Young was "close to moving into uncharted actuarial territory, and yet he could still plausibly claim to be at the top of his game."[10] Dinneen, at age 27, was a five-year veteran of the major leagues. By installing Hughes as his third regular starter, and judiciously using Winter and Gibson as spot starters, Collins was able to get more high-level production from both Young and Dinneen. Both pitchers started eight fewer games in 1903 than they had in 1902, and threw fewer innings (in Dinneen's case, 80 fewer innings). With the added rest, both Young and Dinneen were much fresher during the summer months, as well as for the unanticipated postseason series in October. Young won 28 games to lead the American League in victories in 1903. During the two-month period from May 24 to July 25, Young won 13 of 14 games he started, including four consecutive shutouts during one stretch. Besides the added rest, the newly enacted foul-strike rule in the American League also was a boon to Young and Dinneen as both increased their number of strikeouts.

As Boston was battling to hold onto first place in the American League during the summer months, in the National League the Pittsburgh Pirates were on their way to winning a third consecutive pennant. In late July, Barney Dreyfuss, the president of the Pittsburgh ballclub, announced that if Pittsburgh won the National League pennant, the winner of the American League pennant "will be challenged to a series of 11 games to decide the championship of the world." Among the three most notable conditions that Dreyfuss placed upon his proposed championship series were (1) the winner receive 75 per cent of the gate receipts and the loser 25 per cent, (2) the entire 11 games be played, no matter how many games one club should win, and (3) the location of each game to be mutually agreed upon.[11]

However, there was no provision for sharing the gate receipts from these postseason games with the ballplayers. "I shall insist that the gate receipts, be Pittsburg winner or loser, go to the club employing the players, and not to the players," Dreyfuss said. "The Pittsburg players are under contract to me until October 15 ... My players know me well enough to feel that they will lose nothing in winning for Pittsburg the championship of the world. I will make each and all a handsome present of money."[12] The lack of a compensation provision for the ballplayers was consistent with the general intent for why the National League ballclub owners had entered into the National Agreement with the American League just a few months earlier — to reduce the amount of money going to the ballplayers (generally through lower salaries) and thus increase the amount of money retained by the owners. Acknowledging that ballplayers were entitled to more than their usual salaries for participating in a postseason series would defeat that purpose.

As manager of the Boston Americans, the likely pennant-winner in the American League, Collins said at the time of Dreyfuss' announcement, "I guess our boys will be willing to meet the Dreyfuss team if it wins the pennant, and we manage to land it, but it is a bit too early to discuss terms and conditions."[13] His mention of "terms and conditions," rather than winning the games, indicates that Collins was already considering the financial potential that he and the players on his team might gain from this series of games, since the contracts of the Boston players expired on September 30. While the Pittsburgh players had to play in the postseason games, the Boston players were not so obligated. Another difference in philosophy that can be extracted from Collins' statement is that Collins considered these to be purely exhibition games to generate income, while Dreyfuss was out to settle "the question of base ball supremacy" between the two leagues.

Dreyfuss was highly motivated to stage such a postseason series because he saw the money-making opportunity in marketing the postseason series as a contest to determine the superiority between the two leagues. Secondarily, since he was an active supporter of the January 1903 peace agreement (having received assurance that no American League team would be located in Pittsburgh among other concessions), Dreyfuss felt such a postseason series would further good relations between the two leagues. With his intense desire to stage such a championship series, Dreyfuss was willing to make major concessions to his original proposal. He just needed someone to negotiate the deal with.

Dreyfuss did not meet with Boston owner Killilea until mid-September to discuss the terms and conditions for the postseason series. Killilea seemed to put off meeting with Dreyfuss until after Boston clinched the pennant (which occurred on September 16). The two owners were supposed to meet in Buffalo in late August, where Killilea was at a meeting concerning minor league matters, but a telegram asking Dreyfuss to come to Buffalo was reportedly received too late for Dreyfuss to get there.[14] When Pittsburgh played a Sunday game in Chicago on September 6, the two owners couldn't get together then either. The delay allowed Killilea to negotiate more favorable terms for Boston.

The agreement to play the postseason series (actually an untitled document, but hereafter called the "World Series agreement") that Dreyfuss and Killilea signed on September 16, 1903, shows numerous concessions granted to Killilea. Whereas Dreyfuss had originally envisioned a traveling tour to include several neutral-site cities, all the games were to be played in either Boston or Pittsburgh. Instead of the winning ballclub getting the majority of the net receipts from the series, the receipts were to be equally shared, as conveyed in the stilted language of point 5 of the World Series agreement: "The minimum price of admission in each city shall be 50 cts. and the visiting club shall be settled with by being paid 25 cts. for every admission ticket sold." To Killilea, the series was to be strictly about making money and thus equally sharing the revenue, not about determining a better team that would be rewarded with a greater share of the revenue. The proposal for eleven games, all to be played, was whittled back to a nine-game format with the series ending after one team won five games. Boston had the advantage in the scheduling of the nine games, with the first three and last two in Boston, with the middle four in Pittsburgh. Boston also got the two most favorable dates for attendance — the two Saturday games — where Killilea could maximize revenue that he didn't have to share with Dreyfuss, from the sale of grandstand seats and other ancillary items at the ballpark. There was one last-minute detail agreed to, which was handwritten as point 4½ into the otherwise typewritten text: "No player to participate who was not a regular member of team Sept. 1, 1903." Killilea seems to have asked for this to limit Dreyfuss's use of late-season acquisitions as substitutes for his ailing pitchers; Gus Thompson was thus deemed eligible (he first pitched on August 31) but not Jack Pfiester (who first pitched on September 8). One concept that Dreyfuss did not concede was that the

In his third year as player-manager of the Boston Americans, Jimmy Collins led the team to the American League pennant in 1903 and to victory in the first modern-day World Series after Boston accepted the challenge to play a postseason series with National League champion Pittsburgh. Collins demonstrated his business skills by negotiating a highly favorable agreement with Boston ownership to compensate the ballplayers, since the games were played after the expiration of their contracts for the 1903 season (National Baseball Hall of Fame Library, Cooperstown, New York).

net receipts were to be paid to each ballclub, as there was no explicit provision to pay the ballplayers.[15]

Although the contracts with the Boston ballplayers expired before the postseason series with Pittsburgh was to begin on October 1, Killilea obviously believed he had a strong position to determine what the players would be paid, and wouldn't need to negotiate with them, since he went ahead and signed the World Series agreement on September 16 without concluding a financial arrangement with the Boston ballplayers. Killilea felt that he had the makings of an agreement in his preliminary discussions with Collins when they met in Chicago in mid–August when the Americans were in town to play the White Sox on August 19–21. Collins later said that at that meeting Killilea "did make a proposition to pay us two weeks' salary during the series, but he was to take all of Boston's share of the receipts."[16] Killilea contended that he gave Collins two alternatives, either two weeks of salary or half of Boston's share of the receipts.[17] In any event, there was no conclusion reached at the mid–August meeting between Collins and Killilea about how the ballplayers would be paid for the postseason series.

After he signed the World Series agreement on September 16, Killilea sent a letter to Collins with details about the postseason series. Collins received this letter on September 18.[18] Killilea said that in that letter he "authorized Collins to offer the players one-half of the Boston club's share of the gross receipts from the entire series."[19] Collins contended that was the first time that the 50/50 division was proposed.[20] Collins didn't immediately respond to Killilea's proposed payment arrangement.

Killilea had a problem and Collins knew it. Killilea had foolishly entered into a contract with Dreyfuss to play the postseason series with Pittsburgh, but had no contractual arrangement with the Boston ballplayers to play the series. The day the World Series agreement was signed, Dreyfuss had publicly declared that the postseason series was on — "Dreyfuss Says Boston Games Are Certain," the *Philadelphia Inquirer* headlined.[21] On September 23, Killilea met with Ban Johnson in Chicago to discuss his options.[22] Even with one week until the postseason series was due to commence, and pressured by Johnson to get a deal done with Collins — the man that Johnson would "never forget the loyalty of"— Killilea didn't budge from his initial position.

Following his conference with Johnson, Killilea wired Collins that his original 50/50 offer still stood. On September 23, after talking it over with the players after the team's game with Detroit, Collins wired Killilea to reject the 50/50 offer and seek 100 percent of the proceeds. Collins explained the bargaining rationale: "Now the position of the players is this: In the old Temple Cup series the players divided the net receipts and the owners of the clubs got nothing.... We do not think the situation is at all different now. We have worked hard for the championship and feel that we are entitled to special consideration.... The Cincinnati and Cleveland clubs are to play for the championship of Ohio, and the players are to get half the profits. Neither team won a championship. We feel that there should be a good bonus in winning the pennant, and that we deserve more consideration than the Cleveland and Cincinnati players."[23] Killilea was steadfast in the defense of this position. "The demands of the players seem to me unjust," Killilea said in Chicago. "No expense has been spared that might add to the strength of the club or to help to win the pennant, and while I appreciate in full the excellent work which landed the prize, I do not feel the players deserve all the reward."[24]

The newspapers on September 25 reported apologies from both Collins and Killilea that the postseason series would have to be cancelled. "I am sorry that there are to be no games, as I would like to please the public," Collins said. "But the players are very sore and there is no help for the situation. I don't know as they would be inclined to give Mr. Killilea a one-eighteen share now."[25] After Johnson urged Killilea to try once more to get a deal done with Collins, a deadline (likely established by Dreyfuss) was set for 6:00 P.M. on September 25 when the postseason series would indeed have to be cancelled. Johnson added some spice to the discussion by sending Collins a telegram saying "the press and the public demand these games and you should impress this fact upon your players." Since Johnson sided with Collins, the telegram was more for public consumption and offered Killilea a small face-saving gesture.

Because Killilea had far more to lose than Collins and the Boston ballplayers, Killilea wound up caving in to the ballplayers shortly before the 6:00 P.M. deadline. Finally the letters and telegrams were discarded and the last-minute negotiations were conducted over a long-distance telephone call among Killilea, Collins, and business manager Joe Smart. At 5:45 P.M., the two parties finally agreed on how to split the profits of the postseason series. "What the new terms are is not announced," the *Boston Transcript* reported, "but it is believed that the players will receive seventy-five per cent and the club twenty-five per cent of the receipts."[26] This belief proved accurate when the final distributions were made following the postseason series. Collins had negotiated a great deal for the Boston ballplayers. They got not just 75 per cent of Boston's portion of the shared revenue under the World Series agreement, but 75 per cent of *all* of Boston's net revenue from the series.

Less than a week later, on October 1, Collins was standing at third base for the initial pitch of the opening game of the first modern-day World Series.

Chapter 14

The First World Series

In the basic contours of the first modern-day World Series in 1903, the Pittsburgh Pirates won three of the first four games in the best-of-nine match before the Boston Americans, led by player-manager Jimmy Collins and motivated by the Royal Rooters' incessant singing of the song "Tessie," forged a comeback to win the next four games to become world champions. According to most chroniclers of baseball history, including the authors of the four books published in 2003 to celebrate the 100th anniversary of the World Series, the upset victory by the American League over the firmly entrenched National League forever altered the landscape of major league baseball.

From the retrospective of a century later, the more interesting aspect of the 1903 World Series is whether or not all eight games were played on the up-and-up, and whether Collins was actively involved in the rigging of any of the games. Both teams had substantial motives to not play certain games on the level. Pittsburgh had a shortage of pitchers, and was nearly completely reliant on its ace, Deacon Phillippe. The nature of the financial arrangement with the Boston ballplayers to share in the net proceeds of all the games encouraged them to extend this postseason series as long as possible. There was no risk of impunity, since at the time *all* postseason games were merely meaningless exhibition contests designed to attract and entertain spectators, so that the ballplayers could augment their regular-season salaries and the ballclubs their financial bottom lines. Wagering on the outcome of these games was also prevalent, conducted in public, and reported openly in the newspapers.

Certainly, Collins believed postseason games were merely exhibitions, based on his experience. The 1897 Temple Cup series clearly fit the meaningless category, given its celebratory banquets each evening, the other exhibition games interspersed among the Temple Cup games, and Frank Selee's dubious pitching choices during the series. Most of the games of the All-America tour in the fall of 1897 were played for spectator entertainment value rather than purely on a competitive basis. The local postseason tours in 1896 and 1901 were even more in the meaningless category. In 1903, there had not been a postseason series with serious competitive consequences for the past dozen years.

In their book *Red Sox Century*, authors Glenn Stout and Richard Johnson provide a compelling argument that the first two games of the 1903 World Series were intentionally lost — Game One by Boston and Game Two by Pittsburgh — based on an analysis of the substantial circumstantial evidence in the on-the-field play of both teams. Game One on October 1 at the Huntington Avenue Grounds was overtly curious when Pittsburgh scored four runs in the top of the first inning. "The Boston Americans, the pride of the American League, played the absolute worst baseball of their three-year existence, handing the game to Pittsburgh in a manner that seemed suspicious then and seems even more so now," Stout and Johnson concluded, adding, "The very first game of the very first 'world's series' was, in all likelihood, thrown by Boston."[1]

In Game One, after retiring the first two Pittsburgh batters, ace pitcher Cy Young suddenly lapsed into mediocrity. After Tommy Leach reached Young for a ground-rule triple and Honus Wagner touched Young for a run-scoring single, "things got strange fast." Wagner stole second when Criger, "easily the best defensive catcher in the game at the time," made an off-target throw to second. Kitty Bransfield then hit a grounder to Ferris at second base, "who first bobbled the ball, then fell down, then threw late to first" as Wagner took third. Criger then tossed the ball into center field on an attempted steal by Bransfield, allowing Wagner to score and Bransfield to take third. Young then walked Claude Ritchey, who stole second on a non-throw by Criger. Jimmy Sebring singled to left to score both baserunners. Young was seemingly out of the inning when he struck out Eddie Phelps, but the usually sure-handed Criger "suffered his fourth defensive lapse of the inning and let strike three pass by" and Phelps to take first base. Phillippe finally did strike out, with Criger holding on to the third strike, to end the inning.[2] Pittsburgh went on to win, 7–3, with one run resulting from another Ferris error.

Boston's suspicious play was duly noted in the contemporary press. The *Boston Post* openly reported that "many around town last evening asked if Boston lost on purpose."[3] The *Boston Globe* was more oblique, noting that Criger's play was like "a fur overcoat in July" and that Ferris ought to wear "toe weights for the rest of the series," implying that he "lay down" in the game to allow the Pittsburgh batters to reach base.[4] Since there was substantial betting taking place on the Boston-Pittsburgh games, the substandard play by Boston in Game One was all the more suspicious.

In Game Two on October 2, it was Pittsburgh's turn for suspicious behavior. After Boston scored two runs off Pittsburgh starter Sam Leever in the bottom of the first inning — the first on a home run by Patsy Dougherty on Leever's first pitch of the game — manager Fred Clarke replaced Leever with young, inexperienced Bucky Veil, who had pitched in only 12 games all season. "As if not expecting to win and giving credence to those who later thought the game was fixed, he chose twenty-one-year-old Bucky Veil to relieve Leever," Stout and Johnson analyzed the Pittsburgh pitching change; they added that "curiously" Clarke didn't tap either of the two veteran pitchers on his bench, Brickyard Kennedy or Gus Thompson.[5] Boston proceeded to win, 3–0, as Bill Dinneen shut down the Pittsburgh lineup to even the series. As Tim Murnane observed in the *Boston Globe*, "Large sums of money changed hands, the Boston sports winning back what they lost the day before and a little more."[6]

Perhaps the best circumstantial evidence that the outcome of Games One and Two was fixed came to light sixteen months later when the official rules governing an annual World Series were established in February 1905. These rules precluded the most egregious elements that impacted competitive play throughout the 1903 World Series, by shortening the length of the series from nine games to seven (thereby minimizing the possibility of throwing the first two games), having the players share in the proceeds only from the first four games (thereby eliminating the incentive to extend the series), and providing for a 75/25 split of the proceeds (thereby providing an explicit incentive for the players to win as soon as possible).[7]

What role did Collins have in arranging the suspected thrown Game One? The intensely private Collins never said much about the inaugural 1903 World Series, of course, never mind publicly providing any hint of duplicity in the outcome of Game One. In the only extensive interview about his baseball career, conducted in 1943 just weeks before his death, Collins focused on the financial elements of the ballplayers' pay in the World Series.[8] There were no quotes from Collins in that article about his reaction to winning the 1903 World Series, which was perhaps being unusually mum about such a perceived historically important event in baseball history. However, at the time Game One was played, where was the outrage by Collins over his team's abysmal play in the first inning? Yes, he was a quiet leader, but surely he would have had some reaction. Based on the lack of reports that Collins had any on-the-field objection to his team's terrible first-inning play in Game One, he very likely knew why the pitching and fielding miscues were occurring, and had his advance approval, since intentionally losing the first game helped to extend the series and thus garner the Boston players more money. There, of course, was the possibility of earning additional income by collecting on Game Two wagers placed on a player's behalf by a friendly Royal Rooter.

Exactly how Collins convinced the Boston players to go along with his last-minute negotiation with owner Henry Killilea about the monetary split of the series receipts has never been revealed. One likely explanation is that the educated, negotiation-wise Collins devised an easy win-win solution for the players to make more money in the deal but yet still allow Killilea to save face — plan to play seven or eight games rather than strive to play the minimum of five. Newspaper reporters focused on the percentage split between the owner and the players in the deal while Collins was absorbed behind the scenes in the actual mechanics of how the size of the player payment would be more impacted by the number of games played than by the increased percentage of the receipts. Collins may have even hinted to Killilea at how the players might make this happen, which would explain why the owner didn't bother to attend Game One of the World Series and made his first appearance at Game Two.[9]

Collins' attitude about the nature of the 1903 World Series changed somewhat at Game Three. At the time, the usual pattern for attendance at postseason games was large crowds for the first one or two games followed by a decline at the later games. That pattern held for the first two games in Boston, as there were several thousand fewer spectators at Game Two than were at Game One. However, 20,000 people jammed into the Huntington Avenue Grounds for Game Three on Saturday, October 3. Ticket sellers and police were overwhelmed by the demand to see the ballgame. Newspaper hype had trumped any concern over gambling, ballplayer malaise in the first two games, or spectator desire to watch football rather than baseball. Speculators sold a $1 ticket for grandstand seats for $3. An hour before game time, a huge throng had already ringed the outfield. The 1903 World Series became important at the time because the newspapers, the only trusted public communication medium in those days before radio, deemed the 1903 World Series to be important. The public believed the games were legitimate, if perhaps the ballplayers didn't always think so, as reflected in the demand to attend the ballgames and gamble money on their outcome. At this point, Collins no longer considered the Pittsburgh series to be merely an exhibition. While he now believed the ballgames had a more serious implication, he never lost sight of the financial aspect.

Boston pitcher Tom Hughes may have also been involved in a limited conspiracy to throw Game Three, when he yielded several walks to Pittsburgh batters and grooved a number of pitches for "cheap" hits that allowed Pittsburgh to take a 3–0 lead in the third inning. This time there was evidence that what transpired wasn't an organized fix, since Collins had an overt reaction to the putrid pitching of Hughes and unexpectedly called for a timeout in the third inning after Clarke hit the latest easy ground-rule double. Collins called for Cy Young to replace Hughes, but it took a few minutes for Young to get onto the field since he was in street clothes (not expecting to pitch that day) and needed to change into his uniform in the clubhouse under the stands. Boston lost Game Three, 4–2, even as the more motivated Collins had two of the team's four hits and scored both runs.

Hughes never pitched another inning that fall, and was traded before the beginning of the 1904 season. "For some reason, Collins didn't like him by Series time," shortstop Fred Parent explained years later. "He must have crossed Jimmy somewhere along the line in the season. Collins was a quiet, nice man, but you couldn't cross him. He started Hughes one day after Tom had spent a night on the town. I think Tom did it because he wasn't being pitched. Naturally he was whacked and never appeared in the Series again."[10]

With Boston down two games to one, the two teams, and the Royal Rooters via an organized excursion, moved on to Pittsburgh for the next four games. Boston left on the 10:15 train Sunday morning that went to Pittsburgh via Buffalo, where Anthony Collins met his son on the train platform during a brief stop there. The Boston team did not get to the Monongahela Hotel in Pittsburgh until Monday morning, but rain that day cancelled Game Four. With the game postponed, the Royal Rooters had time on their hands Monday afternoon. They visited a local music store to check out some songs to sing at the next day's game and came across "Tessie" from the musical *The Silver Slipper*, then playing in a Boston theater. The Rooters spent the rest of the rainy day crafting parodies of the lyrics to annoy the Pittsburgh players, between sips of their potent malt beverages.

When Game Four was played on Tuesday, October 6, at Pittsburgh's Exposition Park, Pirates' ace Phillippe shut down the Boston hitters once again as Pittsburgh rolled up a 5–1 lead going into the top of the ninth inning. The Rooters burst into singing "Tessie" for the first time when Collins led off the ninth inning. He responded with a single to center field to ignite a Boston rally. Stahl and Freeman both singled, the latter scoring Collins; Parent then hit into a force out that scored Stahl to narrow the score to 5–3. LaChance singled to send Parent to third, who then scored on pinch-hitter Charley Farrell's fly ball to left field, making the score 5–4. With the tying run on first base, and the Rooters yelling their rendition of "Tessie," pinch-hitter John O'Brien popped out to end the game.

The ninth-inning rally in Game Four was the first indication that the Boston Americans were taking the match more seriously. "The tenor of the series changed. The unsavory play that marked the first three games in Boston magically disappeared in Pittsburgh, lending credibility that one or more of the first three games in Boston had been arranged," Stout and Johnson remarked in *Red Sox Century*. "The desired effect had taken place. Interest in the games in Pittsburgh was high, and reasonable crowds assured. Now Boston could play to win."[11] Following the gamblers' logic, Boston had Pittsburgh exactly where they wanted them, even though Pittsburgh led the series, three games to one. Phillippe was tired after pitching three of the first four games, and Pittsburgh had little in pitching reserves since Ed Doheny was not with the team due to his mental breakdown. Boston feasted on Pittsburgh's depleted pitching corps in the next two games to tie up the series. In Game Five, Boston pummeled Kennedy for an 11–2 victory, and in Game Six they vanquished Leever for a 6–3 win. The Rooters naturally claimed that their singing of "Tessie" had inspired the Boston comeback.

On Friday, October 9, Pittsburgh, looking to get Phillippe an extra day of rest, invoked the weather clause of the World Series agreement to postpone Game Seven due to cold weather, even though the air temperature was in the 60s. The postponement was arguably good for the Boston players, from a financial perspective, as a much larger crowd would attend a Saturday game than one on Friday. Collins expressed an unusual volume of anger about the postponement. "What's the matter with you people?" the *Pittsburgh Press* reported that Collins yelled at Clarke in office of the Pittsburgh ballclub. When Clarke replied that it was too windy and cold at the ballpark, Collins replied, "We're willing to take a chance. What's the use of waiting a day? It's likely to be just as bad then. We want to finish these games and get away."[12]

Collins, whose outward demeanor a Pittsburgh writer described at the time as resembling "a prosperous magnate rather than the captain of a baseball team," sounds far too voluble and out of character in this exchange.[13] Coupled with earlier reports that he had conversations with both Dreyfuss and Clarke *before* Game Six about the possibility of moving Game Seven to Saturday, it appears that the shouting match was just a publicity stunt to appease the public that the game wasn't being moved simply to make more money. In fact, it was moved for exactly that reason. If Game Seven had been played on Friday, then both teams would have had two days off before the next game, since Saturday would have been a travel day back to Boston and there could be no game on Sunday due to the legal prohibition on Sunday baseball. By playing on Friday, both teams would have exchanged a big payday on Saturday for a small one on Monday. Collins was too astute of a businessman not to go along with the postponement. The day off gave Boston fans and newspapermen more time to devise creative ideas. On the day off in Pittsburgh, Collins received the following telegram at the Monongahela House from Charles Taylor, the owner and publisher of the *Boston Globe*:

> James J. Collins, manager and captain of the Boston Baseball Team:
>
> The Boston Globe, believing that victory is within the grasp of you and your comrades, offers to present to each player of the Boston team of the American

League, if it brings to Boston the world's championship, a valuable gold medal, which can be worn as a watch charm, and be treasured as a reminder of the most notable achievement upon the diamond.

Chas. H. Taylor, Editor[14]

With the text of the telegram printed on the front page of the next day's *Boston Globe*, Taylor created more hype to capitalize on the World Series games, setting the stage for his family to take an increased interest in the fortunes of the Boston ballclub.

On Saturday, October 10, the large crowd that spilled onto the outfield grass at Exposition Park, combined with the tired arm of Phillippe, did in Pittsburgh in Game Seven. Collins started the first-inning rally with a ground-rule triple, and scored on Stahl's ground-rule triple. Stahl later scored on an error to put Boston ahead 2–0 before Pittsburgh came to bat. As Cy Young shut down the Pittsburgh batters, Boston sailed to a 7–3 victory to take the series lead for the first time as both team headed back to Boston for Game Eight. After rain postponed the game on Monday, Bill Dinneen notched his third victory of the postseason series in Game Eight on Tuesday, October 13, in a 3–0 shutout of Pittsburgh to make Boston the 1903 World Series champions.

There was widespread publication of the amounts paid to the Boston and Pittsburgh players as their share of the net proceeds of the World Series. Collins and the other victorious Boston players each received $1,182.18 while the losing Pittsburgh players actually received a higher amount at $1,316.25 each. Boston president Killilea received $6,699 while Pittsburgh president Dreyfuss allegedly kept $0 by his well-chronicled gesture to give the ballclub's entire share of the net proceeds to the players.[15] There was far less publicity about how these payment amounts were calculated, which requires knowing the total net proceeds from the gross general admission revenue (shared 50/50 under the World Series agreement), gross grandstand revenue (retained by each ballclub), and expenses (determined by each ballclub to reduce its share).

Since the pool of net proceeds for the Boston players was divided among 17 people (16 players and business manager Smart), the total net proceeds on the Boston side of the ledger equaled $26,796 — computed as $1,182.18 multiplied by 17 ($20,097) plus $6,699. The allocation percentages work out perfectly as 75 percent to the players and 25 percent to the owner. These figures validate Collins' negotiation with Killilea for the players to not only get 75 percent of the general admission revenue covered explicitly by the World Series agreement but also 75 percent of the grandstand revenue from the four games in Boston. The baseline for general admission revenue to be equally shared by each ballclub was approximately $25,000, based on 25 cents per ticket from the combined attendance of about 100,000 at the eight games. Since the $26,796 figure above is *higher* than the starting point in the World Series agreement before expenses are deducted, grandstand revenue had to have been included in the calculation. No Boston newspaper published the backup needed to determine how the $1,182.18 player payment was calculated, but one Connecticut newspaper did publish some details, buried within a story about the Pittsburgh payments. The *Meridan Journal* reported that total gross receipts for Boston were $29,811 and expenses were $3,015.[16] Netting these two figures equals the $26,796 net proceeds number determined above. This demonstrates that grandstand revenue of approximately $4,800 was included in the Boston player computation.

As it turns out, Dreyfuss was not as magnanimous as he made himself out to be. While he was generous with the Pittsburgh players, he did keep some money for himself. The *Pittsburgh Press* reported that the Pittsburgh share of the net proceeds was $21,060, which foots exactly to 16 player shares of $1,316.25 each.[17] The computation of the $21,060 figure was never revealed. However, $21,060 is more than $5,000 lower than the $26,796 total in the Boston pool, when the two figures should have been roughly equal. This indicates that Dreyfuss retained 100 percent of the grandstand revenue (as he was entitled to under the World Series agreement), which approximated $5,000 based on the Boston calculation above. This also indicates that Dreyfuss netted out higher expenses, approximately $4,000 to the $3,000 level for Boston. Unless Pittsburgh's expenses were far higher than those of Boston and grandstand revenue far lower, Dreyfuss did not give *all* of the net proceeds to his ballplayers, just the net proceeds amount as determined under the World Series agreement. Nevertheless, Dreyfuss did score a publicity coup by having the Pittsburgh players take home more money than the Boston players did for their efforts in the first modern-day World Series.

Collins used his $1,182.18 check to invest in more real estate in South Buffalo. "Jimmy Collins is the banker of the [Boston] aggregation," one writer described the manager of the heralded World Series champions. "He has, by judiciously investing his money in Buffalo real estate, insured a handsome income. His winter pastime is collecting rents and keeping his property in shape."[18] Although Collins had originally viewed the job with Boston in the American League as a short-term venture, he could now see how he could use baseball to enhance his burgeoning real estate business.

The Sunday edition of the *Boston Globe* on October 11 provided some unusually explicit insight into Collins' initial and subsequent beliefs about this postseason series, when writer Tim Murnane quoted Collins as saying, "It has surprised me to see the amount of interest that is being taken in this series. I never thought that it would arouse so much enthusiasm."[19] Collins now believed these postseason ballgames rose above being merely exhibitions to generate some additional income, but he wasn't quite sure exactly what they were, other than an enhanced money-making opportunity.

Collins certainly didn't subscribe to Dreyfuss' original thesis of the games to determine baseball supremacy. When asked later in October his thoughts on whether a postseason series between the pennant-winners of the two leagues would now be an annual event, Collins said: "I should not be surprised to see post-season games each fall as long as there are two big leagues. There is no reason, when the games are played out on their merits, as they were in this case, why they should not be successful. They give the public a high article of base ball and enable the championship teams to pick up a bit of prize money for the cold winter."[20] Collins focused on the monetary aspect to the ballplayers and never hinted that the postseason series produced an overall champion, just happy spectators and fans. He still considered these postseason games to be just a series of ballgames designed to provide increased income for the ballplayers, albeit with the games played at a higher level than the meaningless games of the old Temple Cup series. To Collins, each league had a champion, and the postseason games did nothing to diminish those titles by "proving" that one champion was better than the other.

However, the public did believe, at the coaxing of the newspaper publicity, that the postseason series did produce an overall champion in major league baseball. Although Collins did not agree with that assessment, he took advantage of the national belief in the legitimacy of the 1903 postseason series to determine baseball supremacy. Indeed, the vast majority of the wealth that Collins gained from baseball between 1904 and his retirement as a ballplayer in 1911 was the direct result of the national acclaim he received from Boston's victory in the 1903 World Series.

CHAPTER 15

Spring Training in Macon

After Boston won the World Series showdown with Pittsburgh to give the upstart American League an enhanced degree of respect in the Organized Baseball world, Jimmy Collins was in an enviable position to negotiate a new contract with owner Henry Killilea to replace his original three-year deal that expired at the end of the 1903 season. Given Collins' significant negotiation leverage via his walkaway position — he could focus full-time on his burgeoning real estate business in Buffalo if he and Killilea couldn't agree on a new deal — Killilea wasted no time in securing Collins' name on a new contract.

Killilea met with Collins in Milwaukee in early November, only a few weeks after the end of the 1903 World Series. Unlike most of Collins' salary negotiations, though, only very sparse details can be located in the contemporary newspapers regarding the three-year contract that Collins entered into with the Boston Americans for the 1904 through 1906 seasons. In mid–November *Sporting Life* ran a headline that announced the deal: "Chieftain Collins' Royal Reward: A New Three-Year Contract with the Boston A.L. Club." Jake Morse's accompanying article provided few details. Collins summarized the deal to Morse very succinctly: "By the way, my contract ran out this year, and during my visit in Milwaukee I renewed it for three years more at a substantial advance." While no specific salary figure was provided by Collins, Morse did add that the amount was "certainly for not less than $6500 per annum, his old figure."[1]

Collins' annual salary for 1904 and the next two years was actually $10,000. In addition, Collins negotiated a profit-sharing arrangement in this three-year contract, at least for the 1904 season and possibly for the next two seasons as well. In his later years, during an interview with the *Buffalo Evening News*, Collins proudly noted that his highest annual income during his ballplaying days was $18,000. Collins recalled that this amount was "based on a salary of $10,000 and 10 per cent of the club's profits over $25,000."[2]

While he didn't mention the exact year he received this payment, it was clear from his other remarks that this payment occurred in one of the years between 1902 and 1908, since he named far lower salaries for his years in the National League and his first year in the American League in 1901. The year 1904 seems most likely, since that was the high-water mark for ballpark attendance for the Boston Americans, and therefore its profits. According to the formula specified by Collins, the Boston ballclub profits would have had to have been at least $105,000 to trigger the $8,000 bonus payment amount ($105,000 less $25,000 multiplied by 10%). Estimated profits for the Boston ballclub in early September ranged from $60,000 to $75,000, before the big crowds at the season-ending games.[3]

The motivation for Killilea to extend such a potentially lucrative deal to Collins was to keep him in the Boston fold, along with signing all the other ballplayers to contracts for the 1904 season, so that he could collect a top price for selling the ballclub. Besides being in a hurry to sign all the ballplayers after the 1903 World Series, Killilea also extended the term of his lease on the land underneath the Huntington Avenue Grounds through 1910, to further solidify the ballclub's financial structure.

Collins used Macon, Georgia, as the spring training site for the Boston Americans from 1903 to 1906. Macon was "by all odds the best town for training I know of," Collins once told *Boston Post* writer Fred O'Connell.[4] Macon was not only in a warm-weather climate that was conducive to getting the ballplayers prepped for the season, but it was also a place that was conducive to hosting the team in a low-cost manner. Collins, who was now sharing in the ballclub profits, had to front travel expenses for four weeks before the big paydays would arrive from the exhibition games in New Orleans and the finale in his hometown of Buffalo. Macon was recommended to Collins by Joe Kelley and his other friends that had played for the old Baltimore Orioles, who had trained in Macon prior to their championship seasons in the 1890s.

Charles Fountain, author of *Under the March Sun: The Story of Spring Training*, credits Baltimore manger Ned Hanlon with the idea of having extended training sessions in one place in the South rather than the former approach to simply barnstorm through several cities to play exhibition games on the way north to begin the regular season. "The results of Hanlon's innovative spring training were immediate and decidedly dramatic," Fountain writes about Hanlon's training regimen in Macon, since "the Orioles won the 1894 pennant and the next two thereafter."[5]

Besides the Hanlon legacy, Macon was one of the few cities in Georgia at the time that satisfied all five of the desired criteria for a great spring training site: sunny skies and warm weather, convenient transportation, decent hotel accommodations, available baseball diamonds, and other squads to compete against.⁶ Unlike other Georgia cities then used for spring training that were located near the coast (e.g., Augusta and Savannah), Macon was located inland, which gave the city a greater probability of avoiding rainy weather and cool temperatures. In fact, during the three weeks of 1904 spring training, it did not rain one day and the temperatures ranged in the 70s and 80s each day. Macon had good rail connections and adequate hotel accommodations (although not quite as good as nearby Thomasville, where the Boston Nationals trained at this time). The city offered two available baseball diamonds, one owned by the city where the Macon minor league ballclub played and the other at Mercer University. The baseball team at Mercer provided competition for practice games.

As the reigning World Series champions, the Boston Americans were especially welcome to Macon for their training prior to the 1904 season. In January Collins had telegraphed the Hotel Lanier in Macon to make reservations for 15 ballplayers to arrive on March 6. "Manager Collins is of the opinion that the climate of Macon is second to none when it comes to working out Charley horses," the *Macon Telegraph* commented in its report of the Boston team's expected arrival in the city for spring training.⁷ While the weather in Macon was great for the ballplayers, Collins no doubt also secured a good deal from the hotel proprietor, emphasizing the additional business (lodging as well as dining) that the hotel would generate from Boston visitors during the team's three-week stay. The city also provided the baseball diamond in the city park for free.

Besides good weather and inexpensive accommodations, Macon also had a sixth feature that appealed to Collins: there weren't many other activities to distract the ballplayers from their primary goal to get in shape for the regular season. "Some of the boys think the town pretty slow at times," O'Connell wrote in a profile of Macon in the *Boston Post*, but "they appreciate the Southern hospitality" too. For night life, there were only three one-night shows at the local opera house; instead "the boys find lots of pleasure in taking an easy chair in front of the Lanier and watching the Southerners parade up and down each night." Additionally, each night at the hotel "a band of colored minstrels give a concert, singing plantation songs, and the players join in the chorus." On their off-day on Sunday, the players visited an old Confederate fort five miles from the hotel or went fishing in the nearby Ocmulgee River. Some players attended the sessions at the local courthouse before morning practice, where they were bemused by the courtroom antics of Southern lawyers and witnesses, which "beats any burlesque show for genuine fun and amusement."⁸ There wasn't much trouble that the ballplayers could get into in Macon.

Collins had 12 other players with him in Macon, which comprised the bulk of his expected 16-man squad for the regular season. The entire infield was there, first baseman LaChance, second baseman Ferris, and shortstop Parent to complement Collins at third base. Outfielders Stahl and Dougherty. Catcher Farrell. Pitchers Winter, Gibson, and Jesse Tannehill. Reserves Doran, O'Neil, and Wolfe. The four missing players were training on their own at Hot Springs, Arkansas — Young, Dinneen, Criger, and Freeman. They were known as the Hot Springs Quartette. Only Roland Wolfe would not join the team for the 1904 season. Wolfe, termed "a very lively chap," kept things loose on the team, as he liked to tell humorous stories about what it was like to play baseball in the Texas League during the hot, muggy summers in that state. Wolfe bumped around the minor leagues for ten years, but never made it to the majors.

The daily routine in Macon was nothing too strenuous for the ballplayers. "Manager Collins and his men were up at 8 o'clock, and after some minutes' stroll in the corridors, entered the dining hall, where the stars partook of breakfast," the *Macon Telegraph* reported on activity the first day. "After a short rest, the start for the grounds was made. In order to harden their muscles, the champions went in a slow trot to and from the grounds."[9] The morning workout was conducted at Central City Park, about one mile away from the hotel, with the afternoon workout at Mercer University, about one mile in the other direction from the hotel. Collins had the players run back and forth between the hotel and the ball fields, where they then did some stretching and light ball tossing and batting. "Collins does not believe in driving his men, and does not favor too hard work in the spring," Morse wrote about Collins' approach to training in Macon. "He has had lots of experience in this direction, and he knows that too much work is worse than too little."[10] The mission was to get into playing shape; Farrell dropped 14 pounds during his three-week stay in Macon.

The 13-man crew of the Boston Americans in Macon played a few scrimmage games against the Mercer college boys. On March 12, Boston defeated Mercer, 8–2, as the two teams divided $200 in gate receipts from spectators both white and black. On March 19, Boston won, 13–0, before crowd of 1,500, with the net receipts going to the local kindergarten association, as Collins donated the team's share.

O'Connell, the baseball writer for the *Boston Post*, for some unknown reason, played a prank on Collins, when he wrote a St. Patrick's Day article about how Collins had enraptured the Macon chapter of the Ancient Order of Hibernians in his response to the toast "The Irish in Baseball" at the organization's annual banquet on March 17 at the Hotel Lanier. "In the few minutes allotted to me I will try to recall a few of the famous ball players who cherish Ireland as their birthplace or the birthplace of their beloved parents," Collins was quoted by O'Connell. Collins then supposedly named dozens of other major league ballplayers who had Irish roots, before concluding: "As much as ball players of Irish extraction have done for the game in the past, I look for them to do as much if not more in the future. America needs baseball and baseball will always, I think, need a few players with the O's and the Mac's."[11] However, there is no mention of Collins, or any other ballplayer, in the *Macon Telegraph* account of this banquet, which served Vermont turkey, stuffed chestnuts, shoestring potatoes, asparagus tips with hollandaise sauce, and tutti fruitti ice cream. The name of the toast was also a more generic "Irishmen in America," unrelated to baseball.[12]

Since Collins had assiduously avoided casting himself as an Irish-American since his major league playing debut in 1895, it was beyond belief that he would make such a speech at a St. Patrick's Day gathering of 500 Irish-Americans. In addition to the completely uncharacteristic nature of Collins to talk about Irish-American heritage, the old-time ballplayers he named had nothing to do with his youthful days in Buffalo, when O'Rourke, Galvin, and Brouthers played for his hometown team. If there was any Irish sentiment still left in Collins, he would have named them at the top of his list, not Tim Keefe and Kid Madden. He would have also highlighted McGraw, Jennings, and Kelley from the old Baltimore Orioles, rather than only mention them in passing in their current managerial roles. Collins soon had to issue his own retraction to reclaim his dignity, by saying "it was a fake."[13]

To help compensate for the fictitious story that he no doubt thought would be taken as humorous, O'Connell ghostwrote an article under the byline of Collins that was published soon thereafter in *The Illustrated Sporting News*. This new weekly sporting magazine, first published in 1903, was aimed at a college-educated readership and featured photographs and topical articles about improvements in training and new equipment in sports such as rowing, college football, hunting, and polo. Collins felt that the upscale nature of the publication enhanced his image, well beyond what the conventional sporting weeklies, *The Sporting News* and *Sporting Life*, could do for him. However, with a limited audience and lack of coverage of the daily events in sports, *The Illustrated Sporting News* soon perished in 1907. While not many people read the 1904 article, it did portray Collins as a thinker and not just an athlete, such as this excerpt about the benefits of training in Macon:

> The South is the proper place to train a team, as you must have warm weather to work the stiffness out. Especially is this so with arms, and I find the most trouble in keeping the boys from working too hard at the start. This spring we worked for nearly two weeks before the boys took chances in throwing the ball across the diamond, and the consequence is that all are in shape to throw the full limit of their strength. I fully believe in fast practice work, as it makes you faster in the games, and speed counts in the winning of ball games.[14]

One side benefit to training in low-key Macon was team building. Besides the aches and pain of working out, the players bonded in the Southern city, becoming "the life of the hotel with their everlasting 'kidding,'" as O'Connell described it, adding, "Put a bunch of healthy ball players in a small Southern city and there is sure to be something doing all the time."[15]

When the Boston Americans left town on March 27, Collins declared the three weeks in Macon a success: "I am highly pleased with our practice here and believe my men have benefited greatly from their practice here in Macon. Sore limbs and legs are things of the past and their muscles are ready for the work that awaits them. My team is as strong or stronger than last year's, and I feel no hesitancy in saying we will be 'right there' when the umpire says 'play ball.' I am highly gratified with the attentions we have been shown while here and am honestly sorry to leave Macon."[16]

The team played ten exhibition games in the South, at Atlanta, Montgomery, Mobile, and New Orleans, before heading north to Buffalo for a final exhibition game before Opening Day on April 14 in New York City. On the Southern swing, Boston won nine of the ten games (three in Atlanta, one in Montgomery, two in Mobile, and three of the four in New Orleans).

Collins used the 13-man squad that trained in Macon for the three games in Atlanta, before the Hot Springs Quartette joined the rest of the team in Montgomery. After two games in Mobile, the team devoted a week to staying in New Orleans. The capstone game in New Orleans was a Sunday game that attracted 8,000 spectators to see Cy Young pitch Boston to a 5–1 victory over the local minor league team, the Pelicans. "The trip has been a financial success," Collins said after the final game in New Orleans, "owing to the fine attendance in this city."[17]

After a 36-hour train ride from New Orleans to Buffalo, Collins discovered that it had snowed in Buffalo. The weather diminished the attendance at the April 13 game to 1,400 spectators who braved a bitterly cold wind to watch Boston edge Buffalo, 2–1. The snow storm dashed the hopes of Collins to add significantly to the profits of the six-week spring excursion. Additionally, the team was tired for the first game of the regular season, as they had to take the overnight train from Buffalo to New York City to open the 1904 season on April 14 against the New York Highlanders at American League Park.

CHAPTER 16

Another Championship Season

The Boston Americans opened their home schedule for the 1904 season at the Huntington Avenue Grounds on April 18. This date was an important moment in Jimmy Collins' life, as he personally raised the championship pennants for the 1903 season on the center-field flagpole. More infamously, though, a new owner of the Boston ballclub was announced that day, John I. Taylor. Collins would soon clash with Taylor about how the team should be run, which eventually led to his departure from the Boston Americans three years following his hoisting of the championship flags.

Taylor, the 29-year-old son of *Boston Globe* publisher Charles H. Taylor, was Ban Johnson's answer for local ownership of the Boston Americans to replace absentee-owner Henry Killilea. Publisher Taylor invested around $100,000 to buy the ballclub from Killilea to keep his wayward son occupied, since the younger Taylor showed little interest in the newspaper business.[1] Fred Lieb in his history of the Boston ballclub described John I. Taylor as "something of a playboy," a man "without the drive or ability" of his father, and someone who "knew quite a bit about the game, had a pleasant side to his many-sided nature, and had many friends in Boston and the suburbs." Perhaps Taylor's best qualification to be owner was his frequent appearance as a spectator at the Huntington Avenue Grounds.[2]

Johnson had just days earlier spurned the offer of politician John Fitzgerald to buy the Boston ballclub, citing as his excuse that "the terms of the agreement were not lived up to by Fitzgerald."[3] As was later revealed, money was not the most significant element to determine who would be the new owner; "restoring cordial relations between the owners of the rival Boston clubs" was at the top of the list.[4] In other words, soothing the ruffled feathers of Arthur Soden, the president of the Boston Nationals, was high priority, in addition to being a person that Johnson could easily influence. Clearly, the Irish-American Fitzgerald did not come close to fulfilling that need in the mindset of Soden, a dyed-in-the-wool Brahmin. It is not clear if Collins was a potential investor in the Fitzgerald purchase offer; if so, the inclusion of a renegade former employee would have been another reason for Soden to disapprove of the Fitzgerald offer in talks with Johnson. Collins likely knew of the underlying motivation to mollify Soden in selecting a new Boston owner, which is why he negotiated the profit-sharing arrangement into his new three-year contract for the 1904–1906 seasons, to serve as a quasi-ownership provision.

Taylor said all the right things upon being introduced as the new owner. "I have the utmost confidence in Jim Collins and consider him as good a manager as there is in the country," Taylor complimented his field manager, "and shall co-operate with him so far as it lies in my power to give Boston as good ball as it has had in the past, and will spare neither money nor effort in that direction."[5] While Taylor maintained a hands-off attitude for the 1904 season, he did not fully appreciate that he was "fortunate in having as his manager the great Jimmy Collins, the most graceful ballplayer of all-time, and a successful leader of men."[6] The seeds of discontent had been sown. For the first time in his life Collins was working for a man younger than he, but worse, a man who lacked the inner soul to achieve success. Thankfully, the green shoots of discontent didn't surface until after the 1904 season.

At the April 18 home opener against Washington, Collins was at the center piece of the ceremony to raise two championship flags to commemorate the victorious 1903 season. As his Boston teammates looked on, wearing sweaters in the chilly weather, Collins, in his fresh white uniform, first hoisted a large blue flag with white lettering decrying "Boston Americans 1903 World's Champions," which was a gift from Arthur Dixwell, the Boston baseball fan responsible for encouraging others to abandon the Boston Nationals in 1901 in favor of the Boston Americans. Below this flag, Collins then raised the league pennant in a similar blue color with white lettering reading "Boston Champion Club American League 1903," which had been provided by the American League office.[7] By winning the home opener on April 18 and both games of the Patriots Day holiday twin bill on April 19, Collins and his Boston Americans team settled into first place in the American League standings.

Boston continued to hold onto first place for the next three months, as Collins' teamwork approach translated into victories. Collins was also lucky in that there were no injuries to his starting lineup in the field or to the pitchers; in 1904 he needed to use few reserve players and no one beyond the five-man pitching staff that began the season — Young, Dinneen, Gibson, Winter, and Jesse Tannehill, who came to Boston from New York in the offseason trade to exile Hughes. However, Collins couldn't shake the New York Highlanders, managed by Clark Griffith who had recruited Collins to the American League in 1901, which had moved up to second place by mid–June.

The neck-and-neck competition in 1904 between the Americans and Highlanders was the first installment of what turned into a longstanding rivalry between the Boston and New York teams, which eventually were renamed the Red Sox and the Yankees. The heated battle in 1904 was flamed by the intense competitive spirit of the two opposing managers, Collins and Griffith. Although some baseball researchers point to the start of the rivalry as an incident in May 1903 when New York runner Dave Fultz crashed into Boston pitcher Winter covering first base on Fultz's ground ball, the June 1904 trade engineered between Collins and Griffith was far more controversial and the apt place to commence the genealogy of the storied rivalry.

On June 17 Collins traded outfielder Pat Dougherty to Griffith in exchange for little-used utility infielder Bob Unglaub. On the surface, there was no doubt that the trade seemed overly one-sided in favor of New York. Dougherty was the starting left fielder for Boston, and had led the league in base hits the preceding season; Unglaub was a rookie that Griffith had used in just six games. While there was some disbelief expressed by the contemporary press in the wisdom of the trade, historians have excoriated the inexperienced Taylor for making the lopsided trade as he was said to acquiesce to Ban Johnson to benefit the New York Highlanders in their quest for a pennant to increase their popularity compared to the established New York Giants team in the National League. According to one retrospective account, "It was one of the worst trades ever in team history and precipitated a decline on the field far worse than that which was later blamed on the sale of Babe Ruth sixteen years later."[8]

Although Dougherty was a talented ballplayer on the field, he was a negative influence in the clubhouse, so Collins got rid of him in the best deal he could get at mid-season. At the time of the trade, the public remarks by both Taylor and Collins indicated that they both were in agreement that the trade would benefit Boston and that the trade was Collins' idea. Taylor announced that "the trade was made only after consultation with manager James Collins and on his advice." Collins said that Taylor made the trade "with my sanction, and I think the deal with prove to the best interest of the Boston club."[9] Collins would not have capitulated to a Johnson demand to undermine his own ballclub, since in Collins' mind Johnson needed him, and owed him, far more than Collins needed or owed Johnson. Collins even touched on these rumors at the time: "I have always done the best I could for Boston, and I have never injured the club to benefit any other one."[10] Indeed, there was a good reason why Collins traded Dougherty.

Three weeks after the trade in an article entitled "Necessity of Discipline in a Ball Team — Dougherty Was Moody and Insubordinate," Tim Murnane of the *Boston Globe* explained why Collins had to trade the left fielder. "Dougherty on several occasions refused to obey orders and openly refused to listen to manager Collins' suggestions, until it got to be a case of Collins or Dougherty for leader," Murnane wrote, adding that Dougherty was let go "to maintain discipline in the Boston Team" since "a bad example will soon have followers."[11] The source for this article was most likely the other Boston players, not Collins, since it would be out of character for Collins to discuss details of a private matter. Another source could have been John L. Sullivan, the famous boxer, who was a friend of Collins who had arranged a benefit game for Sullivan at the Huntington Avenue Grounds on May 2 that season. Sullivan later remarked about Dougherty, "I didn't see the battle, but the story is that Pat tackled his captain and soaked him good [with his fists], and Jimmy was helped out by another player — Dinneen, I believe."[12] Dougherty had to go because not only did he not respect the word of Collins as law, but also because he didn't respect him personally.

As for why he did the deal with New York and not another ballclub, Collins explained that at a banquet after the season ended. "Several clubs wanted him, but the New York Club, my friends, offered so much more for him that we sold him to that club as a pure business proposition," Collins said. "It was not sentiment, it was not friendship [with Griffith], it was not animosity, it was a pure business deal. New York wanted him, I wanted to sell him, and I did, and there you are."[13]

Replacing Dougherty took a little time. First, Collins used reserve outfielder Tip O'Neil in left field. When that didn't work out, Collins obtained Al Selbach from the Washington ballclub. With Dougherty patrolling the outfield for the New York Highlanders during the second half of the 1904 season, the pennant race tightened up and came down to the final series of the season, which pitted the two rivals together. The pennant race culminated with a season-ending doubleheader to decide the American League pennant. This doubleheader became the cornerstone for the storied rivalry between the Boston and New York ballclubs, which is still hotly contested one hundred years later.

Originally, the American League schedule called for four games to be played in New York during the final series of the season between Boston and New York, including an innovative season-ending doubleheader on Monday, October 10. With a postponed game added into the mix, the final series expanded to five games, with a single game on Friday, October 7, and doubleheaders on Saturday, October 8, and Monday, October 10 (with Sunday as a day of rest, due to the Sunday law in New York that prohibited professional baseball on that day). At mid-season, the five-game, season-ending series in New York certainly looked to be an advantage for the Highlanders, who were jostling with Boston in the neck-and-neck race for the American League pennant.

However, the owners of the New York ballclub apparently had little faith in their own team, as they reached an agreement during the summer to rent out the team's Hilltop Park for college football games in September, October, and November. In mid-July, Columbia University announced that it would play its football games there rather than at the Polo Grounds, where the school had played the past several years. Five games were slated for late September and early October when the Highlanders would be on an extended road trip, and several more games were scheduled after the conclusion of the baseball season. There was just one minor problem. "There will be a conflict in the early part of October," the *New York Times* reported. "On Oct. 8, the day on which Columbia is due to play Williams, the baseball team has a game at home with the champion Bostons. This will probably be shifted to some other city."[14] The lure of a few dollars of rental income from college football had obliterated the Highlanders' scheduling advantage.

Perhaps the New York owners believed the Highlanders would clinch the pennant before the final series with Boston. But the upshot was that the Saturday doubleheader was transferred to Boston. It was a decision that would haunt the ballclub for years. Instead of five games in New York, the two teams played a Friday afternoon game in New York, jumped on a train to Boston for two games on Saturday, and then returned to New York for two games on Monday. As writer Ed Linn noted in his book *The Great Rivalry: The Yankees and the Red Sox 1901–1990*, the season-ending series was eventually defined as "the pennant that was lost on Jack Chesbro's wild pitch," but it could be more aptly labeled as "the pennant that was lost through the stupidity of the Yankee front office."[15] The lure of rental income was too much to resist for the ballclub owners, who gave away a date on which the team could possibly clinch the pennant in order to host a college football game.

Jack Chesbro, New York's star pitcher and a future Hall of Famer, turned out to be the goat rather than the hero of the final series, as Boston captured the American League pennant in the decisive doubleheader on Monday, October 10. Chesbro pitched and won the opening game of the five-game series on Friday, defeating Boston, 3–2, on a chewed-up playing surface for his 41st victory of the season. Columbia had defeated Tufts in a football game at Hilltop Park just two days earlier, in the last of five football games played there during the Highlanders two-week road trip. The victory vaulted New York into first place, a half game ahead of Boston. Chesbro only faltered from there, though.

Chesbro, a spitball pitcher, claimed that throwing the pitch put less pressure on his arm than a fastball, so that he could pitch with fewer days of rest than other pitchers. Manager Griffith had used Chesbro frequently in 1904, starting him in one-third of the team's games that year. Chesbro completed 48 of his 51 starts in 1904, pitching 454 innings. However, Chesbro pushed himself beyond his limits in the final series. In an ill-advised move, Griffith started Chesbro in the first game on Saturday.

Before a crowd of 30,000 people that jammed into Boston's Huntington Avenue Grounds, Chesbro lasted just three innings in the first game on Saturday, as he was knocked out of the box in the fourth inning when Boston scored six runs. It was just the third time all season that Chesbro had failed to complete a game that he started. Boston clobbered New York, 13–2, in the first game and then took the second game, 1–0, behind the shutout pitching of Cy Young. Boston was in first place by one and a half games; New York needed to sweep the doubleheader on Monday in order to win the pennant. Back at Hilltop Park on Saturday, Columbia defeated Williams, 11–0, in a football game played before a crowd of 3,000. That was about 25,000 shy of the anticipated attendance for a pennant-deciding baseball doubleheader that day.

At the Saturday game in Boston, when Collins came to bat in the second inning he was presented with a silver loving cup by Royal Rooter Charlie Lavis. The 26-inch-high cup on an ebony base was the result of a subscription campaign started by Lavis and publicized in the *Boston Journal*, to honor Collins for his contribution to Boston baseball. The inscription on the cup read:

PRESENTED
TO
CAPTAIN JAMES COLLINS
OCTOBER 8, 1904

This cup subscribed to through the *Boston Journal*
is intended as an evidence of the admiration
of the Boston public for a great third baseman,
a great captain and a good fellow.[16]

The fund for the loving cup closed at $306.60 in contributions. While some baseball fans contributed a few dollars, most fans sent in mere cents. Many,

Opposite: Spectators sitting in the inexpensive first-base bleachers at the Huntington Avenue Grounds helped to fuel Jimmy Collins' popularity in the city of Boston. At the last home game of the 1904 season, baseball fans presented Collins with a loving cup as an expression of admiration "for a great third baseman, a great captain and a good fellow" (Library of Congress Prints and Photographs Division, LC-USZC2-6131).

like Fred Eaton, sent in just a penny: "I am a baker but on a strike, so I can only afford one cent to Jimmy. But everything helps to make Jimmy work harder for the second pennant."[17] Collins had certainly done his part to spark interest in newspapers.

On Monday Chesbro was back pitching in the first game, making his third start in four days. The game was tied 2–2 when Boston mounted a rally in the top of the ninth inning. Lou Criger, Boston's weak-hitting, slow-footed catcher, stroked a single to lead off the ninth. He advanced to second base on a sacrifice and to third base on a ground out. With Fred Parent at bat with two outs and Criger on third base, Chesbro cemented his future legacy when his spitball sailed several feet over the head of catcher Red Kleinow to the backstop, which allowed Criger to score the go-ahead run. Boston won the first game, 3–2, to capture the pennant when pitcher Bill Dinneen shutdown a New York rally in the bottom of the ninth by striking out ex–Boston player Pat Dougherty for the final out. The second game of the doubleheader, now meaningless in the standings, was rapidly completed in one hour and ten minutes, with New York eking out a 1–0 win. The 300 or so Royal Rooters who had traveled from Boston to New York, led by Charlie Lavis, commenced celebrating after the first game concluded.

The October 10 doubleheader became legendary partially because of its impact on the 1904 pennant race, but more importantly because it was the initial major confrontation in the storied, longstanding rivalry between the American League ballclubs in Boston and New York. "There is no rivalry on the face of the earth that can compare with the Yankees vs. Red Sox," Linn wrote in *The Great Rivalry: The Yankees and the Red Sox*. "It's everything a rivalry ought to be. Us Against Them. It's not only New York against Boston. It's New York against New England. The canyons of Wall Street and the caverns of Madison Avenue vs. the White Hills of New Hampshire and the Green Mountains of Vermont. We the People vs. the Barons of Entrenched Priviledge. The spacious expanse of Yankee Stadium against the looming monster of Fenway Park."[18] The fame of Collins was eventually elevated by his participation in the early years of the rivalry.

The sale of Babe Ruth by the Red Sox to the Yankees in 1920, following Boston's winning of five World Series titles in two decades, triggered a cataclysmic turn of events in the rivalry. New York went on to win 26 World Series championships before Boston finally eluded "The Curse of the Bambino" to win another World Series title in 2004. During the intervening years, there was plenty of excitement, and heartbreak for Boston fans, during the era of Ted Williams/Joe DiMaggio, Mickey Mantle, and Carl Yastrzemski/Reggie Jackson. There were several last-day-of-the-season showdowns, highlighted by Bucky Dent's home run in the 1978 playoff game and Aaron Boone's walkoff home run in the 2003 American League Championship Series. It all started with Jack Chesbro's wild pitch in a doubleheader on the last day of the 1904 season, when Jimmy Collins claimed victory for the Boston Americans.

Unlike 1903 when Boston participated in the first modern-day World Series, the 1904 championship had no similar culminating event. The champions of the National League, the New York Giants, had earlier refused a challenge issued by the crosstown New York Highlanders to play a postseason series if the Highlanders copped the American League pennant. At the time, Giants owner John Brush and manager John McGraw were still greatly annoyed with American League president Ban Johnson, Brush for his placing of a competing ballclub in New York City and McGraw for continued general dislike of the man. Brush and McGraw didn't want to play a World Series with the Highlanders that would help elevate that ballclub's standing within the city of New York. However, after the Highlanders dropped three of the last five games to the Boston Americans to give Collins' team the pennant, Brush and McGraw were backed into a corner. As soon as the Americans had won the American League pennant, Taylor issued a challenge to McGraw for the Americans and Giants to play a five-game postseason series. McGraw never responded to Taylor's challenge.

Collins took the high road at the time and didn't publicly comment about the lack of a World Series. Collins continued on the high road a week later when Brush suggested a spring series between the two teams as a substitute for the aborted fall series. Collins put his remarks in the context of baseball fans, not any personal disappointment, saying that Brush saw the "mistake in not giving the public a run for its money."[19] Later in life, though, Collins was more outspoken about the snub by the Giants: "McGraw wouldn't play us — he called us a bunch of bush leaguers."[20]

However, at the time his team won the 1904 pennant, Collins was probably relieved that there was no World Series to be played. His team was tired from the lengthy 154-game season that went down to the penultimate game to decide the league championship (which soon made Collins a huge supporter of a return to the 140-game schedule). Such a postseason series would be played in the chilly weather of mid-to-late October. Because of both factors, there was a distinct chance that the Boston Americans might lose to the New York Giants. Since McGraw never responded to Taylor's challenge, Collins could claim that Boston was the world champion by default.

The one negative to the lack of a World Series in 1904 was that the Boston players didn't receive any extra financial reward for winning the championship. Of the four championship teams that Collins played on during his baseball career, the 1904 team was the only one where players didn't receive a bonus of some kind for their efforts to secure a league pennant. In 1897 and 1903, Collins and the other players participated in a postseason series to generate extra money, while in 1898 the owner simply presented them with a bonus. In 1904, all the Boston players received was a free meal and a few dollars from a hastily arranged testimonial.

On the afternoon of October 13, the Royal Rooters sponsored a testimonial for the Boston Americans at the Boston Theatre, where many baseball fans and various dignitaries such as the governor and mayor attended. Due to the generosity of owner Taylor who paid $500 for a box and the theater manager who paid $50 for a regular seat, the testimonial raised $2,000 to be divided among the players. Mike Regan was the host of the festivities, where he coaxed the soft-spoken Collins into saying a few words on stage:

> "What shall I say about this gentleman?" asked Mr. Regan, turning to the next man. "There is no need to say anything," shouted a fan in the balcony; "we know him well. Three cheers for Jimmie Collins, the man who has led the Bostons to victory for two successive years." Then the crowd let go, and for some moments it cheered for "Gentleman Jim," and a stage attache set off a bomb. "Speech! Speech! Speech!" came from all parts of the house, but the modest leader refused to leave his seat. But the "fans" would not be denied, and then Collins came toward the footlights and said: "Ladies and gentlemen. I thank you and I appreciate your kindness very much."[21]

Immediately following the testimonial, Taylor honored the ballplayers at an informal banquet at the Parker House, where they received a free meal and a few drinks as their official reward for winning the pennant.

Collins did collect some additional money related to the team's pennant-winning season, but not by playing in a postseason series, rather through the profit-sharing provision in his contract. In the fall of 1903, Collins had negotiated a contract with then-owner Henry Killilea that called for a $10,000 salary with an additional payment equal to 10 per cent of the club's profits over $25,000. Collins says the profit-sharing payment amounted to $8,000.[22]

Taylor, whose father had handled the ballclub purchase transaction and did little due diligence, must have been shocked to discover this contract provision when Collins confronted him for payment when the two men met on October 17 before Collins left for his home in Buffalo. Collins returned to Boston on November 15 for a two-week stay over the Thanksgiving holiday, ostensibly to make arrangements for spring training. His first order of business, though, was the profit-sharing payment, as the *Boston Globe* coyly reported, "Capt. Collins will call on Pres. John I. Taylor today at the club's headquarters and close up some important business."[23] Although Taylor honored the contract, the profit-sharing payment stuck in his craw. Like all Brahmin businessmen in Boston, Taylor believed that management exclusively was to reap the profits of business, not share them with labor. Although Collins was the field manager, Taylor still considered him to be part of labor. The $8,000 check was the beginning of a testy feud between the two men, as Taylor got more involved in ballclub operations and Collins didn't like the increased oversight.

On the Sunday after Thanksgiving, Mike Regan of the Royal Rooters hosted a reception in honor of Collins, which was attended by about two dozen people. Other Royal Rooters at the reception included Charlie Lavis and Timothy Crowley. According to the *Boston Globe* account of the reception, three single women also attended: "Miss Sadie Murphy, Miss Mamie McNamara, Miss Julia Harmon."[24] Two of these three young ladies would marry Boston ballplayers, Sadie to Jimmy Collins and Julia to Chick Stahl. Since a two-week stay in Boston during the offseason was a long time for Collins to be away from Buffalo, especially over a holiday, he may have eaten Thanksgiving dinner with the Murphy family, indicating that his courtship of Sadie was well along.

Upon his return to Buffalo, Collins immediately put his $8,000 profit-sharing payment to work by building additional housing units in South Buffalo, consistent with the *Boston Globe* report a few weeks earlier that "Captain Collins will probably construct a few houses" during the offseason.[25]

Chapter 17

Clash with Boston Ownership

An article in the magazine section of the Sunday edition of the *Boston Globe* in mid–January 1905 portrayed Jimmy Collins as an up-and-coming businessman, signaling a change in Collins' perspective about life. Under the headline "His Winter Pastime Collecting Rents" appeared five photographs. In the upper left was a portrait of Collins in suit, white shirt with raised collar, and cravat loosely knotted at the neck. A watch fob draped across his breast. His hair was impeccably combed, parted on one side. He looked like any well-to-do Boston Brahmin, not a baseball player. A photo of his parents' house at 1278 Niagara Street in North Buffalo was surrounded by three photos of his rental properties in South Buffalo, two showing Buffalo doubles on Pomona Place and Seneca Street with the third a three-story, multi-family brick building at the corner of Pomona and Seneca. "For several winters he devoted his time to looking after the new buildings he was erecting," Tim Murnane described Collins' dedication to this business venture, "and even now with several fine pieces of real estate, he has planned for two more new houses."[1] Collins came off as a successful businessman in the making, which was undoubtedly his intent in inviting Murnane to visit him in Buffalo.

Murnane's article also provided rare insight into Collins' personal life, which he religiously shielded from public view. Collins' mother, Alice, told Murnane that her son was an avid reader of books, was fond of the theatre, and was a member of the Buffalo lodge of Elks. A female friend of Collins told Murnane that Collins' internal motivation was his belief "that a man without money is like a lame duck doing an overland route." In that conversation, the same woman asked Collins, who was standing nearby, "Why don't you get married and settle down?" Knowing that Murnane was taking notes, Collins replied, "When I get married, I want to take my wife with me. You see this is out of the question with a ball player touring about the country. In the summer months I am on the go and in the winter months among pretty good friends. I have plenty of time yet for that business."² Collins was already planning to live off the income from his rental properties in his post-baseball days.

Collins' role model for using one's employer to live well after the end of a working career was his father, Anthony, who was superannuated in February 1905 by the Buffalo Police Department after more than 30 years on the police force. Anthony received a retirement pension of $600 a year, half of his annual salary during his prime years as a police captain.³ At the time, pensions were very rare, especially from a government job.

While the hefty $8,000 profit-sharing payment didn't ingratiate Collins with Boston Americans president John I. Taylor, who was surprised to discover such a lucrative bonus clause in Collins' contract, the root of the deteriorating relationship between Collins and Taylor was Collins' increasingly deep-seated belief that the Boston Americans *was* his team, not Taylor's. Collins had run the baseball operation for three years without any direct oversight by ownership before Taylor became the owner, and had successfully engineered a second straight pennant-winning season in 1904 without Taylor's assistance. This was the dark side to the soft-spoken Collins. Not liking Collins' attitude, Taylor took a more active role in the team for the 1905 season.

Spring training in Macon, Georgia, in 1905 wasn't as businesslike as it had been the previous two years, since Taylor joined the excursion and brought along a trainload of people from Boston. The *Macon Telegraph* reported that newspaper writers Murnane from the *Globe*, Morse from the *Herald*, O'Connell from the *Post*, Barnes from the *Journal*, and Mitchell from the *American* journeyed from Boston to Macon with Taylor, along with artist Barthomelew of the *Journal* and photographer Chapman from the *Globe* in addition to baseball fans Fred Doe, a New England League manager, and Mike Regan, an ardent Royal Rooter.⁴ Suddenly, spring training for the Boston Americans was as much about publicity and relaxation as it was about preparation. One day O'Connell convinced Collins to join him and Taylor as they practiced their golf swings. "Collins tried his hand at the game, but passed it up after three attempts to lose one of the gutta percha spheres," the *Macon Telegraph* wrote about the golf outing. "Finding the niblick too small for the purpose, he grabbed a bat and took a swipe at the little white thing."⁵ The lack of preparation for the 1905 season started to become evident when Boston lost a ballgame to the Macon minor league team.

There was a bit more hubris in the comments by the ownership-minded Collins at the end of spring training in 1905 than a year earlier. "I can't see why we can't win again," Collins led off his analysis of the Boston team in his bylined article in *The Illustrated Sporting News*. "We have a stronger team than we had in 1904. The other teams have been strengthened, but so have we."[6] His 1905 remarks were well beyond the typical optimism of a manager, especially when contrasted to the 1904 comments in his initial article published in *The Illustrated Sporting News*: "Having gone the full distance in good form last season and having a shade better team this season, I am confident of holding a position at the top from start to finish. The Boston Americans will play their best ball, and the team that beats them out for first money should be given high praise."[7]

His exuberance, not just the confidence of a year earlier, for a "stronger team," not just "a shade better team," was built on his two changes in the 1905 lineup from that of the championship team of 1904. Collins installed two players that he had acquired himself, rookie Moose Grimshaw at first base in place of LaChance and newcomer Jesse Burkett in left field in place of Selbach. Burkett was a controversial addition to the Boston team. Collins acquired the 35-year-old stormy outfielder from St. Louis, a .400 hitter during the 1890s, in exchange for untried youngster George Stone. After the spring, Collins said of Burkett: "I for one do not think that he has gone back any. He will lead the team off in hitting. He can bunt or hit the ball out, and he can get as many bases on balls as any player in the game."[8] Burkett turned out to be a bust, while Stone went on to win the 1906 batting title. Despite the extreme optimism of Collins, the Boston Americans could not muster the momentum to repeat as American League champions for a third consecutive year in 1905.

Boston lost its first five games before Opening Day at the Huntington Avenue Grounds on April 21, when Collins raised the championship flag in center field before his team lost its sixth game in row. After a month-long stay in last place, Collins finally pulled his team into fifth place by winning a holiday twin bill on Decoration Day. The team lumbered through the summer mired in fifth place with a sub-.500 record. Finally a victory over Cleveland on August 5 propelled the team over .500, though still stuck in fifth place. By early September, in contrast to his usual somber, worrisome mood at the ballpark, Collins was all smiles and joking with the players, since "he knows that his team is out of the race, and there is no use of fretting." Collins put a positive spin on the situation at the time: "We can't win all the time and must be satisfied with our luck."[9] It appeared as if Collins would experience his first-ever second-division finish as a manager when a season-ending eight-game winning streak eked the team into fourth place, with a 78–74 record, 16 games behind first-place Philadelphia. Collins, the 35-year-old player-manager, was the leading batter on the team with a .276 average.

While the makeup of the 1905 team was substantially the same as the 1904 championship squad, the big difference in 1905 was injuries. Collins had navigated 1904 by using just five pitchers and six everyday players who played in 150 or more games. Besides injuries in 1905 to Criger and Grimshaw, age began to show on the Americans, as six of the eight starting players in the field were over age 30, with the other two being a spry 29. Cy Young was now 38, the elder statesman of a starting pitching staff whose youngest member was 27.

Taylor sought to remedy both the injury and age issues, not by providing the resources to Collins so that he could fix the situation, but rather by fancying himself as a recruiter of baseball talent to rescue the team on his own. This was the crux of the feud that brewed between Taylor and Collins in 1905, remaining hidden from the public during the baseball season but eventually spilling onto the pages of the newspapers in late December. While his relationship with Taylor deteriorated throughout the 1905 season, Collins still had the integrity not to air the ballclub's dirty laundry in public. "Gentleman Jim has been as uncommunicative as a cobble stone on the subject," *The Sporting News* later wrote about the bad relationship, "his conduct all through the unpleasant proceedings having been characteristic of the man."[10]

Taylor did little to address the injury situation in 1905, generating not one single trade with another major league team to help Collins try to make a recovery and a run at the pennant. He did sign a few pitchers, but none with the appropriate skill for major league competition. The biggest problem was replacing the ailing Criger at catcher, since that position impacted the pitching staff as well. Taylor drummed up no catching prospects. In early July Collins had Charley Farrell scout out a catcher by the name of Charlie Armbruster who was playing for the New London team in the Connecticut League.[11] Armbruster wound up catching 35 games for Collins that season. Collins was so desperate for catchers that he acquired Yip Owens, who was recommended to him by a friend. In the one game he caught for Collins, Yip "looked light and acted worse than he looked," in a 14–0 loss.[12]

Instead of signing players who could help the team immediately, Taylor concentrated on locating young talent for the 1906 season, although many were put on the major league team for the 1905 season. In late July Taylor signed a pitcher named Ferrias from the South Bend team in the Central League and pitcher Joe Harris from the Fall River team in the New England League; Ferrias never played and Harris didn't join the team until after Fall River completed its season.[13] Players that Taylor signed in August included infielder John Godwin, outfielder Pop Rising, outfielder Bill Clay, pitcher Eddie Hughes, and pitcher Ed Barry.[14] Taylor may have had fun traveling through the minor leagues searching for talent, but with regard to his avowed mission of "leaving no stone unturned to secure the proper talent," he fell far short.[15] Even worse, he pressured Collins to play his newfound "talent," which surely galled Collins.[16] Not only did the new players do nothing to improve

Boston's chances for victory on the baseball field, they intensified the smoldering animosity that Collins had for Taylor.

In October, the Boston Americans played a postseason series of exhibition games with their neighbors the Boston Nationals, the first time the two teams had ever played each other since the Americans were established in 1901. Taylor had agreed to play the series back in July if the Americans didn't win the pennant. The seven-game city series was played entirely at the Huntington Avenue Grounds over the span of six days, with single games on Monday, October 9, through Friday, October 13, and a doubleheader on Saturday, October 14. Although Collins did not play in the city series—Bob Unglaub played third base in all the games—he did participate in the payout as the manager of the Americans, collecting a check for $106.98 along with the rest of the players on his team.[17] After five years with the Americans, Collins still had some residual anger from his playing days with the Nationals. When the Americans won six of the seven games from the Nationals, the *Boston Globe* remarked, "The showing indicated that the Nationals were outclassed, and the only regret Capt. Collins expressed was that his team did not make it a clean sweep."[18] For the usually "quiet and reserved at all times" Collins, as Fred O'Connell termed him in a 1904 profile, this comment was one of the first public indications that all was not well with the management of the Boston Americans.[19]

It wasn't until late December that the season-long tension between Collins and Taylor erupted in public, following a likely disagreement over the amount of Collins' profit-sharing payment related to the net receipts from the 1905 season (it's unclear how much, if anything, that Collins received). First, the *New York Sun* published a rumor, without naming any names, about a controversy involving the owner and manager of a major league ballclub:

> It is stated on excellent authority that one of the biggest and most profitable major league clubs soon will change hands. The owner of the club is said to be now at loggerheads with his players to such an extent that one day last season he actually was hooted out of the dressing room after he attempted to deliver a curtain lecture. Since that time the owner and manager of the team have not spoken, and the tension is so great at present that the sale of the entire stock seems to be the only way out of the unpleasant controversy.[20]

The *Chicago Tribune* soon identified the team and men underlying the *New York Sun* account. Under the headline "Friction in the Boston Club," the *Tribune* reported "the alleged coolness between Manager Jimmy Collins and his chief" and "rumors of dissatisfaction among the Boston players" in addition to American League president Ban Johnson being "far from satisfied [with Taylor] with the way the affairs of the local club were conducted last season."[21]

Taylor denied the accusations. "There is no trouble whatsoever between

Collins and myself," Taylor said. "I have never interfered with the management of the team and never have criticized the way Collins has handled things, nor have I criticized the players." Taylor also said that he had no interest in selling the Boston ballclub.[22]

On December 30, the day that Taylor's denial was published, Ban Johnson and Connie Mack were meeting with Collins at his home in Buffalo, supposedly to discuss a possible trade of pitcher Rube Waddell from Mack's pennant-winning Philadelphia Athletics to the Boston Americans.[23] Just why Johnson, as league president, needed to be on hand for that discussion was never explained. The Waddell trade was, of course, just a poorly crafted cover for a discussion to dethrone Taylor as the president of the Boston ballclub.[24]

Less than a month after Taylor denied there was any problem with Collins, Johnson exiled Taylor to Europe for at least a six-month vacation. The rationale for Taylor's sudden departure from the executive suite in January 1906 has never been adequately explained. Either Johnson wanted to elevate Collins to president-in-training or, more likely, Collins initiated a power play to usurp the office from Taylor. In either case, Johnson exercised his perceived power to take "a direct and personal interest in finding [owners] who had not only money but also the enthusiasm and integrity that he felt were essential to maintain the league's reputation."[25] The way Johnson set up the American League, if you crossed him, you would be replaced. In this case, Taylor crossed Collins, and thus indirectly Johnson, who had Collins' back for having taken the risk to jump to the American League in 1901 and helping Johnson make the new league a success.

Johnson was said to be angry with Taylor for being derelict in his duties by being absent from the American League meeting in December.[26] Collins likely used Taylor's absence at that meeting as a wedge to push Johnson to honor his commitment made back in 1901 for Collins to eventually obtain an ownership interest in an American League ballclub. The meeting of the minds in Buffalo was to discuss ways to make that happen for the 1906 season. Johnson was in a tough position, since he didn't want to alienate Taylor's father, the publisher of the *Boston Globe*, which had the best baseball coverage among the Boston newspapers. On the other hand, the timing was perfect to take advantage of John Fitzgerald becoming mayor of Boston on January 1 as the city's first American–born Irish Catholic to be elected mayor, since the Irish-American population was an increasingly important component of the baseball fan base in Boston. Johnson, in consultation with Mack and Collins, concocted the strategy for Taylor to take an extended vacation. Although the new role for Collins wasn't specifically as owner, he was the acting president of the Boston ballclub, with most of the rights and responsibilities that came with being an owner. The official change in ownership could come at a later date, once Collins had a chance to put together a consortium of men that would be an acceptable ownership group to Johnson.

To reflect the new duties, Collins renegotiated his contract, due to expire at the end of the 1906 season, through Johnson and Hugh McBreen, the new business manager of the Boston ballclub. While Collins took a salary cut for 1906, from $10,000 to $8,500, the new $8,500 annual salary applied for two more years through the 1908 season.[27] It appears that the profit-sharing provision was eliminated from the contract at this time, probably in anticipation of formally obtaining a share of ownership upon Taylor's expected sale of the ballclub. To Collins, it was a $25,000 contract that would allow him to further expand his real estate business in Buffalo. Collins' new contract was announced on January 18.

Taylor arrived in Boston on January 24 and said that he "had put everything up to manager Collins and that he had perfect faith in his manager making good."[28] With little fanfare two days later, Taylor boarded a ship destined for Europe.[29] Technically, Taylor was still the owner of the Boston ballclub, but he had effectively abdicated his power to Collins, as his father looked after his holding while he was in Europe. In his article "The Revolution in the Local American Club: Young Taylor Down and Out and Jimmy Collins in Complete Control," Jake Morse summarized the situation: "The fact of the matter is that John I. has gone and Jimmy Collins is the man who will handle the team without interference at all the coming season with sweeping power to sign and release."[30]

CHAPTER 18

Minor League Magnate

Amidst his tussle with John I. Taylor in January 1906 for control of the Boston Americans ballclub, Jimmy Collins made his first investment in a baseball organization when he purchased a one-third stake in the new Worcester, Massachusetts, ballclub of the New England League for $3,000. His two business partners were Jesse Burkett, the outfielder of the Boston Americans, and Fred Doe, a longtime owner-operator of minor league ballclubs in the New England area.

As early as November 1905 Collins was rumored to be partnering with Burkett in the proposed Worcester ballclub, and met with him several times.[1] The *Boston Globe* signaled Collins's ambition by publishing a short item in late December indicating that "Capt. Collins is willing to put some money into a good minor league city."[2] After he renegotiated his contract with the Boston ballclub to cover his services through the 1908 season, to give him an excellent income base, Collins began meeting in earnest with Burkett about purchasing a minor league ballclub. The two met on January 24 in Boston, and with the prognosis good, he postponed his departure back to Buffalo. A few days later Hugh Duffy joined the discussion, when he met with Collins and Burkett at the Copley Square Hotel. "All three have money to invest and they are anxious to take a chance in the business end of the pastime," Tim Murnane remarked in the *Boston Globe* about the meeting, in which he perhaps participated as a consultant, given his side job as the president of the New England League.[3]

Burkett favored putting a new ballclub in Worcester, since he had lived there for the past 15 years after playing minor league ball there in 1889 and then marrying a local girl. He knew not only baseball but also the potential Worcester spectator base. Duffy, a Rhode Island native, favored buying into the existing ballclub in Providence, in which Pat Powers, the former president of the Eastern League, had just purchased a controlling interest in December

1905. Powers was willing to listen to offers to sell, because Providence was a hot property, as the only professional baseball team in eastern New England that could play Sunday baseball. In addition to the Sunday games at Rocky Point, the Providence ballclub had an inflated value after winning the 1905 Eastern League pennant.

Collins thought Worcester to be a better deal than Providence in the short term, since Powers was unlikely to sell unless the offer contained a hefty premium over his purchase price. He and Burkett brought in Doe as a third partner to pursue a Worcester franchise. Burkett negotiated with the owner of the Concord, New Hampshire, ballclub in the New England League to buy that franchise and move it to Worcester. The owner, the Boston & Maine Railroad, was motivated to sell and Burkett drove a hard bargain. In early February the *Worcester Telegram* announced that Burkett would establish a team in Worcester after purchasing the Concord franchise for $4,000—which included 16 players and the grandstand, bleachers, and fences at Rumford Field, which "will be torn down and the lumber delivered to Burkett in Worcester, that being a condition of the sale."[4]

A new ballpark was built in Worcester on Shrewsbury Street, at the corner of Casco Street, to accommodate a total capacity of 4,500 spectators, 1,500 in the covered grandstand and 3,000 in the bleachers down the left- and right-field lines. Burkett arranged to have the local street railway company extend a trolley line to the ballpark, and for the city to widen the street into a boulevard. The ball grounds were thus dubbed Boulevard Park. Union Station, with railroad connections to Boston and Providence, was just one-half mile down Shrewsbury Street, providing easy access to spectators from locations outside of the city of Worcester.

Collins was a silent partner in the running of the Worcester ballclub. When the ballclub was officially formed as a corporation on March 30, Burkett was listed as the president and treasurer, and Robert O'Toole as clerk, with the board of directors consisting of Burkett, O'Toole, and Doe.[5] Collins provided $3,000 of the reported total paid-in capital of $10,000.[6]

Burkett was a virtual one-man show in Worcester; he was not only the president and treasurer in the front office, but he was also the manager and an outfielder on the baseball diamond. The notoriously tough-nosed Burkett got results on the ball field as he led Worcester to the New England League pennant in 1906, the first of four consecutive first-place finishes in the league. Burkett also achieved results in the treasury, as the Worcester ballclub turned a profit of $8,000 in its first year of operation, enough to pay off the debt incurred to build its ballpark.[7]

The fiery Burkett became renowned for his vocal outbursts and physical intimidation in New England League games. Less than a month into the 1906 season, Burkett had to be removed by policemen from the Fall River ballpark after he punched the umpire. "Burkett came tearing up to the plate with his eyes flashing fire and his tongue adding fuel," the *Fall River Globe* described Burkett's tirade. "He became so abusive in his talk that Umpire Henry ordered him to the bench. Burkett refused to go, then shot out his fist and caught the umpire on the jaw. Quick as a flash the umpire swung his right and landed on Burkett's nose. In a jiffy they were at it hammer and tongs."[8] Burkett's antics were good for business, as many spectators went to the ballpark to see what his temper would lead to next.

For the 1907 season, Burkett (perhaps with Collins' help) showed a flair for promotion, as he used his extensive connections with major leaguers to arrange numerous exhibition games, which often attracted more spectators than did the team's league games. Sometimes Burkett didn't let the league schedule deter his exhibition calendar. In June 1907, Burkett sent a scrub team to Lowell to play the team's scheduled league game (which Worcester lost), while the regulars stayed in Worcester to play an exhibition with the St. Louis Browns of the American League (which pocketed the Worcester ballclub a good sum of money). Burkett also lined up several Sunday games in 1907, when the Providence ballclub wasn't using the Rocky Points ball grounds. While the attendance for the Worcester games at Rocky Point was respectable, at 2,000 to 3,000 people, it didn't measure up to the 5,000 to 10,000 spectators that the Providence club usually attracted to its Sunday games there. The Sunday games weren't a spectacular financial deal for the Worcester ballclub, because Rocky Point was just too far of an excursion for many Worcester patrons.

Burkett also experimented with the novel idea of night baseball in 1907. The Worcester team played a game under artificial lights on September 9 in Worcester against a barnstorming team of Cherokee Indians, who strung 30 gasoline lamps on five poles around the perimeter of the diamond, just outside the base lines. The actual game played under the lights was a modified version of regular baseball, since the lighting system fell short of approximating natural conditions during the day. "The ball used is about one and a half the size of a league ball, and is of soft material, making it well nigh impossible to hit out of the infield," one newspaper described the modifications to the equipment for night play. "Its surface is coated with a glistening white enamel so that it can be plainly seen. The bat used is very small and light."[9] The novelty game attracted a decent crowd. "There were 2400 paid admissions and several hundred small boys who worked in by some means other than buying a ticket at the gate," the *Worcester Telegram* remarked about the audience for the 9–7 victory by the Cherokees.[10] The ballgame at night attracted more than eight times the audience of that afternoon's game with Brockton in the intra-league postseason series. The published attendance for the Worcester-Brockton game was just 381 people.

In 1907 the Worcester ballclub once again turned a profit, enough to pay a dividend of $1,200 to Collins.[11] But that was it for a return on his investment until Collins sold his stock in 1912. Doe sold his stock in the ballclub in the fall of 1907 to O'Donnell, who assumed the treasurer's duties. Partly because O'Donnell paid himself a salary, and Burkett began to take a salary too, the Worcester ballclub finances suffered. "There were no dividends for Collins," the *Worcester Telegram* commented after Collins sold his stock in 1912. "The books showed that the club did not make any money and of course Collins didn't get any $2500 a year salary because he wasn't around to see if the club could afford to pay him that much."[12]

During the summer of 1906, based on the auspicious beginning with his February 1906 investment in the Worcester ballclub, Collins decided his future was in making a larger investment in a higher-level minor league ballclub. He set his sights on the Buffalo and Providence ballclubs of the Eastern League.

CHAPTER 19

Manager Absent Without Leave

By mid–February 1906, with owner John I. Taylor dispatched to Europe for six months by Ban Johnson, Jimmy Collins had virtually unfettered control of the Boston Americans ballclub. Six months later, though, Collins was a pariah, having deserted the ballclub to soak up the sun at a popular suburban Boston beach. What started out as a premeditated effort by Collins to transition into the next phase of his baseball life — as a ballclub executive — instead embarrassingly turned into the lowest moment of his baseball career. What happened?

Collins was highly motivated to be part of an ownership group to buyout Taylor and control the ballclub, with Collins becoming the president. With Taylor out of the way for the 1906 season, Johnson had given Collins a tryout as president. However, just when he was on the cusp on moving from the baseball diamond to the executive suite, three factors combined to derail Collins from achieving his ultimate goal in professional baseball. First, Collins quickly discovered that he just wasn't good at the job of being an executive. Second, the early success of his business partnership with Jesse Burkett in the Worcester ballclub of the New England League nudged him to seek his goal of being an owner-executive in the minor leagues rather than at the major league level. Third, Collins, a 36-year-old bachelor, had fallen in love and was looking to get married in the near future.

Being the top man in the Boston ballclub was not a good fit for Collins. His initial task was to convince the ballplayers to accept cuts in their salary for the 1906 season, which were contained in the contracts that Taylor had approved and sent out before he left for his European vacation. This task changed his relationship with the ballplayers, since he now held four jobs: player, captain, manager, and acting president. He did everything except cut the grass and man the treasury. Since the ballplayers now viewed Collins more as their employer and less as their teammate (as they had for the previous five seasons), they no longer had the same level of respect for him (except, of course, his good friend Chick Stahl). Boston's play on the baseball diamond immediately showed the reduced motivation level of the ballplayers.

After Boston lost its first three games, the team defeated the New York Highlanders in the Patriots Day holiday twin bill on April 19 before splitting the next eight games on the road to end April with a 6–7 record, in fifth place in the American League standings. That was the high point of the 1906 season for the Boston Americans. As Fred Lieb relates in his history of the Boston ballclub, "If the descent from first place to fourth seemed quite a drop in 1905, the great debacle came in 1906, when the Pilgrims plunged through the cellar door into the bottomless pit."[1] Over a two-year span, Collins plummeted from revered hero who led a veteran team to a second consecutive pennant to reviled bum who deserted an aging last-place team.

After Boston lost its final game of the road trip on May 1, the team rattled off 19 consecutive losses on its home turf at the Huntington Avenue Grounds, not winning another ballgame again until the team defeated Chicago on May 25. On May 2 the team sunk into last place, where it stayed for the remainder of the 1906 season. By the end of the 20-game losing streak on May 24, the Boston Americans were 16 games out of first place, and hopelessly out of the pennant race. Boston's 20-game losing streak in 1906 was an American League record that stood for more than eight decades, until the 1988 Baltimore Orioles lost 21 straight games.[2] Collins played third base for the first 18 games of the 20-game losing streak, but he put John Godwin at third in the May 23 game, with "a lame knee keeping him on the bench."[3]

As many a newspaper article made clear at the time, the aging nucleus of the Boston team was the problem. As some writers noted, the more specific problem was "Collins' unwillingness to break up his old champions," particularly replacing second baseman Hobe Ferris and outfielder Buck Freeman.[4] Collins was also criticized for not overhauling the veteran pitching staff headed by Cy Young and his inability to produce an adequate replacement for veteran catcher Lou Criger, since the current crop of new catchers (Charlie Armbruster, Charlie Graham, and Bob Peterson) wasn't nearly good enough. "One can't help but admire Collins for sticking by the men who made him famous. But a change is needed. Everybody wins but Boston," the *Washington Post* summarized the sorry situation in Boston. "As soon as Jimmy forgets old-time friendships and proceeds to clean house, the sport will blossom [in Boston] where it is fast falling to decay."[5] However, attempts to retool the Boston Americans were ineffective during the 1906 season. Over the next century, a number of baseball historians excoriated Collins for staying with graying veterans during the 1906 season as the prime example of his deficiency as a manager.

The big problem for Collins, despite being the acting president in 1906, was that he didn't control the purse strings of the Boston ballclub. Business manager Hugh McBreen controlled the money, and he only took orders from the Taylor family. While nominal owner John I. Taylor was on his European "vacation," his father, the real owner, Charles H. Taylor, made the money decisions. Either because of disinterest, engulfment in his newspaper business, or to spite Collins for embarrassing his son, Charles Taylor did not approve any proposed deals to spend large sums of money to acquire ballplayers. The best Collins could do was sign a few raw recruits, such as catcher Bill Carrigan and outfielder Jack Hoey who both joined the team straight from the campus of Holy Cross College, and outfielder Jack Hayden. Collins couldn't execute a trade for new players, since he had no talent, young or old, to offer in exchange. Even if he could do a trade with some of his friends who were managers in both major leagues, there was a legitimate question whether they would go so far as to help Collins win a third pennant within a four-year span.

Collins' tenure as an independently operating acting president came to an abrupt end on May 17 when Johnson arrived in Boston to "help out" Collins in acquiring some new ballplayers. After a "conference" between the two men, Johnson sent out telegrams "to hunt for new material for Boston." Three days later Collins and Johnson went to New York City to negotiate face-to-face with the management of several visiting teams there, in particular the Chicago Cubs and the St. Louis Browns.[6] Johnson's effort to intercede as an intermediary to improve the Boston situation was not at all unusual during his reign as American League president. As his biographer Eugene Murdock writes, "He was anxious to maintain equality of talent throughout the league, and consequently trades to build up weaker clubs, which would promote close pennant races and increase fan interest, were not unusual."[7] However, Johnson's attempt to twist arms to assist Collins failed to produce any tangible results to inject new talent into the Boston team, and actually exacerbated an already negative situation.

Because Collins resented Johnson's intrusion into his independence to run the Boston ballclub as acting president, his relationship with Johnson began to deteriorate from this point forward. While Johnson had Collins' back during the previous five seasons in gratitude for Collins' role in elevating and solidifying the new American League as a worthy competitor to the National League, Collins severely tested the limits of that gratitude during the summer of 1906.

Collins did not seem to appreciate the preferential treatment that he had

After American League president Ban Johnson ousted John I. Taylor as president of the Boston Americans, by forcing him to take an extended European vacation, Jimmy Collins effectively became the interim president of the Boston ballclub in 1906 (note the subservient position of Taylor to centerpiece Collins in this 1906 team poster). After Collins failed as an executive and then deserted the ballclub in midsummer, Johnson had to orchestrate an ousting of Collins, via suspension, to sever him from all ballclub duties (National Baseball Hall of Fame Library, Cooperstown, New York).

received at the hands of Johnson. His confidence seemed to turn into hubris after his elevation to acting president in early 1906. Yes, Collins did have a significant role in making Johnson the success that he was by 1906, but Collins didn't respect the power that Johnson could wield that he had withheld during the formative years of the league under the guise of loyalty to Collins. Since

Johnson's ego was much larger than Collins' ambition, eventually Johnson would trump Collins when it came to protecting the Boston baseball market. Now that John Fitzgerald was mayor of Boston — the first American–born Irish Catholic to be elected to that office — appeasing the Taylors and other Boston Brahmins became a higher priority to Johnson than keeping happy an ambitious Irish-American third baseman.

Since Johnson couldn't personally supervise Collins, he brought in Charles H. Taylor, the father of John I., to oversee the Boston operation before his son returned from Europe. Since the elder Taylor was publisher of the *Boston Globe*, this move put Collins at a further disadvantage by limiting the positive newspaper coverage that he might otherwise expect from fellow Irish-American Tim Murnane, the baseball editor of the *Globe*. Murnane knew where he stood in the Brahmin-Irish battle in the Boston community. The 55-year-old Murnane had small mouths to feed at home, the children of his second marriage, so he was not about to jeopardize his paycheck to help out Collins. If this were Buffalo, the ethnic situation would have been handled differently, but Collins played baseball in Boston, not Buffalo.

Apparently, Collins' girlfriend, Sadie Murphy, hadn't regaled Collins enough about the stark reality of being Irish-American in the city of Boston. Sadie, who was 27 years old (nine years younger than Collins), grew up in the working class home of her immigrant parents, Patrick and Honora Murphy, who struggled to raise seven daughters.[8] Her father was a laborer who died in 1897 at age 50.[9] Her widowed mother ran a lodging house at 26 Greenleaf Street, which was a short throw from the third-base-line fence at the Huntington Avenue Grounds.[10] Sadie experienced first-hand how tough life could be as an Irish-American in Boston.

Collins played only sporadically following the end of the 20-game losing streak, getting into just 37 games during the entire 1906 season, as he claimed the injured knee prevented him from playing. "My knee will stand all the sudden strains that I can be brought to bear in running ahead or back, but the quick twists to the side are what hurts," Collins explained in early June when the team had a Sunday off in Detroit. However, the apparent bum knee didn't stop Collins from organizing and participating in a fishing trip to a lake 20 miles outside of Detroit where "the plucky sportsmen kept at it till nightfall, coming home hungry and empty handed."[11] Collins seemed to use a small leg injury as an excuse to not play third base, when as a younger man he would have taken the field without question.

Red Morgan and Godwin split the third-base duties for Boston in 1906, as by mid–June Collins was managing the team in street clothes rather than in his baseball uniform, with Stahl as acting captain. Not playing third base highlighted a significant deficiency in Collins' managerial skill set: as a bench manager he was far less effective than he was as a playing manager. On the field he could lead his men through action; on the bench his quiet leadership was lost on the ballplayers. By the end of June, Collins was being paid an $8,500 annual salary to effectively accomplish nothing for the Boston ballclub.

While the Americans were stinking up the Huntington Avenue Grounds, over in Worcester, 40 miles west of Boston, Jesse Burkett was winning ballgames and driving his ballplayers toward the New England League pennant, before good crowds at the newly constructed Boulevard Park. Burkett was in a similar position as Collins, performing as a ballplayer in addition to the managerial duties as captain, manager, and club president. The sticky situation of granting Burkett his release from the Boston ballclub to play for Worcester became a non-issue when Collins was put in complete charge of the Boston ballclub in February. The obvious conflict of interest to grant Burkett his release to improve the prospects for Collins to make money on his investment in the Worcester ballclub wasn't seen as unethical at the time.

On Sunday, July 1, Collins abruptly left the ballclub following the team's return to Boston after a lengthy western road trip, where it was to play one game with the New York Highlanders on June 30 before a short three-day road trip to Washington and a culminating twin bill on the Independence Day holiday. Collins never boarded the train to go to Washington and also never appeared at the Huntington Avenue Grounds for the team's homestand over the next two weeks in July. Stahl was designated as the acting manager in addition to his duties as acting captain. At this point in the 1906 season, Collins made his decision to stop performing all his duties for the Boston ballclub and focus on his next step in baseball. Given his difficult times as the acting president of the Boston Americans, and deteriorating relationship with league president Ban Johnson, Collins decided to abandon his quest to be a major league owner and instead pursue ownership of a minor league ballclub where he felt he could have more control over the ballclub's destiny.

On July 1, Collins and Hugh Duffy resurrected the investment group that they had started back in January with Burkett, which had led to the purchase of the Worcester ballclub by Burkett and Collins (and Fred Doe) without Duffy. For the July 1 discussion, they invited only Doe as a potential investor since Burkett was fully involved in running the Worcester operation. Duffy, then the manager of the Philadelphia team in the National League, was in Boston on July 1 for his team's series with the Boston Nationals that was set to begin the next day. Duffy, in his third year at the helm of the Phillies, was an interested party to pursue ownership of a minor league ballclub for the 1907 season because by June it was already a widespread rumor that Duffy would be fired at the end of the 1906 season.

The three men set their sights on buying into one of two Eastern League ballclubs, either Buffalo or Providence. Both had good income prospects. Collins would help draw crowds in Buffalo, his hometown, while Providence used the Rocky Point resort to be the only Sunday-playing professional baseball team in eastern New England. Shockingly, Collins decided to completely quit doing his duties for the Boston ballclub and take some time off before he began to negotiate his way into a minor league ownership.

Ironically, on the same day that Collins was plotting to mutiny from the Boston Americans, Tim Murnane wrote in his Sunday *Boston Globe* column that "Capt. Collins is looking 50 percent better than when he left with the team for the west."[12] Murnane was referring to Collins' ailing knee and the fact that Collins was walking better, indicating a possibility that Collins would rejoin the team as its third baseman. Of course, unbeknownst to Murnane, Collins looked better because he had decided to jettison all the drama of Boston baseball and move on with his life.

As Collins stayed away from the ballpark for the next two weeks, most Boston baseball writers pretended to ignore the situation that Stahl was running the team and Collins was nowhere to be seen. Even the *Boston American* newspaper, the Hearst afternoon tabloid that specialized in sensational stories to appeal to the lurid interest of the masses, failed to publicize the unauthorized absence of Collins. During his hiatus from the ballclub, Collins was often spotted at Nantasket Beach, a short boat ride from Boston to the town of Hull on the South Shore of Massachusetts, which was a popular summer getaway from the Boston heat.[13] Although she is never mentioned by name in news accounts about the beach exploits, Collins was likely frolicking with Sadie and her family at Nantasket. Her sister Elizabeth (with her husband Thomas Goode, a Boston policeman, and her children) was a frequent visitor to Nantasket along with other members of the Goode family. Thomas and Elizabeth Goode later purchased a summer cottage at Nantasket for their family members to enjoy extended stays during the summer.[14]

In mid-July Collins briefly returned to the Huntington Avenue Grounds to publicize the testing of his knee. As Murnane related in the *Globe*, "His knee was very troublesome, and it did not take long to convince him that he was still unfit to return to the game."[15] Jake Morse in *Sporting Life* was a bit more descriptive: "The sensation of the hour was the sudden departure of Jimmy Collins. It seems that after Collins had made an attempt to get in the game his knee again gave-way and in disgust he took off his uniform and quit the team."[16] After Collins left the ballpark, the ballclub issued a bulletin stating, "Collins' relations with the Boston club are unchanged.... During his continued absence Chick Stahl will be in charge of the club, as he has been for some time."[17]

While Johnson's patience with Collins had worn thin by this point, he urged Charles Taylor not to formally suspend Collins, who continued to be paid by Taylor while he was performing few duties for the ballclub. The club sent him to a doctor to get him into playing shape as soon as possible. Johnson told Collins to "put on his uniform and get out on the coaching lines where his advice would be of much value to the younger players."[18] Pressured by Johnson, Collins did rejoin the Boston Americans for the team's three-week road trip that began in late July. However, on the way to Detroit, Collins got off the train in Buffalo, to spend some time at his parents' house, causing Johnson to tersely announce: "No, Mr. Collins is not with the team. I don't know when he will rejoin it. That is his own affair."[19] Collins caught up with the team at its next stop in St. Louis, where he pinch-hit in the July 29 game. Upon the team's return to Boston in mid–August, Collins "limped a little" on the field and pinch-hit in the August 16 game.[20] Then he disappeared again.

On August 29, the front-page headline in the *Boston Globe* told the whole story: "Capt. Jimmy Collins No Longer at Helm: Indefinitely Suspended by Boston American League Club." After his several absences without leave, Johnson and Taylor decided "that leniency no longer was a virtue, but that the welfare of the team and the interests of the American League in this city demand that drastic measures be taken for competent management of the team. Consequently came Collins' suspension." Stahl was officially put in charge of the team. Murnane, in an uncharacteristically heavy-handed analysis of the situation, no doubt upon the orders of publisher Taylor, wrote: "His repeated absences from the ball field and his absolute desertion of the club a few weeks ago clearly have exemplified not only his lack of interest, but in a larger measure has magnified his incompetency to handle a baseball situation which demanded thought, ingenuity, and baseball brains." Johnson continued the character assassination of Collins by saying, "It is beyond me to explain why he should so grossly betray the confidence and trust reposed to him."[21] Once again lounging at Nantasket Beach, Collins told reporters that he didn't care about the suspension. He also claimed another injury, after suffering a spill in a horse-drawn carriage ride on Sunday, August 26.[22]

After paying Collins hundreds of dollars a month to do absolutely nothing for the Boston ballclub, Charles Taylor stopped paying Collins at the time of the suspension and reportedly docked Collins $3,000 for non-performance of his duties.[23] Collins was infuriated by this act, since he contended that he had an ironclad contract, a "non-forfeitable" one, which required that he be paid whether or not he played and managed.[24] Morse, in his *Sporting Life* column, reported that Collins "has taken legal counsel and has been informed by it that he cannot be traded or sold, according to the terms of his contract,

[and] if the Boston Club cares not to avail itself further of his services it must give him his release." Morse then curiously added, "Collins is satisfied to go elsewhere if he is not wanted."[25] For a man who seemed completely disinterested in playing baseball during the 1906 season, why would Collins be "satisfied to go elsewhere"? Although Morse did not explain any further, Collins needed his release from Boston in order to be an owner-manager-player at the minor league level, just as he had been able to accommodate Burkett to do with the Worcester ballclub.

A frustrated Collins was interviewed by Morse two weeks after his suspension, where Collins was uncharacteristically outspoken about the conditions he had to manage under in 1905 and 1906. In the article subtitled "Collins on 'Inside Affairs,'" Morse quoted Collins as saying:

> I am not a talker and have refrained from discussing my troubles with the Boston Club because I do not believe in spouting one's grievances. I have been accused of insubordination, lack of knowledge of the game, poor leadership and pretty near every other sin on the base ball calendar. It has been a particularly sore spot with me that I should be blamed for the trades that the club made.... At different times I have tried to buy players for the team to strengthen it and invariably was sat on. I tried to secure McIntyre, of Detroit, and McFarland, of Chicago, both of which players I could have purchased. But there was nothing doing. Last year I saw that a number of the players would have to be replaced and I could have got young men who would have delivered the goods, to take their places, but I was not allowed to make the changes I desired. As a result the Boston team has become a huge joke. I am tired of being saddled with the errors of others and want the truth to be known.[26]

However, Morse then took Collins to task for his transgressions: "Granted that what Collins says is true, that did not excuse, under any circumstances, the way he left the club without permission. Certainly that was not granted in the contract.... Few men ever had a better thing than Collins and ever received more princely treatment. It is almost beyond explanation that a young man with such a fine prospect should have so far forgotten himself and what was due from him as Collins did."[27] As a man of the Jewish faith in protestant-dominated Boston, Morse knew how hard it was to ascend within the Boston business community, and thought that Collins, a man of the Catholic faith, had foolishly tossed away an opportunity to get the better of the city's protestant establishment.

As Collins enjoyed the sea and surf at Nantasket Beach, he had already set his sights on becoming part of the ownership group of one of two Eastern League ballclubs, either Buffalo or Providence. Majority owners in both ballclubs were looking to sell out, George Stallings in Buffalo and Pat Powers in Providence. The only question was how large of an investment would be required to purchase the majority interest; could it be low enough to return a sufficient profit on the investment? Then, who would be the partners in the investment group?

When Stallings announced on September 12 that he was leaving the Buffalo ballclub, rumors began to swirl that Collins would replace him. However, underneath headlines like "Collins to Lead Buffalo?" lay a wire service report that was meaningless: "Friends of James Collins of the American League Club of Boston, with the approval of one of the Buffalo Club's prominent officials, telegraphed Collins advising him to bid for Stallings' stock, with the object of succeeding Stallings in management."[28] Through his friends, Collins was manipulating the press to ferret out interest from Buffalo ownership and at the same time attempt to keep Stallings' price low, since the market price was expected to be high since Buffalo had won the Eastern League title during the 1906 season.

However, compounding Collins' plans to obtain a substantial ownership stake in a top minor league ballclub was turmoil in the president's post in both the Buffalo ballclub and the Eastern League office. Collins got along with Jacob Stein, the Buffalo president, but he realized that Stein wanted to step down from the presidency to focus on his law practice. Collins was also friendly with Harry Taylor, the Eastern League president, but he knew from his negotiations to buy the Providence ballclub that Pat Powers wanted to return to be president of the Eastern League after he finalized the sale of the Providence ballclub.

Powers was looking to make a quick buck on his investment in the Providence ballclub, having just purchased his controlling interest in December 1905. Sunday games were a very significant part of the financial equation in Providence, since Powers was not content simply to play Sunday games at Rocky Point during the team's homestands. On road trips, Powers routinely had the Providence team travel back to Rhode Island to play exhibition games on Sunday with major league teams. Distance was no deterrent to get in a Sunday game at Rocky Point. For Providence's August 5 game with the Pittsburgh Pirates, the team took a train on Saturday night from Baltimore to Rhode Island and then immediately after the game boarded a train to Montreal to resume the team's road schedule on Monday.[29] Powers was seeking to capitalize on this money-making opportunity by extracting a high price for the ballclub from the future owners.

Within Collins' three-person investment group, Doe became the lead negotiator with Powers. Since Doe could use only one business partner who doubled as a player-manager, either Collins or Duffy had to drop out of the ownership group. Duffy was willing to go in with Doe at a higher price than Collins wanted to pay, since Duffy had far fewer viable options in baseball after being fired as the Philadelphia manager at the conclusion of the 1906 season. Duffy and Doe were the sole investors that purchased the controlling interest of Powers on November 9, 1906.[30] Although the sale price was not divulged at the time, it was later revealed that Duffy and Doe paid a total of $15,000 for Powers' stock in the ballclub, $7,500 each as equal partners.[31] Collins must have thought that $7,500 was too steep a price.

Powers pulled a power play as the Eastern League owners booted Taylor as league president on October 23, by a vote of five to three.[32] Taylor, tired of baseball politics, focused again on the law and two months later was appointed a judge. Alexander Potter was elected Buffalo president in late December, who would become a thorn in Collins' future quests to become the primary owner of the Buffalo ballclub.[33] With Taylor and Stein stepping out of the picture, Collins backed off from attempting to buy Stallings' stock in the Buffalo ballclub.

Because Collins was insistent on being a majority owner, rather than a less-powerful minority owner as he was in the Burkett–dominated Worcester ballclub, his hubris was an obstacle to ever become an owner of the Buffalo ballclub. He would have been better off buying into the 26-man ownership group that purchased the ballclub prior to the 1905 season, led by Taylor and Stallings, which was structured as a corporation.[34] Even as a minority owner, his stock would have escalated in value and he would have had a shot at being president by working from the inside.

Collins was in a pickle, unfortunately. He had played his two best cards at buying into minor league ownership, and came up empty on both opportunities, but yet he was not ready to retire from baseball to live off his investment income. Although returning to the Boston Americans looked to be the longest of long shots in September, by December Collins was negotiating to return to Boston as its third baseman for the 1907 season.

By late October, Collins was already laying the groundwork to try to return to the Boston Americans. "The controlling interests of the Boston club and myself understood each other. I had a talk with General Taylor, owner of the club, and I think that before long I will know definitely what my position is," Collins said in an interview with the *Buffalo Express*. "It was unfortunate that I hurt my leg as I did. I know a lot of people thought that I ought to be playing when it was a physical impossibility, and that made matters worse. I certainly wanted to get in the game bad enough," he said, trying to deflect criticism that he had deserted the ballclub.[35]

To prop up his value as a ballplayer to entice Taylor to take him back, Collins used his good friends in baseball to publicize proposed transactions involving Collins. In mid–October, Clark Griffith, manager of the New York Highlanders, spread rumors that New York was willing to offer some regular players in exchange for Collins.[36] In early November, Griffith's buddy Joe Cantillon, who had recently left the job as manager of the Milwaukee minor league team to become the manager in Washington, recommended Collins to replace him. "The Milwaukee people, it is understood, are willing to give $7,500 a year with full control of the team," the *Washington Post* reported on the Collins' ploy, "and the berth has caught Collins' fancy."[37] Later in November the *Philadelphia Inquirer* reported that Connie Mack expressed interest in bringing Collins to Philadelphia to anchor the Athletics infield.[38] Jim McAleer, manager of the St. Louis Browns, was said to be interested in acquiring Collins.[39]

Of course, all these expressions of interest in Collins were just fabricated rumors. Collins' no-cut contract was a huge obstacle to any trade actually being consummated, since the acquiring ballclub would be stuck with the 36-year-old Collins for two more seasons at $8,500 per season without any recourse to remove him from the team. Collins even enlisted the help of lawyer Henry Killilea, the former owner of the Boston Americans who was very familiar with Collins' contract from the October 1903 renegotiation, to convince Taylor to take back Collins.[40] Killilea's reasoning likely was that Taylor would be responsible to pay Collins whether or not he played during the 1907 and 1908 seasons, given his ironclad contract with the Boston ballclub, so why not try to get something out of Collins for the money. This was the critical leverage in the discussion; otherwise, why else would Taylor agree to bring back Collins? Even the most teary-eyed, knee-scraping, voice-cracking apology from Collins couldn't make amends for his transgressions.

The icing on the cake were Chick Stahl's numerous public expressions of loyalty to Collins. "Jimmy and I have been pals for ten years. Consequently I am pulling for Collins for his old job as manager," Stahl said that fall. "Taylor should keep him by all means, and if he keeps him Jimmy should be made manager. I don't want the job of bossing my old boss, and I won't undertake the proposition."[41] Despite his loyalty to Collins and misgivings about being his boss, Stahl accepted the job as manager of the Boston Americans for the 1907 season when John I. Taylor, who had returned in mid–November from Europe, offered it to him in early December.[42]

Collins showed up at the American League meeting in Chicago in mid–December, where the theatrics continued with McAleer making a big fuss about the St. Louis Browns acquiring Collins, but then he backed off by saying that Collins' contract was a problem. In the end, Collins apologized to Charles Taylor and then met with John I. Taylor and Stahl to come to an agreement about the conditions of his return to the team.[43] There are no indications that Ban Johnson participated in the discussions related to Collins returning to Boston as strictly a ballplayer.

When he burned his bridges with Johnson during the summer of 1906, Collins gave up any chance of ever returning to be a manager or ballclub owner in the American League. There are no public reports that Collins and Johnson ever met again after the 1906 season. While he paid a large price for the unwise risks he took in 1906, Collins in the end walked away with a deal to be grossly overpaid to play third base for two more major league seasons. It was a generous wedding present for his upcoming nuptials.

CHAPTER 20

Making Sense of "It"

After making amends with President Taylor at their mid–December 1906 meeting in Chicago, Jimmy Collins furiously set about to prepare himself to play third base for Boston in the 1907 baseball season. Now 25 pounds heftier than his normal playing weight after six months of inactivity during his hiatus from the Boston ballclub, Collins worked out at the YMCA in Buffalo over the holidays before he left for Hot Springs, Arkansas, in mid–January to get into "first-class trim." Collins told Tim Murnane of the *Globe* that he would "soon have off the superfluous weight which I now carry," and that he was optimistic about the team's chances with his old friend Chick Stahl as manager.[1]

To demonstrate his motivation while at Hot Springs, Collins challenged Dave Brain, the third baseman of the Boston Nationals, to a five-mile roller skate race on January 25. The race was not only a chance to show he was getting into shape, but it was also an opportunity to make some money, as "considerable money changed hands on the result." Brain, a 5-to-4 pre-race favorite, defeated Collins after taking the lead from him in the fourth mile. Brain offered Collins a rematch for a $100 wager, but Collins declined. He still needed to drop some more pounds.[2]

Collins lost 20 pounds during his four weeks in Hot Springs, through a combination of exercise and steam baths, before he left on February 13 to go home to Buffalo.[3] There, he had two weeks to relax before the Boston team was scheduled to leave from New York City on March 1 to go to formal spring training in Little Rock, Arkansas. Now, Hot Springs is just 50 miles from Little Rock. No one questioned why Collins, still a bachelor, didn't just stay in Hot Springs for a few more days until he needed to be in Little Rock, rather than travel by train 1,000 miles to Buffalo and then need to make a return trip of 1,000 miles back to Arkansas.

When the train left New York City for Little Rock on March 1, Collins was still in Buffalo. He sent Stahl a telegram saying that he would leave Buffalo on March 5 and be in Little Rock "ready and fit for business" on March 7.[4] Once he did arrive, the Boston baseball writers that had traveled with the team to Little Rock marveled at the "happy" and "nothing serious" attitude of the usually stone-faced Collins. Collins had them believing that his renewed zest came from no longer being the team's manager. "I feel like a new leaguer," Collins told the writers. "Being a plain, everyday player is great fun, just go out and play ball and it's all over for the day." He added, "I notice that Chick Stahl has already taken on a careworn look. It's a serious problem with Chick. I know he is in dead earnest to get a winner."[5] The suddenly happy-go-lucky Collins was seemingly a different man. However, increasingly, so was Stahl, in a negative way, as the Boston spring excursion wound its way north from Little Rock.

Stahl committed suicide on March 28 in West Baden, Indiana. Why Stahl took his own life remains a mystery more than a century later. An even bigger mystery, which has been virtually ignored by researchers who have examined the Stahl suicide, is the role of Jimmy Collins, who was Stahl's closest friend on the team and his roommate at the West Baden Springs Hotel.

Just before 10:00 o'clock on the morning of March 28, Stahl stepped from his room into the adjoining room where Collins slept and then drank three ounces from a bottle of carbolic acid, a deadly poison that in those days anyone could easily buy at a pharmacy. Collins soon noticed that Stahl was reeling about the room before he rolled onto the bed. Collins saw Bob Unglaub pass by the doorway and pulled him into the room to try to help Stahl. Seeing the bottle and smelling the distinctive odor, Unglaub asked Stahl, who was writhing in agony, why he drank the poison. Stahl then uttered his final words: "It drove me to it." Stahl died minutes later, still dressed in his Boston uniform.[6] Stahl's use of the vague "it" as the reason for his suicide has created the mystery, which has assumed an aura not unlike the conspiracy theories surrounding Lee Harvey Oswald's shooting of President John F. Kennedy in November 1963.

Collins denied any knowledge of what the "it" was that drove Stahl to suicide. "I know of no reason whatsoever for Chick's suicide," Collins said after he had telegraphed Chick's wife about her husband's death. "I knew that he had not been himself for several days and I suspected that something was preying about his mind, but this knowledge came to me in a sort of intangible way, and I was not certain even of that."[7]

The conventional explanation for Stahl's suicide is that the stress of being the Boston manager, which Collins had alluded to on March 7, was too much for Stahl to handle. Stahl did indeed resign the manager's post on March 25 while the Boston team had stopped in Louisville. But his many odd actions prior to that, including talk of suicide, signal a less obvious explanation. Among the theories advanced to explain the suicide include Stahl being blackmailed by a woman he got pregnant the year before and Stahl being involved in a homosexual relationship. The latter theory has some evidentiary basis, as a man in Stahl's hometown committed suicide two days later by drinking carbolic acid and left a note that read, "Bury me beside Chick."[8] Several sportswriters at the time alluded to non-baseball reasons as the motivation for Stahl's suicide, but without specific details.

One theory never advanced to explain Stahl's suicide, which directly connects to Collins, is that Stahl's "it" refers to "marriage," i.e., that marriage drove Stahl to suicide. Stahl had only been married for four months before his death. Collins was the only person who would know that the unspecified antecedent to the pronoun "it" was marriage, since Collins had made a personal revelation to Stahl around that time that he wanted to remain private for as long as possible. Collins, the apparent confirmed bachelor, had married a friend of Stahl's wife during the winter of 1907 before he left for spring training in Little Rock. This marriage would not become public until after Collins was traded from Boston to the Philadelphia Athletics in June 1907. Which aspect of marriage drove Stahl to suicide is unclear. Perhaps when Collins told Stahl that he had married his wife's friend Sadie Murphy, "a chum of Mrs. Chick Stahl," the statement pushed him over the edge.[9]

Stahl married Julia Harmon on November 14, 1906, at the St. Francis de Sales Church on Vernon Street in the Roxbury section of Boston. The wedding was "a quiet affair" that was conducted in a short ceremony at 10:00 A.M. in the church rectory with the bride wearing "a neat-fitting blue traveling suit" and a "hat adorned with ostrich plumes."[10] Since white wedding gowns and elaborate ceremonies were not yet in vogue in 1906, there was nothing unusual about the occasion. The bride and groom were whisked off to South Station to catch a 10:45 A.M. train for their honeymoon trip through upstate New York, with stops in Syracuse and Buffalo ("where they will spend several weeks with Jimmy Collins, one of Chick's teammates"), on their way to Stahl's home in Ft. Wayne, Indiana.[11]

Stahl and his wife split up during their visit to Collins in Buffalo, according to Glenn Stout and Richard Johnson in their encyclopedic history *Red Sox Century*, with Julia returning to Boston and Stahl continuing on to Ft. Wayne where he "spent the rest of the winter living apart from his new wife."[12] Obviously, something caused the separation. Stahl avoided coming to Boston thereafter. He negotiated his deal to be manager when owner John I. Taylor came to Ft. Wayne, and completed the Collins deal in December at the league meeting in Chicago. In mid–January, he spent less than 24 hours in Boston, arriving late at night on January 9 and leaving the following afternoon.[13]

Perhaps Stahl felt that Julia had suckered him into getting married by alleging that she was pregnant, which would explain why they broke up in Buffalo just days after the wedding. Stahl may have thought that Collins had been tricked into a similar fate by Sadie in order to get the 37-year-old ballplayer to the wedding altar. Collins knew what "it" was, and his obsession with keeping his off-the-field life private led him to take the real reason to his grave without divulging "it." He also did not attend the funeral.

The news of Collins' marriage wasn't reported in the Boston newspapers until Tuesday, June 12. The rumors about his marriage presumably started when Collins was spotted back in Boston on Saturday, after that day's game in Philadelphia, when he departed with a female companion on a train bound for Buffalo. When a Buffalo reporter confronted Collins' mother at the 1278 Niagara Street residence on Monday, she tersely "verified the rumor received here early this morning that her son, James Collins, has been married," but she "absolutely

Chick Stahl, one of Jimmy Collins' best friends, committed suicide in March 1907 just months after succeeding Collins as manager of the Boston Americans. Although the reason why Stahl took his own life remains a matter of conjecture, Collins' secret marriage to a friend of Stahl's wife may have been a factor (Library of Congress Prints and Photographs Division, LC-DIG-ppm-sca-18774).

refused, however, to give any details as to the time or place of the ceremony."[14] While Alice Collins confirmed that her son had dropped off his wife in Buffalo on Sunday and then left on Sunday night for Philadelphia (to play in Monday's ballgame), that was about it for details. "What do you people care anyway about the marriage?" she asked the Buffalo reporter, before adding that "Jimmy's wife will attend the marriage [of his sister Margaret on June 12] and will then leave Buffalo to meet her husband" in Philadelphia.[15]

The *Boston American* estimated Collins' wedding date as "three months ago" after an interview with his mother-in-law, Honora Murphy. "My daughter and Mr. Collins have known each other for almost four years," she said. "They were engaged for several months before they were married. I think they were married in Buffalo, N.Y., but I am not sure."[16] When Collins was interviewed in Philadelphia on June 12, he provided no further details on his marriage, as he "answered all questions in regular Yankee style by either parrying or asking one in return." Asked if he had anything to say about his reported marriage, Collins responded, "I guess there is nothing to say, is there?" As to the date of the wedding," he replied, "Quite a while ago," then laughed and ran onto the baseball diamond at Columbia Park.[17] The *Boston Herald* interviewed a friend of Collins on Wednesday, who bluntly said the postponement of the marriage announcement "was nobody's business but their own." The friend did offer that Collins was married "just before the Boston club left for Little Rock in March."[18] Based on these scraps of evidence, it appears that Collins asked Sadie to marry him in mid–December after he made amends with John I. Taylor and secured his hefty salary for the remaining two years of his contract. That would correlate with "engaged for several months" that Sadie's mother told reporters. The marriage ceremony then occurred between February 13 when Collins left Hot Springs for Buffalo and March 5 when he left Buffalo for Little Rock. Since Collins was delayed in his departure to spring training at Little Rock, the marriage was likely near the end of that timeframe rather than at the beginning of it. The marriage also helps to explain why Collins was so eager to drop 20 pounds off his frame at Hot Springs and why he was so effervescent with baseball writers upon his arrival in Little Rock — it wasn't an apparent attempt to redeem himself from his 1906 transgressions.

Collins was not just extremely secretive in 1907 about his marriage; no documentation can be located today to verify that the marriage actually occurred. There is no marriage certificate filed in either Massachusetts (where such records, and an index, can now be easily viewed by the general public at the state archives) or in the city of Buffalo (where a search at City Hall from 1906 to 1908 turned up empty). The records of the Church of the Annunciation in Buffalo, the home parish of the Collins family, have no such marriage record (although there is one for his sister Margaret who married on June 12, 1907). There is also no such marriage in the records of the St. Francis de Sales Church in Boston, the home parish of the Murphy family.[19] Collins could have been married in a civil ceremony at an unusual location. Alternatively, the arrangement could have been simply a so-called "common-law marriage," which is consummated without a ceremony, civil or religious. It is possible that this was Collins's second marriage, in which case either of the above explanations could apply, since the Catholic Church does not, to this day, countenance divorce and remarriage (unless the first spouse has died). The *Buffalo Express* did speculate back in 1893 that Collins had married before he took a lengthy trip to Chicago immediately after the end of the 1893 baseball season.

In response to Stahl's death, Collins hurled himself into the game of baseball. While Taylor replaced Stahl as manager three times (Cy Young, George Huff, and Bob Unglaub) as Boston plummeted to the bottom of the American League standings, Collins focused on sharpening his game at bat and in the field. In the April 27 game against Philadelphia, the *Boston Globe* reported that "Collins made two beautiful plays, one on a catch with one hand on a throw from Unglaub, and a jumping catch of a liner from Cross."[20] By May 20, Collins was the leading hitter on the Boston team, with a .296 average. His 37-year-old body was still up to the rigors of major league play. On June 6, Collins played his last game in a Boston uniform, when he went 1-for-3 in a 6–2 loss to Detroit at the Huntington Avenue Grounds, as "Collins got in one sensational assist and several plays of an extra quality."[21] Taylor finally had someone to take Collins off his hands to eliminate the ongoing problems he had with his overly ambitious third baseman.

Connie Mack, manager of the Philadelphia Athletics, expressed interest in acquiring his old friend Collins to play third base. On June 6, Mack boarded an evening train in Philadelphia to go to Boston to negotiate a deal with Taylor.[22] Ordinarily such mid-season transactions were conducted by telegram or long-distance telephone call. But Mack wanted to talk to Collins face-to-face first, to assess his motivation to play for the Athletics, before any discussions with Taylor, since taking on the $8,500 annual salary in Collins' contract was a substantial financial commitment for the Philadelphia ballclub.

Mack and Collins had been friends since the nascent days of the fledgling American League, when Mack had negotiated the lease in Boston on behalf of Ban Johnson and Charles Somers to house what would become the Huntington Avenue Grounds. As the managers of two of the eight American League ballclubs for the first six years of the league's existence, their genial relationship extended well beyond simply baseball matters, even though Mack was an owner-manager and Collins a player-manager.

The discussion between Mack and Collins at their meeting on June 7 was never divulged to the public. Collins no doubt told Mack that in addition to his physical fitness to play third base better than the Athletics' current occupant, John Knight, he also had a rejuvenated mental attitude that would enhance his performance on the baseball diamond that summer. Collins certainly confided to Mack that he had secretly married before the 1907 season began and now expected to raise a family, so that he was motivated to earn a World Series check on a pennant-winning team. Collins knew what factors appealed to Mack. He knew that the widower Mack was "a devoted family man," who raised three children on his own and helped to support numerous other relatives in his extended family. Collins likely suspected that Mack, in the words of his biographer, "believed in the stabilizing effects of marriage on established players."[23] When Collins had Mack convinced that he was a former bachelor who now faced greater responsibilities in life, and would play hard on the baseball field to earn more money, the two men went to talk to Taylor. Since Collins now had significant leverage in the negotiation, with Taylor desperate to get rid of him and Mack eager to obtain his services, Collins asked for, and received, a payment of $3,000 to compensate him for his docked pay during his suspensions in the 1906 season.[24] The payment didn't come out of Taylor's pocket, as he simply increased the amount of cash he asked from Mack.

Following the completion of the June 7 ballgame between Boston and Detroit, the trade was announced: Philadelphia sent third baseman John Knight and $7,500 to Boston in exchange for Jimmy Collins.[25] After a hastily arranged farewell dinner that evening at the Hotel Langham, after he packed his belongings and cleaned out his room, Collins left Boston on the 8 o'clock train to Philadelphia. Taylor made sure that Collins didn't get all the baseball headlines in the morning newspapers, though, as that day he completed another transaction, hiring his fourth manager of the season, Jim McGuire. The headline on the front page of the *Boston Globe* the next day was "New Manager and New Third Baseman," accompanied by a large picture of McGuire.

CHAPTER 21

Playing for Mack in Philadelphia

When Jimmy Collins arrived in Philadelphia for his first game with the Athletics on June 8, 1907, Connie Mack's team stood in fourth place in the American League standings, six games out of first place behind the league-leading Chicago White Sox. Mack won his first game with Collins at third base, a victory over the St. Louis Browns, as Collins collected three hits in four at-bats before a Saturday afternoon crowd of 15,000 at Columbia Park. "The reception accorded Collins when he came to bat in the first inning was characteristically Philadelphian," the *Philadelphia Inquirer* described the ovation given Collins. "It was not boisterously demonstrative, but there was no denying its sincerity."[1] Collins would prove to be a fan favorite in Philadelphia as much as he had been in Boston.

Collins provided a spark that ignited the Athletics' push for the pennant in 1907. After the wily Collins arrived from Boston, the Athletics won 11 of their next 15 games to nudge into third place on June 25, three games out of first place. "When Connie Mack secured Jimmy Collins he put his team in the race for the flag," said Detroit manager Hughey Jennings, famous for his "we'll take it easy on you" remark to Collins in 1895 when he played his first game at third base for Louisville. "He may not be the Collins of old, but he is still a great ball player and time will prove that he has added a lot of strength to Mack's team."[2] Collins kept the Athletics in the hunt during the next six weeks in a tight four-way race among the White Sox, Indians, Tigers, and Athletics. "Jimmy Collins has vindicated Manager Mack's judgment," one baseball writer remarked about the impact of the veteran third baseman. "Jimmy has stopped the leak and imbued the team with a feeling of confidence that has been lacking since 1905."[3] Shortly after the Athletics moved into second place on August 10, closely behind first-place Detroit, they took over first

171

place on August 12 with a victory at Detroit. The Athletics remained in first place for ten days, before dropping back to second place on August 25.

In the Labor Day twin bill in Philadelphia on September 2, the Athletics executed a comeback victory in the afternoon game by scoring two runs in the bottom of the ninth inning to defeat Washington, 3–2. However, Collins injured an ankle in that inning, adding to his existing health woes with his wobbly knee. Collins led off the ninth with a walk and advanced to second base on Rube Oldring's single. When Monte Cross laid down a sacrifice bunt, rookie pitcher Walter Johnson fielded the bunt and tried to cut down Collins at third. In his hustle to beat the throw, Collins sprained his ankle when he slid hard into third base. When Johnson's wild throw sailed into the stands, Collins limped home with the tying run and Oldring strolled in behind him with the winning run.[4] In the ensuing celebration, few noticed that Oldring had to help Collins cross home plate.[5] Collins sat out a few ballgames with the injured ankle, but returned to play injury-hampered for the Athletics' stretch run.

With the vast majority of their ballgames at home for the remainder of the season, the Athletics had an edge over Detroit to capture the American League pennant and play in the World Series. The Athletics returned to first place on September 4 and held the top spot for nearly three weeks. However, due to rainouts and ties earlier in the season, doubleheaders began to pile up in September, which crippled Mack's already overworked pitching staff. A loss to the White Sox on September 24 dropped the Athletics into second place with two weeks to go in the 1907 season. The four-game series at Columbia Park between Philadelphia and Detroit on September 27–30 loomed large to decide the American League pennant, with single games on the Friday the 27th and Saturday the 28th, a day of rest on the Lord's Day (Sunday baseball was illegal under Pennsylvania law), and a doubleheader on Monday the 30th.

Collins had helped bring the Athletics to the brink of winning the pennant, but alas it was not a good four days for Connie Mack. On September 27 the Athletics narrowly lost, 5–4. After the September 28 game was cancelled by rain, only one of the two games slated for September 30 was played and it ended in a 9–9 tie after 17 innings. Detroit left town in first place as Philadelphia squandered its opportunity to overtake the Tigers. Only one of the four scheduled games counted in the standings. Unfortunately, those three other games would never be played, along with several others that Mack had deliberately not rescheduled in order to avoid more doubleheaders. League policy at the time was that if games couldn't be made up before the last day of the regular season, they weren't played, even if it might impact which team won the pennant. The three missed games in that Detroit series were crucial to Philadelphia's pennant hopes, since the Athletics wound up with five fewer win-loss decisions than Detroit in the standings.

The September 30 game was an epic in baseball history. "For excitement, drama, and controversy in the crucible of a fierce pennant race, this game rates as great," Mack's biographer Norman Macht describes that game.[6] As an overflow crowd of 24,127 fans watched, with thousands behind a rope in the outfield, Philadelphia led 7–1 after six innings. Collins scored the seventh run in the fifth inning, when he doubled into the overflow crowd and scored on Oldring's fly that was misjudged by Davy Jones at the foot of the ropes. However, the Tigers roared back to tie the game 8–8 at the end of nine innings. The two teams traded runs in the eleventh inning.

In the bottom of the fourteenth inning, the Athletics' Harry Davis hit fly ball into left-center field. As Detroit outfielder Sam Crawford raced along the ropes toward the flight of the ball, a uniformed policeman who was sitting in front of the crowd on a soda crate jumped up to get out of Crawford's way and "ran across him," as the *Philadelphia Inquirer* described the action the next day, before Crawford reached the ball but then dropped it. As Davis stood on second with an apparent double, the packed crowd in Columbia Park roared. However, neither base umpire Tommy Connolly nor home plate umpire Silk O'Loughlin made a call on the play. When the Tigers claimed that the cop had interfered with Crawford, the two umpires talked and then O'Loughlin signaled Davis out. That decision spawned a brawl among the players on the field, which took several minutes to quell. After order was restored on the field, Danny Hoffman hit a single that would have scored Davis with the winning run to end the game with a Philadelphia victory. Instead, Hoffman was stranded on base. After three more innings, the game was called due to darkness.

Nearly a doubleheader was played, innings-wise, but not one win or loss was added to the league standings. "That the Athletics did not win in the regulation nine innings was owing solely to their own fielding misplays," the *Philadelphia Inquirer* opined the next day, referring to the seven Philadelphia errors in the game. "That they did not win out in the fourteenth was due to an outrageous and high-handed usurpation of umpirical authority on the part of 'Silk' O'Loughlin."[7] That devastating tie virtually extinguished the Athletics' hopes for the 1907 pennant. Philadelphia finished the season in second place, one and a half games behind Detroit. Collins batted .272 with 99 hits in his 99 games with Philadelphia. His leg injuries slowed him down to the point where he became essentially a singles hitter, as he stroked 21 doubles but nary a triple or a homer. Most of the Philadelphia players embarked on a barnstorming trip within eastern Pennsylvania to play some local ballclubs to partially replenish their foregone World Series checks. Collins declined to join his teammates on their barnstorming tour, as he immediately left for Buffalo after the last game of the regular season. After all, given his real estate investments in Buffalo, Collins really didn't need the paycheck from either the high-profile World Series event or a low-brow barnstorming excursion.

Collins was financially well off by this point in his baseball career. In early 1908 a syndicated newspaper column named Collins as the third baseman on the Rich Men's Baseball Team, a nine-man all-star lineup of major leaguers who had saved and invested their money wisely. "Jimmy Collins has always invested his coin in Buffalo real estate and collects rents on several pieces of valuable property just now," the article explained the selection of Collins, and went on to estimate the net worth of his properties. "He probably owns close to $40,000."[8] Collins' investment in the Worcester ballclub in the New England League was also doing well in 1907, as the ballclub turned a profit for a second consecutive year and declared a dividend of $1,200 to Collins on his $3,000 investment.[9] Collins was glad that he hadn't invested in the Providence ballclub with Hugh Duffy and Fred Doe, as their disagreements about the operation of the ballclub erupted into a nasty public spat in the fall of 1907.[10] Doe eventually sold out in the spring of 1908 to Royal Rooter Charlie Lavis and his business partner Timothy Crowley.[11]

During the offseason, Collins had surgery to repair his ailing knee. In January 1908 Mack visited Collins in Buffalo on the way back to Philadelphia from Chicago, and found him to be in good shape. "This surgeon performed an operation on the leg and by means of the baking process restored Jim's game leg to its former healthy condition," Mack told reporters back in Philadelphia. "Jim has been practicing in a gymnasium daily to thoroughly test his leg, and is satisfied now that it is sound as it ever was."[12]

For Mack, the 1908 season was a transition year for the Athletics, as he eased out his older ballplayers and experimented with many younger ones to see who would be the replacements. In particular, Mack wanted to find a place to regularly play another Collins, Eddie Collins, an infielder who would go on to a Hall of Fame career after helping the Athletics win four pennants within the five-year span 1910–1914. The Athletics started out strong but then faded after the Fourth of July, finishing in sixth place with a 66–85 record, 22 games behind the Detroit Tigers.

On April 18, 1908, Collins played his first game against the Boston Red Sox, the newly named Americans team that Collins had managed, as his nemesis John I. Taylor had hatched the new name late in 1907. Collins was still a favorite in Boston. "Jimmie Collins was the headliner of the day," the *Boston Globe* reported. "He was given a hearty reception when he walked to the bat and brought out a rousing cheer when he laced the first ball pitched for a fine double to left, tearing around the bases in his best form."[13]

In his last season in the major leagues, Collins was clearly a far less proficient batter than he had been just a few years earlier. He compiled a .217 batting average in 115 games during the 1908 season. He could no longer get the bat around on power throwers like second-year pitcher Walter Johnson of the Senators. "I'll never forget what a shock it was to see the ball streaking by," Collins later recalled about Johnson's fastball.[14] Johnson went on to win 417 ballgames, second best in baseball history, and be an inaugural member of the Baseball Hall of Fame in 1939.

On August 13, 1908, Collins played his last game in Boston as a major leaguer when he participated in a benefit game for Cy Young. Collins played on an all-star team against the regular Boston squad, since it was an off day for all eight teams on the American League schedule. The all-stars won, 3–2, as Collins had two hits and scored the winning run in the eleventh inning after he tripled and crossed the plate on a single by Detroit pitcher, and former Boston teammate, George Winter. A crowd of 18,000 at the Huntington Avenue Grounds gave Young a pleasant sendoff, as he collected $8,000 as the net receipts from the game.[15]

While he enjoyed helping out an old friend and former colleague, Collins took away one lesson from the Cy Young benefit game — there would be no pity party for him in Philadelphia. He would walk away from major league baseball unannounced. Collins played his last major league ballgame on August 29, 1908, when he played in both games of a doubleheader against Detroit at Philadelphia's Columbia Park. Collins went 0-for-2 in the first game and 1-for-3 in the second game (a single in the second inning off the aforementioned Winter) to finish with a .294 career batting average.

With the Athletics on the road for the vast majority of the rest of the 1908 season, Mack relieved Collins of his ballplaying duties so that he could focus on personal business. The time off allowed Collins to concentrate on the next step in his baseball career, to become part-owner of a minor league ballclub. The hiatus from the baseball diamond also permitted Collins to enjoy family time with his newborn daughter Agnes, who was born on August 24 in Philadelphia.[16]

Two weeks after his final game, Mack obliquely announced that Collins was done for the 1908 season. "When the Athletics pull out for Washington this morning, Hartsel, Jimmy Collins, Vickers, Bender and Dygert of the old squad will be left behind," the *Philadelphia Inquirer* reported.[17] But the box scores had already enlightened Athletics fans about the departure of Collins. For the August 31 doubleheader at New York, Mack played two recruits at third base, Frank Manush in the first game and Scott Barr in the second game. Manush lasted just three weeks at third base before his anemic .156 batting average landed him on the bench, in the only major-league tour of duty during his baseball career. On September 21 another recruit, Frank Baker, played third base more successfully. Baker eventually acquired the nickname "home run" and went on to a Hall of Fame career.

Collins certainly departed on good terms with the management of the Philadelphia Athletics. He stayed lifelong friends with Connie Mack and that fall he went hunting with majority owner John Shibe along with teammates John Coombs, Eddie Plank, and Danny Murphy. While they camped on the banks of the Allagash River in Maine, Collins played a prank on Shibe and Coombs as they sat around a campfire while he, Plank and Murphy had supposedly retired to their tent to sleep. A loud animal noise scared Shibe and Coombs, before they looked over at the tent. As Coombs told the story, "Collins, with his cap over his ears, his sweater around his neck, his mackinaw over his shoulders, his feet covered with three pairs of stockings and a number eleven moccasin, and with four blankets wound around him, was uttering sounds which were the cause for the thunder-pealing echo."[18]

Securing his next job in baseball turned out to be more difficult than Collins initially imagined. Since serious changes were afoot in the minor leagues, Collins had to hustle back to Buffalo from Maine to work on securing his next stop in baseball.

CHAPTER 22

Back to the Minor Leagues

After playing his last major league ballgame with the Philadelphia Athletics in 1908, Jimmy Collins had to wait several months for the resolution of a festering feud between the two major leagues and the top two minor leagues, the Eastern League and the American Association, before he could make any progress on his ultimate goal to be the majority owner of a top-flight minor league ballclub. His existing minority interest in the Worcester ballclub of the New England League was just a trial run for something larger.

During the summer of 1908, Collins had heard from old friends like Hugh Duffy at Providence and read in the weekly baseball publications about the rumors that the top ballclubs in the Eastern League and American Association would join forces to form a third major league. The idea was less a real plan and more a negotiation tactic to get the two major leagues to agree to more favorable terms for these two minor leagues than would apply to the other minor leagues under the National Agreement. Representatives of both minor leagues met on November 18 at the Hotel Lafayette in Buffalo, just two miles from Collins' home in North Buffalo. This was the perfect place for Collins to network with ballclub owners in both of the two top minor leagues to assess ownership and managerial opportunities for the upcoming 1909 season, presuming, of course, that the owners could iron out their differences with the major leagues.

At the November 18 meeting, the representatives agreed to a list of seven proposals. At the top of the list were the creation of a separate classification for the Eastern League and the American Association and equal footing with the two major leagues regarding the drafting of minor league ballplayers. They selected a negotiating committee to present these proposals to the National Commission, then the governing body for Organized Baseball, at its December 7 meeting in New York City. They also agreed to hire Henry Killilea, the former owner of the Boston Americans, as their attorney.[1]

Buffalo of the Eastern League and Minneapolis of the American Association were two of the bigger instigators within the two minor leagues. Alexander Potter, president of the Buffalo ballclub, wanted to be in a third major league so that he could get top dollar to sell the ballclub. Mike Cantillon, who co-owned the Minneapolis ballclub along with his brother Joe who was the manager of the Washington Senators of the American League, was constantly at odds with Organized Baseball's hierarchy. Most recently Cantillon caused a ruckus when his Minneapolis team played a few exhibition games with the semi-pro Logan Squares of Chicago, owned by his old pal Jimmy Callahan, the former White Sox manager, who Collins also knew from their days together with the Players Protective Association. The problem was that some of the ballplayers on the Logan Squares were on baseball's ineligible list, thus invoking the cardinal sin that any ballplayer in Organized Baseball couldn't participate in a ballgame that involved an ineligible player.

When the proposal presentation at the December 7 meeting seemed to go well, it appeared that the two minor leagues would get their wishes and avert a war with the major leagues.[2] Collins must have had positive indications of a potential owner-manager-player role in either minor league, perhaps as result of a conversation with either his friend Duffy or his old boss Killilea who were both at the meeting, since he then asked Connie Mack for his unconditional release from the Philadelphia Athletics. On December 11, Mack granted the request.[3] The National Commission formally consented to many of the proposals at its January 5, 1909, meeting, primarily the creation of a new AA classification for both the Eastern League and the American Association (as well as the Pacific Coast League, which hadn't asked to be included).[4] However, the National Commission rejected all the proposals where these two minor leagues would be on equal footing with the major leagues. Since the Eastern League and the American Association now knew what they were — not a quasi third major league, but the highest level of the minor leagues — ballclub owners could now realistically talk with Collins about where he might fit in.

Plan A for Collins was always to buy into the Buffalo ballclub, if the price was right. However, in December 1908 Potter was already asking $50,000 cash to sell the ballclub.[5] When the National Commission agreed to establish the AA classification, Potter upped the price even more. While it had always been the dream situation for Collins to own his hometown ballclub, the price was too high, given what the cautious investor Collins saw as the potential return on the investment. While rumors were rampant in the newspapers that Collins would become an owner-manager of the Buffalo ballclub, it never materialized. Collins "failed in an effort to secure the Buffalo franchise," *Sporting Life* reported. "He made an offer for the local club, but would not pay the almost prohibitive price put on the local team."[6]

Collins got an offer from the Toledo ballclub in the American Association, where one of the minority owners was Charles Somers, the initial owner of the Boston Americans whose financial inducements had lured Collins to jump to the American League. The Toledo offer was just to be a player, not also be the manager. While it was a courtesy offer, it was evidence to the baseball world that someone was interested in the services of the 39-year-old veteran ballplayer.[7] As a last resort, Toledo might do. To become merely a minor league ballplayer was a decided step back for Collins, though, as not only would he not be the manager (a job he had held in the major leagues for six years) but he would also be far from a path to ownership. While Collins realized that sometimes you need to take one step backward in life in order to take two steps forward — he had the example of his father's acceptance of a demotion on the Buffalo police force back in 1885 to lean on — taking two steps backward was another matter.

Plan B was Minneapolis, based on a very preliminary conversation Collins had with co-owner Mike Cantillion at the November meeting in Buffalo. In mid–January 1909, Collins went to Chicago under the guise of being a potential marathon race promoter, ostensibly to observe a marathon race between two runners on January 22 that was sponsored by Jimmy Callahan. When a *Chicago Tribune* sportswriter ran into Collins at the race, he wrote an article that put a positive spin on Collins' employment situation. "Collins has not decided where he will play ball next season," the *Tribune* reported. "He may not be a player at all, being willing to act as a bench manager. He has had offers from various clubs of classes AA and A, and is sure of a good minor league berth." The *Tribune* then noted one of the obstacles facing Collins: "Jimmy is accused of having enough money saved up to kiss baseball goodby."[8] This latter aspect limited the opportunities for Collins, since some people were skeptical that Collins had sufficient motivation to lead a ballclub.

Collins, leveraging his connections, was really in Chicago for a meeting that Callahan had arranged with his buddy Mike Cantillon at Cantillon's office in Chicago, which offered more anonymity than trekking to Minneapolis. Mike also had been the field manager of the Minneapolis team the previous two years. Knowing that the headstrong Cantillon wanted a championship team in 1909, Callahan greased the wheels for Collins to convince Cantillon that he could continue to play third base. Of course, the straightforward Collins also mentioned his desire for a role in running the team. Collins walked away from the meeting with a deal to play third base for the Minneapolis Millers and a vague commitment to run the Millers on the field. At this late stage, it was the best deal Collins could get with any of the ballclubs in the new AA level of the minor leagues.

There was a chasm of misunderstanding, however, between Collins and

Cantillon. Collins, who wanted the title "manager," leaked the deal to eastern newspapers, which wrote that Collins "will manage the Minneapolis team of the American Association."[9] However, because Cantillon had no intention of relinquishing his role as manager and thought Collins would just be field captain, Cantillon denied the rumor that Collins would be manager. The *Minneapolis Tribune* reported that the rumor was not confirmed by local team headquarters, a telegram to Cantillon in Chicago "failed to elicit any light on the deal," and that E.N. Dickinson, Cantillon's secretary, said the idea that Collins would be manager "can be stamped as an absurdity for Mike Cantillon will surely be on the bench this season."[10] The next day, the *Minneapolis Tribune* wrote that Collins had been signed to play third base, and nothing more, based on a telegram confirmation from Jimmy Callahan, "Mike Cantillon's right-hand man in Chicago."[11] A week later, the *Tribune* finally was able to report the accurate statement that Collins "was signed as third baseman and field captain of the Millers."[12] Collins had indeed agreed to take two steps backwards, since being manager was not part of his original deal with Minneapolis.

Collins traveled to Hot Springs, Arkansas, in mid–February to start getting ready for the 1909 season. Tim Murnane of the *Boston Globe* saw Collins working out in Hot Springs and remarked that he "looks better than he has for three years, wearing his old smile" and "seems just as happy as when he handled the Boston champions."[13] From Hot Springs, Collins traveled to Galveston, Texas, where Joe Cantillon was conducting spring conditioning for his Washington Senators players that March.[14] Since it rained nearly continuously in Galveston, Collins had the opportunity to talk to Joe Cantillon about how he and his brother Mike envisioned the future of the Minneapolis Millers.

One immediate problem for the Cantillon brothers was their continued ability to stage Sunday games in Minneapolis, which represented a significant portion of their revenue and basically generated the profit for the ballclub. Sunday games were now in question, since a local minister had threatened to have Minneapolis police enforce the Minnesota state law that prohibited professional baseball games on Sunday. Collins was familiar with this situation, having seen the consequences of such a law in both Boston and Philadelphia. While the Minnesota legislature was considering a new law to allow Sunday baseball, the issue was taking up a lot of Mike Cantillon's time.[15] Another problem for Joe Cantillon was that he was in the final year of his three-year contract as the Washington manager. Given his lack of success with the Senators, Joe realized that American League president Ban Johnson would likely pressure the Washington owners to hire a new manager.

Collins had a solution to handle both problems. If Collins were named manager of the Millers, Mike Cantillon could focus on the Sunday baseball issue and the more significant aspects of the manager's job (while Collins handled the on-the-field aspects of the manager position) and he'd relinquish the position at the end of the 1909 season if Joe Cantillon wanted to manage the Millers if he indeed was forced out in Washington. The latter was not a problem for Collins, since he eventually wanted to go back east anyway, and was a benefit to the Cantillon brothers as they would avoid an intra-family squabble if Mike stayed as the Millers manager. Under this temporary arrangement, both sides were aware that Collins would keep the manager's seat warm for Joe Cantillon and that Collins wanted to return to the East Coast in the long run.

In late March, *Sporting Life* reported that Mike Cantillon "has about made up his mind to give Collins full charge of the Millers and quit dabbling in field generalship himself."[16] By early April the decision to do so was made. The official resolution of the Millers manager position was to split the job into two segments, with Cantillon handing the business and player acquisition aspects and Collins the on-the-field duties. The important matter to Collins was that he had the manager title for the 1909 season and a chit for future assistance after the season.

The Sunday baseball situation cleared up for the Cantillon brothers when the Minnesota legislature passed a law on April 19 to legally permit the Millers to splay ballgames on Sunday. The Cantillons could now play Sunday games at downtown Nicollet Park, rather than have to use the smaller, out-of-the-way location at Minnehana Driving Park, which they had previously used to skirt the law. On April 25 on overflow crowd watched the first-ever Sunday game at Nicollet Park, against cross-town rival St. Paul.

Less than three weeks into the 1909 season as the Minneapolis manager, however, Collins suffered an off-the-field tragedy when his eight-month-old daughter Agnes died in Buffalo on May 2 of tubercular meningitis.[17] The circumstances back in Buffalo had not been ideal. When Collins left Buffalo to go to Hot Springs in February, he left behind at his Niagara Street home his wife, Sadie, who was six-weeks pregnant with their second child, to care for their five-month-old daughter Agnes. Collins had left his wife in a challenging position without much of a maternal support system. Sadie's family was all back in Boston. Collins' mother, Alice, had her hands full caring for her aging husband, Anthony, who was in fading health now four years into his retirement from the Buffalo police force. Collins' sister, Margaret, who had married in 1907, now had her own toddler to look after.

When he received word of his child's death, Collins left Minneapolis to return to Buffalo to console his distraught wife, who was now four months pregnant. He also lay to rest his infant daughter, who was the first to be buried in the newly purchased Collins family plot in Holy Cross Cemetery in the town of Lackawanna, located just over the city line from South Buffalo.[18] He next made arrangements for Sadie to return to Boston, so that she could be with her family for the next five months of her pregnancy. Her mother and two sisters all lived under the same roof at 95 Calumet Street in Boston, the home of her oldest sister, Elizabeth, and brother-in-law, Thomas Goode, who was a police lieutenant.[19] Collins returned to Minneapolis for the team's May 7 game with Toledo.

While Collins was away from baseball attending to family concerns, the National Commission nullified the deal it had agreed to in January to establish a separate AA classification for the Eastern League and the American Association. In a statement released on May 4, the National Commission contended that since neither league had signed the legal documents, it was revoking the decision.[20] Rather than give the top minor leagues a little latitude to run their organizations, the two major leagues decided to clamp down harder on their relationship with the minor leagues to minimize the independence of what they considered to be subservient organizations. Astutely reading between the lines, Collins probably determined then that owning a minor league ballclub was not going to be his destiny.

As Collins carried out the terms of his contract for the remainder of the 168-game season in the American Association, Joe Cantillon's future as the Washington Senators manager started to appear shaky. "He wants time to decide whether it is to his best interests to continue here as the manager of the team, or take charge of the Minneapolis club, which he and his brother own," the *Washington Post* reported. "It seems that the Minneapolis club is paying Jimmy Collins a princely salary to manage it, and Cantillon could do this himself and save the amount being paid to Collins."[21] With Joe Cantillon now likely to want to manage the Millers for the 1910 season, Collins spent more time contemplating a more immediate baseball future somewhere in the Boston area.

Newspaper reporters must have spotted the pregnant Sadie Collins back in Boston, as rumors soon swirled that Collins was destined to be the next manager of the last-place Boston Nationals, to replace Frank Bowerman. Collins had to continually deny that he was interested in the Boston job. In late June, John Dovey, president of the Boston Nationals, who had purchased the ballclub from Arthur Soden, issued a statement saying that "there is no foundation for the rumor a few days ago that Jimmy Collins was likely to be secured as manager."[22] When Bowerman was fired in July, he was replaced by Harry Smith, not Collins.

Following the death of his daughter, Collins focused completely on baseball, as he had done after the suicide of his friend Chick Stahl two years earlier. In early July, Minneapolis moved into first place in the American Association standings. With a largely veteran lineup, which included outfielder Tip O'Neil who had played for Collins back in 1904, the Millers fought to hang on to first place through the summer in a hotly contested pennant race with Louisville and Milwaukee (managed by John McCloskey, Collins' manager at Louisville back in 1895). Collins had no problem improving his team, since Minneapolis operated as a virtual farm club for the Washington Senators, as the Cantillon brother exchanged players between Minneapolis and Washington throughout the season. In June, Gravvy Gravath arrived from the Senators as did Nick Altrock in July. Tom Hughes (of 1903 World Series infamy), Otis Clymer, and Orth Collins were sent to the Millers in August by Washington for the September pennant drive, when the Millers had to play the final three weeks of the season on the road.

However, the Millers faded down the stretch and finished in third place with an 88–79 record, four and a half games behind first-place Louisville. Collins injured his right arm in the September 22 game at Columbus when he slid into second base in the seventh inning; by the tenth inning he couldn't lift his arm. He was out for the rest of

COLLINS, MINNEAPOLIS

Experiencing difficulty buying into a ballclub in one of the two top minor leagues, Jimmy Collins accepted a job as player-manager of the Minneapolis team in the American Association for the 1909 season. However, the death of his daughter Agnes early in the season motivated Collins to exit Minneapolis and return to the Boston area for the 1910 season (Library of Congress Prints and Photographs Division, bbc 1152).

the season, which concluded with a doubleheader in Toledo on September 27. However, the *Minneapolis Tribune* already believed that it had seen the last of Collins with the Millers. "I doubt very much if he returns to Minneapolis, for he is hoping to buy a franchise for himself," Frank Force wrote that week in his "Sport Gossip of the Day" column.[23]

As he managed the Millers in street clothes and nursed his ailing right arm, Collins received word that Kathlyn Collins was born on September 24 in Boston.[24] The birth of his second daughter erased some of the angst surrounding the death in May of first-born Agnes Collins and helped to bring some joy into his family. After speaking to reporters, Collins left Toledo after the season-ending doubleheader to go to Boston. "All things considered, we cannot complain of the way we finished at all," Collins told the Minneapolis baseball writers. "We have played around the top all season, and but for the unfortunate accidents we encountered during the last month, I honestly believe we would have copped the bunting. At that we had a most successful season from both a player's standpoint and a financial one."[25]

Collins proved himself to be a capable manager during his brief tenure in Minneapolis, although the one knock on him was that he was too quiet and wasn't aggressive enough in arguing with umpires and baiting the opposition team. Collins maintained his passive managerial style to put the players on the field and simply try to win the ballgame with their physical skills. He continued to be a respectable third baseman at nearly 40 years old, as his .273 batting average landed him just outside the list of the top ten hitters in the league (O'Neil of the Millers was the batting champion with a .296 average in the pitching-rich league). With his aging legs, though, he was covering much less territory at third base and thus made far fewer dazzling plays in the field.

Less than a week after his last game with Minneapolis, Collins was seen at the Huntington Avenue Grounds, where the Boston Red Sox were winding up their season. "I ran across Jimmy Collins here in the last double-header of the season, Saturday, October 2, and Jimmy was as chipper as a lark and looked about as well as he did six years before," Jake Morse reported about Collins' chat in the umpire's room with his former pitcher and now umpire Bill Dinneen and Tommy Connolly, "both of them on earth and very much so in the year 1903, the memorable year when Jim landed the World's Championship here. Of course there was a lot of chaffing about Bill's new job."[26]

It didn't take long for Collins to secure his next job in baseball, which fit perfectly with his need to be closer to his family in Boston. On October 30, Collins agreed to be the new manager of the Providence ballclub of the Eastern League, which was located just 40 miles south of Boston.[27] The vacancy at Providence was created on October 20 when Hugh Duffy accepted the offer extended by Charlie Comiskey to be the manager of the Chicago White Sox in the American League.[28]

Collins signed his contract to be player-manager of the Providence Grays at the Boston office of one of the ballclub's owners, Charlie Lavis, a former Royal Rooter, on Saturday evening, October 30. "After negotiations lasting but two days I have secured Jimmy Collins to manage the Grays for next season," Lavis told the *Providence Journal*, "and believe I have landed one of the best pilots outside the big leagues." Lavis added that Collins "will make an ideal successor to Mr. Duffy." After Collins met Lavis on Friday night and announced, tipping his hand about his deal with the Cantillon brothers, "that he would have no difficulty in getting away from Minneapolis," the two men quickly consummated the arrangement.[29]

That Collins was able to obtain a manager's job in an ideal geographic location just one month following the end of the 1909 season does seem incredulous, however. The fact that Lavis struck a deal with Collins within 10 days of Duffy's departure as manager is plausible, since Collins did a decent job with Minneapolis and he still had some name recognition from his Boston playing days. The fact that Duffy was still a part-owner at Providence (although in a constant quarrel with his partners Lavis and Timothy Crowley), and would have given an unqualified recommendation to hire his old buddy Collins, adds further credence to a reason for the rapid hiring of Collins. However, the sudden hiring of Duffy by the White Sox is a bit fishy.

Duffy was an odd choice by Comiskey. His previous record as a major league manager was unremarkable during his stints with Milwaukee (1901) and Philadelphia (1904–1906). He did not have a Chicago connection or a strong link to Comiskey, other than their common involvement in ramping up the American League in 1901 (which lasted just one year before Duffy was managing in the minor leagues). The best reason for Comiskey to hire Duffy was to nurse along rookie shortstop Slats Blackburne, whom Duffy had managed at Providence when Comiskey reportedly paid $10,000—"the highest price ever given for a minor league fielder"— to get him.[30] Comiskey's concern was legitimate, since Blackburne turned out to be a dud, hitting just .124 in 75 games for the White Sox in 1910.

It is not inconceivable that Comiskey had some prodding to hire Duffy by one of his hunting buddies, Joe Cantillon, who went on an annual winter hunting expedition with Comiskey.[31] Cantillon needed the Providence managerial position to be open, so that Collins could take that job, in order to free up the Minneapolis managerial position for Cantillon. Of course, Mike Cantillon could have fired Collins to open up the job, but that would have been seen as tacky after the successful season the Millers had in 1909. Later that fall, Joe Cantillon announced that he would, indeed, manage the Minneapolis Millers for the 1910 season.

Collins was happy to be back in the East, although his public comments were the usual many words with little insight. "It will be like old times to be in the same circuit with Buffalo," Collins told a Buffalo writer that November. "It was a great surprise to me when I received the offer to come East again, and I am sorry to leave Minneapolis, where I have many friends. I am not sorry to be in the East some more."[32] When writer Jake Morse ran into Collins in January, he reported: "Collins is satisfied to remain about these diggings. He says he never felt better in his life than he does at the present time, and he is confident of his ability to play his old-time game."[33]

After observing the aggressive financial management of the Providence Grays by its owners during the first several weeks of the 1910 season, Collins confirmed to himself that he had made a good decision not to invest in the ballclub with Duffy and Doe back in the fall of 1906. Because of their hefty investment in the ballclub, Crowley and Lavis had to be both tight-fisted in managing expenses and aggressive in generating revenue, primarily by scheduling Sunday ballgames at Rocky Point, in order to eek out a profit.

The demanding quest for revenue began with a whirlwind preseason exhibition schedule, which spotlighted Collins as the main gate attraction. On Tuesday, April 12, Providence played the Boston Nationals at the South End Grounds in a heavily advertised match pitting "Jimmy Collins vs. Fred Lake," each of whom was the new manager of their respective team. "Jimmy Collins was given a splendid reception on his first appearance at the South End Grounds since 1900," Melville Webb, Jr., wrote in the *Boston Globe*. "He was the recipient of a handsome horseshoe of flowers, the gift of the Providence owners, C.J. Lavis and Timothy J. Crowley."[34] About 2,000 fans saw the 40-year-old Collins play third base "with his old-time grace," but strike out twice at bat.

Providence then toured several cities in eastern Massachusetts, which were home to franchises in the New England League. The team started north of Boston in Lawrence and then progressed south to Brockton, Fall River, and New Bedford, where only a few hundred fans came out to see each game. On Sunday, April 17, Providence played the Boston Red Sox at Rocky Point, where only 1,100 fans braved a very cold day to venture out to the ocean-hugging ball grounds. The big payday for Providence was the Patriots Day holiday twin bill on April 19 in Worcester, when 6,500 people attended the separate-admission event, 2,500 for the morning game and 4,000 at the afternoon game.

The marketing of Collins continued at Providence's home opener on April 21, when a record 11,000 spectators paid to see Collins' team defeat Toronto, 2–1. "Jimmy Collins made a great impression with the Providence fans today. He didn't get a hit, but his expert fielding saved the game," the *Providence Journal* reported. In the seventh inning with the bases loaded and two outs, Collins "made one of his wonderful one-hand stops behind third, throwing himself full length at the bag and getting his forceout play not an instant too soon."[35] Collins was a hit with fans on the road as well, particularly in his hometown of Buffalo, where the Bisons' opening game on May 9 against Providence drew 13,000 fans to establish a new record.[36]

The most ridiculous revenue-raiser that Providence engaged in during the 1910 season was a Sunday, May 22, exhibition game against the Chicago White Sox at Rocky Point, an eight-inning affair that the Grays lost 9–5. "The Sox made the journey of 100 miles [from Boston] for this purpose, but that was not a marker to what the Grays covered in the way of distance to get licked," the *Chicago Tribune* reported. "They jumped from Montreal to play this game, arriving about noon, and had to catch a 6 o'clock train for a night's ride to Rochester to play tomorrow."[37]

After the initial hoopla, though, attendance dropped precipitously for the ballgames in Providence as the Grays sunk to the lower half of the Eastern League standings. Things didn't improve over the summer, as Providence battled Jersey City to see which team could avoid holding the cellar position in the standings.

For the second time in two years, a death in the family disrupted Collins' life during the baseball season. On September 1, his father, Anthony Collins, died at the Pierce Sanitarium in Buffalo. Collins, who had been injured in the August 30 game at Toronto, hopped a train to get to Buffalo in time to be at his father's bedside before he passed away. Some 250 people attended the funeral service at the Church of the Annunciation, where eight police captains served as pallbearers. To honor the former police captain, a police detail of twelve patrolmen in full dress uniform escorted a funeral cortege of fifteen carriages from the church to Holy Cross Cemetery, where Anthony Collins was laid to rest in the family plot near his granddaughter Agnes.[38]

Collins was away from baseball for ten days, not returning to the Providence Grays until September 9 for the team's series with Jersey City to determine last-place in the Eastern League standings. The Grays sunk to last place in a doubleheader loss to Jersey City on September 10, and stayed there for the remainder of the season. Collins finished a very mediocre year as a player (.224 batting average, .931 fielding average), but as a manager he was extremely ineffective. Many observers throughout the league thought Collins would be fired as the Providence manager before the 1911 season. "Jimmy was a great third baseman in the big league and a pretty able general, but he had a bad year in Providence," the *Baltimore Sun* commented in the fall of 1910. "It is said that the fans think him too quiet," and that Duffy would return to pilot the Grays.[39]

Crowley and Lavis, perhaps unwisely, gave Collins a second chance to demonstrate his competence as manager, this time as a bench manager, not as a playing manager. However, when the Grays didn't perform any better in 1911 than they had in 1910, Collins was fired six weeks into the 1911 season on June 10. Crowley was the bearer of the bad news to Collins, handing him his unconditional release. "Dissatisfaction with the way the team has been directed is understood to have caused the owners to make the change," was the way *Sporting Life* termed the release of Collins in a front-page article.[40] The *Providence Journal* was more blunt, assessing Collins as too passive to manage a professional baseball team: "Manager Collins ceased to have authority over his men long before the season was half completed last year and ever since he has been only a figurehead."[41]

Collins must have had an inkling that the end was near, since he inserted himself into the Providence lineup at third base in both games of the Sunday doubleheader at Newark on June 4. Before those two games, Collins had appeared in only six games for the Grays. In the last ballgame he played in his professional baseball career, Collins had one hit in four at-bats, and had four putouts, one assist, and one error in six chances at third base.

"I gave baseball everything I had and when I quit, I was like the guy who died with his boots on," Collins said later in life about the physical pain he endured in his last years on the baseball diamond. "My arches had broken down, my legs ached, I had Charley horses, and I couldn't lift my right arm."[42]

Collins spent the summer of 1911 with his family in Rhode Island, in "a pretty little cottage at Longmeadow, a stone's throw from the beach at Rocky Point, and is not worrying about baseball."[43] The Collins family would soon increase in size, as Sadie Collins discovered that summer she was pregnant once again.

CHAPTER 23

Real Estate Mogul

In 1912, just seven years after leading Boston to its second consecutive American League pennant, Jimmy Collins was effectively unwanted by Organized Baseball. "He is one of the grandest men the game ever produced, a thorough gentleman, universally liked, and was always a credit to the game," the *Baltimore Sun* described Collins during February 1912. "Today, in the prime of life, he is looking for a position as manager of a minor league club, and finds no one after his services." The *Sun* then added rhetorically, "Did the Red Sox win Collins his managerial fame, or was it Collins who made the Red Sox famous?"[1]

Collins' hope to become the majority owner of a minor league ballclub had been dashed, as prices continued to skyrocket at what turned out to be the height of popularity of minor league baseball. "Ten years ago almost any franchise in the Eastern League could have been bought for $5,000," Pat Powers explained in 1910 about the inflation in franchise values. "Now $50,000 would not buy any of our clubs."[2] Hugh Duffy and his partners in the Providence ballclub sold out in December 1911 to Frank Navin and Bill Yawkey, the owners of the Detroit Tigers, who paid $72,000 for the Providence ballclub and its ballpark.[3]

Collins had no regrets that he hadn't paid inflated prices to buy into either of the Buffalo or Providence minor league ballclubs, since the dynamics of making money in the minor leagues had drastically changed. The business model of minor league baseball had changed in the previous ten years from generating income from spectators attending games at the ballpark to developing ballplayers for the major league teams (often acting as a farm for players on option). In purchasing the Providence ballclub, Navin and Yawkey looked to lower the Tigers' player development cost by owning the minor league ballclub rather than acquire players piecemeal. Another advantage to ownership was to avoid uprisings by the minor league ballclub owners like the one experienced in 1909. Since Collins wanted to be his own boss, an independent businessman, as the owner of a minor league ballclub, not be an affiliate of the major league ballclubs, his plan to be the majority owner of a minor league ballclub was now dead.

Since it looked to be an auspicious time *to sell* a minor league ballclub rather than buy one, Collins sold his one-third interest in the Worcester ballclub in late January 1912 to Paul McHale, who had financing assistance from the other two owners, Jesse Burkett and John O'Donnell. "How much Collins got wasn't given," the *Worcester Telegram* reported. "But the price was probably $8000, as that's the amount Collins wanted for it. Burkett and O'Donnell tried to buy it from him at $4000. But Collins said nay to the proposition."[4] The $8,000 price would have yielded a healthy return for Collins, nearly a tripling of his original investment of $3,000 in 1906. Collins had good leverage to get his price because he was a roadblock to Burkett and O'Donnell in trying to get their $25,000 asking price for the Worcester franchise in order to liquidate their two-thirds share. Collins got out at the right time, since the New England League crumbled three years later and faded from existence when it merged with the old Connecticut League.

Luckily, Collins, the businessman in a baseball uniform, was not dependent on baseball to make a living, because he had developed an extensive network of rental properties in South Buffalo during the previous decade to provide a more than adequate income to support his family. As the *New York Sun* noted in the spring of 1912, "Jimmy Collins, once Boston's star third baseman, has dropped out of the game. He owns a row of tenements in Buffalo and is well off."[5]

In 1912, Collins continued to divide his time between Buffalo and Boston. When in Buffalo, he checked up on his rental properties while he stayed with his mother at the Niagara Street homestead in North Buffalo. His wife, Sadie, stayed in Boston to care for their growing family—which now numbered two daughters with the birth of Claire Collins on January 17, 1912—in their own apartment at 107 Calumet Street, just a few doors down from Sadie's mother and sister Elizabeth and her family at 95 Calumet.[6]

Collins kept his hand in baseball during the 1912 season as a scout for old friend Clark Griffith, the new manager and part-owner of the Washington Senators in the American League.[7] Being a scout was an unpaid position, but it gave Collins an excuse to watch a variety of ballgames at the amateur (college and summer league), semi-pro, and minor league levels. If he came across a potential prospect, he'd call in senior scout Mike Kahoe, who coordinated scouting activities across the country for Washington, and pick up a finder's fee if Griffith signed the prospect.[8]

One of Collins' missions for the Senators was to keep tabs on two pitching prospects that Griffith had signed and optioned to ballclubs in the New England League — Joe Boehling at Worcester and Guy Johnson at Haverhill.[9] Boehling was a keeper, going 14–8 for Worcester in 1912. He then teamed up with Washington's ace pitcher, Walter Johnson, to compile a 17–7 record in 1913 to help Washington to a second-place finish. Boehling pitched three more seasons for Washington until he was traded to Cleveland late in the 1916 season. Guy Johnson (no relation to Walter) went 9–14 for Haverhill in 1912 and never pitched in the major leagues.

With the Boston Red Sox under new ownership — John I. Taylor had sold the ballclub to James McAleer in September 1911 — Collins made several trips to the team's new steel-and-concrete ballpark, Fenway Park, which replaced the wooden Huntington Avenue Grounds for the 1912 season. Collins, who never played in the steel-and-concrete American League ballparks such as Shibe Park that opened in 1909 and Comiskey Park that opened in 1910, was astounded to see the investment committed to building these large stadiums to accommodate the growing interest in baseball. Collins had easy access to Fenway Park because he knew a number of influential people at the ballpark. Besides McAleer, who had been the St. Louis Browns manager when Collins was still an active third baseman, Jake Stahl was now the Red Sox manager; Stahl had played for Collins on the 1903 World Series team. There was also his brother-in-law Thomas Goode, who was captain of the police precinct in charge of patrolling the area around the ballpark.[10]

As the Red Sox rolled to the team's first American League pennant since Collins led them there in 1904, Collins saw enough ballgames at Fenway Park to render a thoughtful opinion on the team's chances to win the 1912 World Series against the New York Giants. "I think it is an even thing. All this talk about the great superiority of the Boston team sounds well to the fans in this city [Boston], but you have got to show me where they are going to have any cinch," Collins bluntly told sportswriters. "The Red Sox are a faster team than New York, but they have not the experienced players McGraw can show. They have been through one series, and this counts for a whole lot. Looking at it from any angle, I can't see anything but a toss up between Boston and New York."[11]

Collins was accurate in his assessment. It was a tightly contested World Series, with the Red Sox defeating the Giants four games to three, with one tie, to cop the World Series title. However, his comments lacked the optimism of a hometown booster, like the commentary by the Royal Rooters who continued to stoke spectator interest with their rabid favoritism of the Sox. Collins' thoughts were printed in a few out-of-town newspapers, but received little space on the Boston sports pages, which wanted to print hometown hype, not objectivity.

The Red Sox victory in the 1912 World Series was the genesis of a rapid decline in Collins' fame in Boston, as the Red Sox captured three more World Series titles in the next six years, with championships in 1915, 1916, and 1918. Jimmy who? The new baseball heroes in Boston were Smoky Joe Wood, Tris Speaker, and a pudgy pitcher by the name of Babe Ruth. The 1903 World Series title was a distant memory, and Jimmy Collins was just another old ballplayer. In December 1912 the *Brooklyn Eagle* reflected on his rapid fall from fame: "When he led the Boston Americans to a pennant he was lauded to the skies. Newspapers devoted pages to telling how he parted his hair and what he thought of the crop prospects, yet when Old Man Time got busy with the scythe and cut his team from under him, Jimmy fell so far there was none so poor as to do him honor. The hordes of sycophants and lovers of reflected glory fell away from him and today Collins is but a memory."[12] Perhaps if Collins had slanted his comments to favor the hometown Red Sox he could have sustained a more lasting public image, but that wasn't his style.

Rather than live in Buffalo to oversee his real estate holdings, Collins made a commitment to stay in Boston. In 1913 he moved his family to an apartment at 36 Fenwood Road, where his in-laws the Goode family were just down the street at 73 Fenwood.[13] His nephew Eddie Goode, then a 14-year-old budding ballplayer, got the opportunity to work out with the Red Sox players at Fenway Park through the connections of his famous uncle.[14] Before Eddie entered the Boston High School of Commerce in September 1913, Collins probably also took him to see a few college games in the Boston area as he scouted the local athletes, such as the traditional opening game between Harvard and the Red Sox at Fenway Park on April 8 and the Bunker Hill Day holiday game on June 17 between Holy Cross and Boston College at the South End Grounds.

However, after only four years as full-time residents of Boston, the Collins family moved back to Buffalo in 1914. Settling into Boston had been more challenging than expected for Collins. During his days as a popular ballplayer, Collins had managed to navigate the relatively impermeable divide between Boston's Brahmin society and its Irish-American underclass. Although he never openly promoted himself as an Irish-American, Collins was now just another middle-aged Irish-American to many Bostonians, albeit one with a large bank account and enough income from rental properties that he didn't have to work at a job for a living. He just couldn't make enough connections in Boston to establish himself in business in the city.

With Irish-American John Fitzgerald in his second term as Boston's mayor, Collins probably thought he could overcome the Brahmin-Irish divide to leverage a business opportunity or two as Irish-Americans gained more influence in Boston. However, it was exactly the fact that Fitzgerald had been able to win a second mayoral term that Boston's business and social elite now detested Irish-Americans even more than during Fitzgerald's first term. When Fitzgerald was out of office between his two terms, the Republican establishment in Boston (under the guise of the Good Government Association) reformed the basic structure of city government, in the words of historian Thomas O'Connor, "to make certain that neither Fitzgerald nor any other machine Democrat out of the wards would get back into the mayor's office again."[15] The city charter was modified to make it more difficult for an Irish-American to become mayor (elections were now non-partisan) and reduce the influence that an Irish-American mayor could have if elected (especially to parcel out jobs via patronage). Even with a wholesale change in the way that Boston city government was run, Fitzgerald managed to win election to a second term as mayor.

Collins couldn't even secure a baseball opportunity with an Irish-American institution, Boston College, which had been founded in 1863 by the Society of Jesus, the Jesuit sect of Catholicism, to provide higher education for the sons of the Irish-American working class in Boston. In early January 1914 the *Boston Globe* reported a rumor that Collins was negotiating with the athletic board of Boston College to coach its baseball team that spring, concluding that "Collins will probably coach the team."[16] Collins likely was the source of the rumor, to ferret out how serious the college was about hiring him. However, the article's remarks, loosely linked to the source of the rumor, about "the engagement of Collins ought to mean much to B.C. athletics" and that a first-class baseball team would increase the college's "athletic prestige," indicated a bit too much of an empire-building mentality for the Jesuits. Instead of Collins, Boston College hired Joe Monahan, who was a BC alumnus and had played minor league ball with the Lowell ballclub of the New England League.

By March 1914, it was clear that Collins was not going to be able to duplicate in Boston the success he had obtained in Buffalo. The election in mid-January of James Michael Curley as mayor of Boston was only going to make Irish-American relations with Boston's elite even worse, since Curley was an Irish-American with an avowed mission to shake up the established Boston community. On his first day in office, Curley "sent Yankees into fits of apoplexy by proposing to sell the Public Garden for $10 million" and use the money to create smaller public gardens in the neighborhoods where more people could benefit from the scenery. Curley had no shortage of ideas to change Boston. As historian O'Connor writes, "The Brahmin aristocracy and the conservative elements of Boston society would never cooperate with a political leader who openly mocked their institutions and trifled with their proud sense of family heritage."[16] Boston was going to be a very hostile place to be during the Curley administration. With their two daughters to consider, Collins and his wife, Sadie, made the decision to return to Buffalo where they believed their girls' educational opportunity and general future would be brighter. The decision to leave Boston was made a bit easier since Sadie's mother had died in November 1913, so they no longer had to be near her in her failing health.[18]

Curiously, in March, Collins initiated a rumor through the Associated Press wire service, which was published in newspapers across the county, that he was negotiating to become the manager of the Buffalo ballclub of the Federal League, a third major league that was challenging the status quo of the American and National Leagues. Collins was also said to be "a candidate for third base position if he became manager."[19] There were obvious problems with the story, including the efficacy of a comeback for an overweight 44-year-old former ballplayer and the fact that Buffalo already had Larry Schlafly under contract as its manager. Collins seemed to want to exact retribution against the Buffalo management, headed by real estate developer Walter Mullen, for unknown reasons, perhaps as a favor to the owners of the Buffalo ballclub of the International League, the new name for the old Eastern League. Certainly, Collins would not have wanted to be part of the management group for an enterprise very likely to fail, since the Buffeds management had yet to build a ballpark and had to resort to selling shares of stock to the general public in order to raise capital to run the team. "Wish to deny emphatically Associated Press rumor," Mullen telegraphed the *Buffalo Express*, while the newspaper also reported that Schlafly "considers it a joke ... circulated by the opposition," i.e., the existing Buffalo minor league ballclub.[20] It's not likely anyone took the rumor very seriously.

Back in Buffalo, Collins purchased a house, using a mortgage, at 30 Edson Street.[21] The house was located in the southeastern part of South Buffalo, about two blocks from Cazenovia Park and very near the Buffalo city line with the town of West Seneca. The house on Edson Street was a "Buffalo double," similar to the houses that Collins had built as rental properties in South Buffalo. While the family was living in Boston Collins had continued to report his occupation as "ballplayer," even though he was no longer active in baseball, but upon his return to Buffalo he changed his reported occupation to be "real estate," which served as a perfect demarcation for his new life in Buffalo.[22]

The last national publicity Collins received upon his move back to Buffalo was a report in early December 1914 that he was dying. Headlines such as "At Death's Door is the Former Famous Third Baseman and Team Leader, Jimmy Collins" appeared in newspapers across the country.[23] Collins did suffer from a severe bout of pneumonia, contracted while outdoors too long in the cold November air, but he soon recovered. Following his highly publicized near-death experience, Collins retreated from public life to focus on his family and manage his real estate investments.

Privately, Collins assisted his friends and relatives when he could. He hired his nephew Harry Collins, his brother Henry's son, to work on his properties as a carpenter.[24] He also helped nephew Eddie Goode back in Boston to further his baseball career by playing college baseball at Harvard, where old friend Hugh Duffy was now the baseball coach. Goode prepped at Exeter Academy to satisfy the Harvard admissions staff (a Boston High School of Commerce diploma wasn't good enough back then), then played three years of varsity baseball for coach Jack Slattery, who replaced Duffy at Harvard for the 1920 season.[25]

When America entered World War I in 1917, Collins' real estate business had probably reached its zenith of prosperity, nearly 20 years after its inception around 1900. Collins had achieved his goal to be an independent businessman by deploying many of the Irish-American values imparted to him by his father, not to duplicate his father's Irish-American ideals but rather to embellish them. Collins wasn't nearly as rich as the millionaires who resided in the mansions along Buffalo's prestigious Delaware Avenue, but he was a successful American businessman — not an Irish-American businessman — another aspect of his goal.

The war provided one last surge in high-quality tenants to rent the flats in Collins' properties, as exemplified by the tenant in the other flat at 30 Edson Street in 1920, William Kaufman, who was a machinist at a local auto plant.[26] The war brought many workers into Buffalo, since the city played a prominent role in supplying defense equipment for the U.S. government's war effort. For example, the Curtiss Aeroplane and Motor Company in Buffalo supplied the bulk of airplanes to the U.S. government to fight the war, hiring 10,000 new workers to help build the government's fleet of airships.[27] While the influx of thousands of new laborers into the Buffalo economy helped to prop up rents, given a shortage of available housing, the impact was just temporary as many companies laid off the workers after the war once the demand for the war-related supplies evaporated.

With Collins settled into his quiet life as a real estate mogul in South Buffalo, few sportswriters sought out his views on the success of the Boston Red Sox and their pitcher-turned-home-run-hitter, Babe Ruth. When Boston owner Harry Frazee sold Ruth to the New York Yankees after the 1919 season, there were no quotes from Collins in the newspapers commenting on the transaction. Since Collins believed that the home run was bad for baseball, he probably would have supported Frazee.

One of the reasons that Collins faded from the baseball landscape, in addition to being an intensely private person, was that a new generation of baseball writers now staffed the Boston newspapers. Collins had outlasted all three dominant baseball writers in Boston who had observed him as a player and manager. Fred O'Connell of the *Boston Post* died in 1907 while Collins was still active in baseball.[28] Tim Murnane of the *Boston Globe*, who had written that extensive article in 1905 about Collins' real estate activities, died in 1917 when he collapsed from a heart attack at the Shubert Theatre in Boston.[29] Jake Morse, who wrote for the *Boston Herald* but more importantly also for the weekly *Sporting Life*, left the business in 1912 after struggling to make his creation *Baseball Magazine* an economic success as well as a literary hit.[30]

Other than these three Boston writers, few people associated with Organized Baseball had an incentive to perpetuate the name recognition of Jimmy Collins during the postwar era. If it weren't for a corruption scandal in the Buffalo Parks Department that erupted in February 1922, Collins probably would have remained out of the public eye for the rest of his life and would likely never have been inducted into the Baseball Hall of Fame.

CHAPTER 24

Muny League President

On February 21, 1922, Albert Febrey, director of recreation in the Buffalo Parks Department, was arrested by the police and charged with the theft of public money. Febrey was also president of the Buffalo Municipal Baseball Association, a post he had held since the organization's formation in 1913. While a scandal in the Parks Department was unavoidable for new commissioner John Meahl, he moved quickly to forestall any semblance of impropriety in the baseball league by asking Jimmy Collins to replace Febrey as the president.

Less than three weeks after the arrest of Febrey, Meahl had convinced Collins to be the new president of the Buffalo Municipal Baseball Association. "Dissipating all doubt as to the prospect for baseball in the city parks under the new administration of parks and public buildings this summer, the Buffalo Municipal Baseball Association was reorganized last evening," the *Buffalo Express* reported. "The new president of the association will be James J. Collins, Buffalo's famous big-league player of other days."[1] A much younger Collins might have smirked broadly at the thought of Meahl, a German-American from the East Side aristocracy, asking him, an Irish-American with roots in the First Ward, for his help, but in 1922 the request was just business as usual for Collins. He had friends and connections throughout all income levels and neighborhoods in Buffalo.

Meahl was a new City Council member, having defeated incumbent John F. Malone in a wave of voter enthusiasm to elect Francis X. Schwab as mayor in November 1921. Meahl also assumed Malone's position as commissioner of the Parks Department. When Meahl had his staff comb through Malone's operation, he discovered numerous instances of larceny and forgery. Febrey had forged vouchers for paychecks for a man named Charles Taylor, who had a no-show job, and Thomas Mercer, whose checks went to Malone's campaign fund (as thanks for Malone giving him a job). Febrey had also authorized vouchers to purchase suits of clothes for Malone's personal use. The scandal ran deeper than just Febrey. Frederick Kull, the department's auditor, stole money from the city by conspiring with the president of the Eastern Oil Company to bill the city for gasoline that was never delivered, and splitting the money with him. All these transactions had been certified by Malone, who was also arrested for graft along with Kull and several other Parks Department staffers.[2]

Febrey pled guilty, as did everyone else except Malone, who demanded a trial. At the October 25, 1922, trial, Febrey testified in great detail about how he and Malone bilked the city of Buffalo for thousands of dollars. Febrey testified that Taylor came to his house every Sunday morning to collect his pay for the no-show job. Malone's defense attorney made Febrey look bad, by getting him to acknowledge that his son often saw him give the money to Taylor, and that Febrey went to church immediately after giving Taylor the swindled money. "Who checked Taylor to make sure that he worked," the defense attorney asked Febrey. "I supposed that he was not to work," Febrey replied about Taylor's $3 a day job as the night watchman at the administration building in Delaware Park. Trying to pin some blame on Malone, Febrey added about Taylor's real value, "I understood that he handled sailors along the waterfront and was supposed to be useful around election time."[3] After the jury took less than an hour to find Malone guilty, the judge sentenced him to three and a half years in Auburn prison. Febrey received a sentence of two to five years.[4]

By the time of Febrey's testimony at Malone's trial, Collins had completed his first baseball season as the new president of the muny league, as Buffalo residents referred to the Municipal Baseball Association, the first of 22 consecutive terms as league president.

Why did Collins agree to take the position as president of the muny league? The position was largely ceremonial and Collins never accepted a stipend to perform the duties (probably to avoid an appearance of Febrey-style impropriety). As a result of his comfortable life in the ten years since he was last associated with Organized Baseball, an explanation of "to get back into baseball" is far too simplistic. From a business perspective, there were some benefits for Collins to have a higher civic profile within Buffalo. He could perhaps charge higher rents for the flats at his rental properties or attract better quality renters that would stay longer. The local bankers could also view him as a more attractive credit risk and offer him lower interest rates when he refinanced the mortgages on his properties. But these business reasons are too arcane. The best explanation for why he became muny league president is that Collins was interested in public service because that's what rich people like John D. Rockefeller and Andrew Carnegie did after they created their wealth. Rockefeller and Carnegie weren't just capitalists; they gave back to the community.

One of the biggest benefits to Collins of being the muny league president, unbeknownst to him at the time he accepted the post, was the spread of his reputation as a great ballplayer among a new generation of baseball fans in western New York. Meahl, who was also a part-owner of the local Buffalo Bisons ballclub in the International League, was a prominent spokesman at many Buffalo athletic events. Meahl was often profuse in his praise and admiration for Collins' baseball heritage. "He is the president of the biggest baseball league in the country and there is no one better qualified to instruct and direct the future stars of the diamond than Jimmy Collins," Meahl said at the muny league's award banquet in December 1922, and urged the players to emulate Collins. Most importantly, Meahl was not bashful about characterizing Collins as baseball's "greatest third baseman of all time," a label that stuck long after Meahl retired in 1926 from his four-year stint in Buffalo city politics.[5] Meahl's promotion was instrumental in perpetuating Collins' reputation among sportswriters in western New York, which eventually led to his election to the Baseball Hall of Fame.

Meahl was a showman when it came to public events concerning the muny league. At the opening of the 1922 baseball season, Meahl and league officials toured the city to stop at each playing field to participate in a ceremony marking the start of the season. At diamond number one at Cazenovia Park, the players and officials lined the foul lines as Joseph Suttner, the director of recreation (who had replaced Febrey), introduced Meahl and Collins — "intra-dooo-cing the greatest third baseman of all time" — as thousands of spectators applauded and newspaper cameras clicked. Both men donned baseball caps as Meahl headed to the mound with a ball and Collins to the batter's box with a bat, to perform an act for the crowd. "The commissioner shot an underhanded shoot at Jimmy, who bent and missed badly," one newspaper reported of the commissioner's commanding pitch that eluded the bat of the game's greatest third baseman.[6] Each year, Collins would participate in this annual stunt to amuse the crowds and increase interest in the muny league, with "Jimmy doffing a player's cap, digging his toe into the turf and awaiting the famous curve, which no one can solve."[7]

The Buffalo muny league played on two dozen baseball diamonds carved out of the grasslands of the city's park system, with diamonds at Delaware Park, Riverside Park, and Cazenovia Park in Collins' newly adopted South Buffalo neighborhood. Collins' Edson Street home was only two blocks from Cazenovia Park. In 1922 the muny league consisted of 11 separate leagues in three classifications (AA, A, and B), with 88 teams and 1,100 players aged 12 to 35. Ballgames were only played on Sunday afternoons.[8]

As was the case in most urban areas, the city of Buffalo now controlled amateur baseball rather than the former loose confederation of athletic clubs in the City League, which had now morphed into semi-pro status. Muny baseball completely changed how youngsters played baseball since Collins' days as a youth on the vacant lots of the Second Ward and in City League games. As Harold Seymour points out in *Baseball: The People's Game*, "As muny ball waxed and sandlot ball waned, the voice of the bureaucrat sounded across the diamond." The informal nature of boys' games, "with little or no adult intrusion or help," had been replaced by organized game schedules assigned by adults on crowded parkland to make maximum use of available space and with awards and trophies presented to players for their efforts. Adult supervision of these leagues was supposed to develop character in the players, such as honesty, obedience, and citizenship.[9] Collins realized that while he had developed his full baseball potential in the old anything-goes sandlot system, the muny league greatly improved the chances that many more youngsters could develop their talents to further their baseball exploits, either in the adult muny leagues or possibly in the professional ranks.

As president of the Buffalo Municipal Baseball Association, Jimmy Collins kept his hand in baseball after his playing career was over and his dreams of minor league ballclub ownership had expired (National Baseball Hall of Fame Library, Cooperstown, New York).

In his role as president of the muny league, Collins became an ambassador for Buffalo sports. In 1922 he helped to organize two benefit baseball games. In June he recruited a team of former ballplayers in the Buffalo area to play Rogers Hornsby and the St. Louis Cardinals in an exhibition game in Buffalo. St. Louis defeated the Buffalo squad, 13–2, as Collins played third base and went 1-for-4 at bat.[10] In September he participated in an old-timers game at Braves Field in Boston to benefit Children's Hospital. Collins managed the team of American League old-timers, while Fred Tenney directed the National

League old-timers. The Collins team crushed the Tenney team, 28–7, as 20,000 spectators enjoyed seeing nearly 50 former stars perform. Collins went 0-for-2 at bat, but flawlessly handled two chances in the field.[11]

In the week preceding the 1922 old-timers game, Collins watched several Red Sox games at Fenway Park and afterward talked to umpire Billy Evans. In an article published several years later by umpire-turned-writer Evans, the outspoken Collins was candid about his dislike for the changes in major league baseball since his playing days. "It looks to me as if the players' passion for long drives has taken much away from the game," Collins said. "Not a single player in all the games I saw choked up on his bat and tried to place his hits. Not one player tried to beat out a bunt. I saw only two bases stolen in six games." Collins did not like the dependence on the home run to score runs in bunches, rather than try to play for one or two runs. "I have always believed that playing for one run called for much more inside stuff than trying to get runs in clusters," Collins said about baseball strategy, declaring that a player like Babe Ruth only came around once every 25 years. "Baseball is still a great game, but no better. It has newer and different thrills, but no more than in our day."[12]

Collins began working a part-time job in the early 1920s, as a boxing judge, to supplement the income from his rental properties, in the first sign of rough times ahead for Collins. He had received a judging license in October 1920 from the New York State Boxing Commission, as the *New York Times* reported that "James J. Collins, famous third baseman of the old Boston Red Sox, now living in Buffalo, was authorized to act as a judge."[13] Collins' name could often be found in the agate type of newspaper reports of boxing results in Buffalo and Niagara Falls. His decisions were usually routine, but every once and a while he would be involved in a controversial decision. In a 1926 bout between boxers Schoell and Rosenbloom, the *Niagara Falls Gazette* reported that the fans booed when the fight was called a draw, since Schoell was seen as an easy winner, with one judge scoring in favor of Schoell "while Jimmy Collins gave it to Rosenbloom," with the referee determining it to be a draw.[14]

Collins' income from his rental properties began to suffer in the 1920s as the texture of the South Buffalo neighborhood where his buildings were located began to change. Whereas the streetcar had brought Irish-Americans from the First Ward in the first two decades of the twentieth century, the affordable mass-produced automobile now permitted their movement further east into the town of West Seneca or northeast into the new suburbs of Amherst and Williamsville. Accelerating the exodus of upwardly mobile Irish-Americans from South Buffalo was the changing nature of the East Side neighborhood immediately to the north. The original German-American population of the lower East Side had been largely replaced by Jewish immigrants from Russia and Poland, beginning around 1910. Another transformation of that neighborhood occurred after World War I. "During the 1920s many of the Jewish residents of the East Side, some of whom had been there for less than ten years, began to move to newer and nicer neighborhoods in the more northerly sections of Buffalo," urban studies professor Mark Goldman wrote in his history of Buffalo. "Blacks, migrants from the rural South, had since the labor shortage of World War I been moving in in increasing numbers ... virtually all of them moved onto the lower East Side." As Goldman observed, "the surrounding white world was hostile" to these new inhabitants of the lower East Side.[15]

Changes in the Buffalo economy in the 1920s also contributed to a different nature of Collins' tenants in his South Buffalo flats, with lower incomes and more menial jobs. The city's economy no longer depended on locally owned companies that produced goods and services related to Buffalo's strategic location at the midway nexus of "the agricultural and industrial heart of America in the Midwest and the cities of the East." Cheap power from Niagara Falls fostered the development of new industries.[16] General Motors built a factory, displacing the Pierce Arrow Company as local automaker. Petrochemical companies emerged. The now-antiquated plant of the Lackawanna Steel Company, located near the western edge of South Buffalo, was acquired by corporate giant Bethlehem Steel in 1922. Other mergers and concentrations changed the face of commerce in Buffalo. Even local movie theaters were bought and incorporated into the Fox Movie Company.

While Collins survived on his real estate investments during the early 1920s, his income from rents was probably lower than before the war and the refinancing of his mortgages done at less favorable terms and interest rates. Living off the rental income became more challenging around 1927. Although his daughter Kathlyn had graduated from Mt. Mercy Academy in 1926, Collins could no longer afford private-school tuition, so his younger daughter Claire went to public high school.[17] Collins seems to have sold the home at 30 Edson Street in order to raise cash, since in 1927 the family began renting an apartment at 10 Tuscarora Road.[18]

These two significant changes in Collins' life indicate not only a reduced income but also the beginning of the demise of his real estate business. The value of his rental properties would have reached its peak in 1926, according to the results of the 2011 study "Real Estate Prices During the Roaring Twenties and the Great Depression." While many people believe that real estate values, like common stock prices, topped out just before the stock market crash in October 1929, real estate values actually peaked in the second quarter of 1926 — coinciding with the peak of the Florida housing bubble — and then declined over the next three years with a very brief absolute peak in the third quarter of 1929 before dropping precipitously thereafter by 67 percent at year-end 1932.[19]

The decline in his rental-property values impacted Collins' ability to pay off the short-term balloon mortgage payments on his properties, since banks at the time would only finance at best 50 percent of the current value. Collins had to ante up cash to replace the mortgage amount he couldn't refinance. At some point in the refinancing of the balloon mortgage payments, he depleted his savings and had to sell properties to raise cash (if he could locate a buyer). Until 1929, Collins was probably able to cope with the refinancing challenge during this vicious downward spiral of shrinking real estate values, but after the stock market crash in 1929, when property values plummeted (by 20 percent per year in the above study), he was no doubt unable to avoid foreclosure on many, if not all, of his remaining rental properties.

In 1929, Collins moved his family again, this time to a flat in a Buffalo double at 257 Richmond Avenue, which they shared with Dr. Willard Schwartz.[20] Interestingly, his new residence was just several blocks north of the original site of Olympic Park, at the corner of Richmond Avenue and Summer Street, where Collins as a teenager had watched the ballgames of the Buffalo ballclub in the National League.

By the late 1920s, the Collins family was taking an annual extended vacation around Labor Day to visit Sadie's sister Elizabeth Goode at her family's cottage at Nantasket Beach in Hull, just a short distance from Boston. Sadie would often stay a month or so, arriving in August with her daughter Claire and then departing after Labor Day once her husband arrived.[21] In early September 1929, Collins was spotted in the press box at Braves Field watching a Sunday game between the Red Sox and the Yankees (the Sunday law in Massachusetts then prohibited games at Fenway Park because the ballpark was within 1000 feet of a church). New York won, 6–4, as Babe Ruth hit a home run.[22] The annual trips to Nantasket Beach lasted until 1933, when Collins' brother-in-law Thomas Goode, then the assistant superintendent of the Boston police force, died.[23]

Collins was occasionally back in the national baseball news. One of the earliest tributes to Collins was an article written by Fred Lieb in 1923, which was distributed by a wire service and appeared in numerous newspapers nationwide. In the article, Lieb summarized his thoughts about the third base position: "Jimmy Collins was the greatest third baseman of all time. That is a statement which few will contradict. In picking an all star team for all time, several positions may be in doubt but there is practical unanimity among baseball men in selecting Collins for the so-called hot corner of the infield." Lieb described Collins as one who "ranged a little more territory than any others," and characterized him as "a hard, dangerous hitter getting many base-knocks of the extra-base type."[24] Another accolade was written in 1926 by George Trevor of the *Brooklyn Eagle*, who began his lengthy article on Collins' achievements by writing: "Just as Hal Chase overshadows his fellow first basemen, so does the incomparable Jimmy Collins tower above the great third basemen of all time. Jimmy Collins is first — there is no second."[25]

Collins' name regularly surfaced as the third baseman picked for the various all-time teams selected by famous ballplayers and sportswriters. Collins was named on numerous all-time teams, including those chosen by Ty Cobb in 1926, Grantland Rice in 1929, Connie Mack and Honus Wagner in 1930, and Babe Ruth in 1931. The rage of naming all-time teams in the late 1920s and early 1930s eventually spawned the idea of establishing a Baseball Hall of Fame to officially recognize the game's great players, rather than rely on the fading memory of older observers.

The *Boston Post* capitalized on this trend of honoring former major league baseball stars by sponsoring an old-timers game at Braves Field on September 8, 1930. Bill Carrigan was the manager of a team of older Boston players. Carrigan started Cy Young on the mound, with himself at catcher, the 1903 infield of Candy LaChance, Hobe Ferris, Fred Parent, and Collins, and an outfield of Tris Speaker, Harry Hooper, and Duffy Lewis. The Boston team defeated the All-Stars, 6–4, before an audience of 22,000 fans. The 60-year-old Collins cracked a single up the middle into center field in his only time at bat. Two things were different for Collins and his teammates from their former playing days. The first was that their uniforms sported numbers so the spectators could identify them from the stands (Collins wore number 21). The second was that the ballgame was broadcast on radio station WNAC in Boston, so fans not at the ballpark could also enjoy the game by listening to the action through their radio sets.[26]

When *The Sporting News* published a long biographical sketch of Collins in 1933, the baseball weekly reinvigorated the story surrounding his 1895 fielding of bunts by the infamous Baltimore Orioles, complete with Hughey Jennings' statement that the Orioles would go easy on Collins and Collins' retort, "That's all right, bunt 'em down to me and I'll show you something."[27] Ten years later this story would become the centerpiece of a campaign to put Collins in the Baseball Hall of Fame, which at the time was still on the drawing board to be built in Cooperstown, New York.

Times were tough in Buffalo during the Great Depression, as they were in other large cities across the country, with high unemployment and a painfully slow economic recovery. The New Deal policies of Franklin D. Roosevelt, the new U.S. president whose administration began in March 1933, did little to deter the grim situation in Buffalo. "The New Deal did not bring prosperity to Buffalo. Nor did it bring an end to unemployment and hard times," Goldman concluded in his history of Buffalo entitled *High Hopes*. In Buffalo, the Great Depression "left in its wake a permanent and dependent class of workers forever unable to support themselves" through jobs with companies in the private sector; instead, many lived off wages from jobs in the federal, state, or local governments.[28]

Collins was one of those Buffaloians who were "forever unable to support themselves." By 1935 Collins was collecting a paycheck from the city of Buffalo as an employee in the Parks Department.[29] To cutback on expenses, Collins and his wife moved in with their oldest daughter, Kathlyn, and her husband Frank Walsh, at their home at 300 Crestwood Avenue.[30] Younger daughter Claire married George McCall and left Buffalo to live in suburban Williamsville.[31]

In December 1935, the name of Jimmy Collins was included on the list of 33 former ballplayers for the first balloting of those to be included in the inaugural induction into the Baseball Hall of Fame. Collins was one of three third basemen, along with Pie Traynor and Bill Bradley. However, the Associated Press, in its nationally distributed article, felt compelled to append the Collins name with the parenthetical "(former Brave and Red Sox star)" to distinguish him from the current St. Louis Cardinals first baseman named Jimmy Collins.[32]

To educate a new generation of baseball fans that only knew the St. Louis infielder to be Jimmy Collins the ballplayer, an Associated Press writer interviewed the 66-year-old former third baseman in early 1936. While the subsequent nationally distributed article was only sporadically published in local newspapers, the article does contain several quotations attributed to Collins, a rare commodity, to provide a glimpse into his thoughts. While the AP writer focused on Collins' acclaim as the manager of the 1903 World Series champions, Collins not surprisingly offered the writer few words of wisdom regarding those 1903 exploits, as the article quoted Collins as changing the subject: "No, sir, I guess I'm not anxious to be running one of those sixteen clubs now, even if I were younger. But I'd take my old Red Sox and put 'em against anything in the field today." To supplement a lengthy recounting of his fielding exploits in 1895, Collins was quoted simply as saying: "That was just 'heads up' baseball, the kind of ball you've got to play if you're to get to the big show."[33]

Collins was much more animated when the subject turned to the Buffalo muny league, as the AP writer quoted Collins as saying: "I like to watch those kids play baseball. You can't tell me the game has lost its grip on the youngsters. Why we have so many applications from teams that we can't possibly take care of all of them." Collins was an evangelist for municipal ball, saying that muny leagues were "the best thing" for the game. "You get a lot of youngsters playing the game under supervision and some of them are bound to be good enough to go up."[34] He cited Frankie Pytlak, then a catcher with the Cleveland Indians, as the most famous graduate of the Buffalo muny program, and noted many others had played in the minor leagues.

There was also another ballplayer then pitching in the Buffalo muny program who would go on to become not just a major leaguer, but also a Hall of Famer — Warren Spahn. Before he signed with the Boston Braves in 1940 and pitched his first major league game in 1942, Spahn played as much baseball as he could in Buffalo, by playing on high school, semi-pro, and muny league teams.[35] Spahn's first stop in Organized Baseball was at Bradford, Pennsylvania, in the local Class D PONY League, which had been organized in 1939 by *Buffalo Evening News* sports editor Bob Stedler, partially to take advantage of the Buffalo muny league as a feeder system. Spahn went on to become the left-handed pitcher with the most victories in major league history.

As America went to war in 1941, Collins worked his job with the city and oversaw the muny league during the summer, but cut down on his activities in the colder months, when he used to attend numerous sports banquets in the Buffalo area. In his later years, though, Collins wasn't able to spend much time tossing a ball with his grandchildren.

In January 1943, after Collins fell on some ice near Kathlyn's house at 75 Wilbury Place, he recuperated for a few days before returning to work. On February 21, though, he stayed in bed, saying he was tired. After Kathlyn called a doctor, Collins was admitted to Millard Fillmore Hospital on February 24. He was diagnosed as having pneumonia, but his doctor was not optimistic, saying Collins had only a "very slight" chance of recovery. "He is putting up a good fight," the doctor said, "but his age and his heart are very much against his getting better."[36] Collins never left the hospital to return home.

Collins died on March 6, 1943, after a two-week battle with pneumonia. "He was game to the last and never complained," his daughter Kathlyn told newspaper reporters.[37] A simple burial mass without a eulogy was celebrated at the Holy Spirit Church on March 9, where the six directors of the Buffalo Municipal Baseball Association served as the pallbearers.[38] The muny league paid for a large portion of the funeral expense. Collins was buried at Holy Cross Cemetery in the Collins family plot along side his parents (his mother Alice had died in 1935, joining his father who died in 1910) and his infant daughter Agnes, who had passed away a year before his father.[39]

Bob Stedler wrote a long article about Jimmy Collins in the March 6 edition of the *Buffalo Evening News*, based on interviews with Collins just a few weeks before. Large portions of Stedler's article reappeared the following week in *The Sporting News* in his colleague Cy Kritzer's article entitled "Late

Jimmy Collins, the 'King of Third Sackers,' Became Hot Corner Star by Ability to Handle Bunts." Stedler and Kritzer were the only ones able to crack through the intense privacy of Collins to provide a few aspects of him beyond baseball.

It was difficult for other sportswriters to get beyond his baseball career. "Anecdotes concerning the late Jimmy Collins, original king of third basemen, are as hard to come by as shipyards in the Gobi sands," *Boston Globe* sportswriter Jerry Nason wrote soon after the passing of Collins. "Veterans of the press box recall him vividly in an academic sense — his fielding grace, agility, and daring distances he played away from the bag. But rare is the Collins anecdote." When Nason interviewed Fred Tenney, the first baseman who played with Collins on the championship Boston teams of 1897 and 1898, the most interesting thing that Tenney could say about Collins was "he was the first third baseman I ever saw who turned his back to the plate, without a glance back, and took a fly ball over his head."[40]

With the insight gained from the interviews with Collins, Stedler was the best person to pursue the one item lacking on Jimmy Collins' baseball resume: enshrinement in the Baseball Hall of Fame.

CHAPTER 25

Hall of Fame Selection

Two months before Jimmy Collins passed away in 1943, *Buffalo Evening News* sports editor Bob Stedler executed a press campaign to get Collins elected to the Baseball Hall of Fame. Stedler's first action was an article in the *Evening News* that touted the highlights of Collins' baseball career. "He revolutionized the art of playing third base," Stedler wrote. "Oldtime writers said day in and out he gave a grand opera performance in the field." Stedler speculated that Collins hadn't yet been elected to the Hall of Fame because "the modern generation of writers haven't been sufficiently refreshed on his career." Stedler tried to rectify that situation by writing to all members of the Baseball Writers' Association of America (BBWAA). He included a highlight sheet of Collins' career and a short biography that had been published in 1933 in *The Sporting News*, which gave details on his legendary fielding of the bunts by the Baltimore Orioles.[1]

Judson Bailey of the Associated Press immediately wrote an article based on Stedler's mailing, which was printed in newspapers nationwide in mid-January 1943. "Although baseball's Hall of Fame at Cooperstown has enshrined 26 of the game's immortals, it still lacks a third baseman," Bailey opened his article to help advance Stedler's argument that Collins should be in the Hall of Fame. "The case made out for Collins is a good one," Bailey concluded. "Perhaps when another election is suggested by the baseball writers they will fill the third base vacancy."[2] In addition to the widely distributed Associated Press article, Stedler's mailing inspired several syndicated sportswriters to write columns that advocated the enshrinement of Collins. Arthur Daley ended his "Sports of the Times" column with: "The secretary will please cast one immediate Hall of Fame ballot for Jimmy Collins."[3] Likewise, Grantland Rice concluded his "Sportlight" column with: "In my opinion it would be a crime to leave Jimmy Collins off the roster that belongs to baseball's Hall of Fame."[4]

Stedler's campaign to educate current-day sportswriters, nearly all of whom had never actually seen Collins play third base, was necessary because Collins had fallen far short of achieving the required 75 percent of votes to be enshrined in Cooperstown during the first five Hall of Fame elections. In the inaugural 1936 election, Collins was named on only 58 of the 226 ballots cast by the baseball writers, to capture just 26 percent of the vote. His percentage of the vote increased slightly in the 1937 and 1938 elections, to 30 percent, but then dipped to 26 percent in 1939 and 29 percent in 1942. In each of the first five elections, Collins placed among the top 15 vote-getters, but never higher than tenth (in 1937 and 1938).[5]

In their 1943 columns advocating Collins for the Hall of Fame, both Daley and Rice noted that Collins had been "just short" of making it into Cooperstown in the first election in 1936, with Daley more specifically writing that it was a "picayune margin of three votes." Clearly, this selling point was an error. The lowest vote-getter among the five Hall of Famers elected in 1936 (Walter Johnson) garnered 189 votes, while the minimum needed for the 75 percent threshold was 170. Collins generated just 58 votes, good only for 13th place. Under this standard for a near-miss, seven other players besides Collins were also "just short" of election to the Hall of Fame. The myth of the margin of three likely derived from the basic principle of the initial Hall of Fame election in 1936 for the writers to select ten worthy modern-day players, while an Old-Timers Committee picked five notables from the nineteenth century. Collins, in 13th place in the writers' voting, finished three spots away from being in the top ten in the 1936 election.

Collins never publicly divulged his thoughts about being included in the Hall of Fame. Given the timing of Stedler's promotional campaign — the next Hall of Fame election wasn't slated for another two years — Collins must have indicated such a desire to Stedler since he began the campaign soon after an interview that Collins gave the *Buffalo Evening News*, the only lengthy interview Collins ever granted following the end of his playing days. Collins did go out of his way to attend a number of events in the late 1930s that would expand or reinforce his reputation among the current-day baseball writers, such as attending the New York baseball writers' dinner in New York City in January 1938 and several old-timers games in 1939 that were conducted to celebrate the baseball centennial.[6] Even though there was no business angle in it, Collins must have been at least not averse to his potential selection as a Hall of Fame ballplayer, perhaps considering it an extension of his public service duties that originally led to his taking the position as president of the Buffalo Municipal Baseball Association.

The passing of Collins in March 1943 served as a sympathetic springboard for his selection to the Hall of Fame, as many baseball writers over the next two years adopted the stance taken by writer Charles Young, an advocate for Johnny Evers, in the following passage:

> Jimmy Collins, one of the greatest third basemen of all time if not the greatest of them all, died without getting the recognition he was entitled from the baseball men who are entrusted with the task of electing players to the Hall of Fame at Cooperstown. Like our adopted Johnny Evers, famed second baseman, Jimmy Collins should have been in the Hall of Fame years ago; both contributed greatly to baseball, just as much as some of the stars who have been voted in. The names of Jimmy Collins and Johnny Evers will be added to the list some day. Of this we have little doubt. Jimmy Collins, however, won't be able to enjoy the thrill that must be enjoyed by a player so honored.[7]

Momentum built among BBWAA voters for Collins to be a posthumous choice for the Hall of Fame in the 1945 election. Days before the ballots were to be counted on January 20, the early favorites for the Hall of Fame were Collins and Roger Bresnahan, since both had recently died. The *New York Times* ran an Associated Press account of the handicapping under the headline "Collins Is Closer to Hall of Fame." The story went on to conclude that both players "have been just under the border line in previous polls, but stand the best chance to enter the charmed circle this time."[8] However, both men fell short of the required 75 percent plateau.

In the 1945 election, Collins finished eighth in the balloting, when he was named on 121 of the 247 ballots. This 49 percent of the vote was the highest rate he attained in six Hall of Fame elections. However, the 1945 election was the first one where no ballplayer reached the 75 percent threshold for election. Collins finished behind Frank Chance, Rube Waddell, Ed Walsh, Johnny Evers, Bresnahan, Miller Huggins, and Mickey Cochrane.[9]

"There will have to be some revision of baseball's electoral college, or the very purpose of the Hall of Fame balloting will have defeated itself," Daley commented on the barren 1945 election. "So great is the spread of names submitted—there were ninety-four candidates this time—that it now looks impossible for any single hero to attain the necessary three-quarters of the votes."[10]

Clearly, even with a heavy dose of electioneering by Stedler, Collins faced an insurmountable task to be chosen for the Hall of Fame. Fortunately, another avenue opened up for the Collins proponents. The Old-Timers Committee had been resurrected in 1944, after serving back in 1939 to choose the five pre–1900 selections for the Hall of Fame. In August 1944, Judge Landis, the baseball commissioner at the time, added new members to the Old-Timers Committee (which later became the Veterans Committee). The death of Landis in November 1944 spurred the committee into action, as they met at the judge's funeral and selected him to the Hall of Fame. With no selections by the BBWAA in the January 1945 election, the Old-Timers Committee met in the spring of 1945 to try to break up the logjam that was hamstringing the ability of the baseball writers to effectively select candidates for the Hall of Fame.

The Old-Timers Committee in 1945 was comprised of Ed Barrow, chairman of the board of directors of the New York Yankees; Connie Mack, the owner-manager of the Philadelphia Athletics; Bob Quinn, former president of the Boston Braves; Mel Webb, sportswriter for the *Boston Globe*; Stephen Clark and Paul Kerr, both of the National Baseball Museum; and Sid Mercer, sportswriter for the *New York Journal-American*.[11] Of these seven men, Collins had clear advocates in Mack, Webb, and Quinn. Mack was an old friend from their days in the fledging American League. Webb had actually seen Collins play third base in a Boston uniform, albeit late in his playing career. Quinn had been an executive in both the Red Sox and Braves organizations.

On April 25, three months after the barren 1945 election, the Old-Timers Committee selected Collins along with nine other ballplayers for inclusion in the Hall of Fame. Collins was one of three men who were unanimous choices by the committee, along with Fred Clarke and Wilbert Robinson.[12] However, given the recent death of President Franklin Roosevelt and the anticipated surrender of Germany to end the war in Europe, the public response to the Old-Timers Committee's action was very understated. Most newspaper announcements, like the following lead in Mel Webb's article in the *Boston Globe*, were mundane: "Ten famous old-time players, including Hugh Duffy and the late Jimmy Collins — outstanding performers of yesteryear — were elected to baseball's Hall of Fame today."[13] The timing was simply not right for extensive fanfare related to baseball.

Because of wartime travel restrictions, the annual Hall of Fame exhibition game had already been canceled for 1945, so there was no opportunity to stage an induction ceremony for Collins and the other selections by the Old-Timers Committee.[14] While the Hall of Fame exhibition game resumed in 1946, there was only a limited induction ceremony that year (to honor the plaque of Judge Landis) since no ballplayer had been named on 75 percent of the ballots in that year's BBWAA election.[15] Collins' plaque was eventually quietly placed in the Hall of Fame, with contents that read simply:

CONSIDERED BY MANY THE GAME'S
GREATEST THIRD BASEMAN. HE
REVOLUTIONIZED STYLE OF PLAY AT THAT
BAG. LED BOSTON RED SOX TO FIRST
WORLD CHAMPIONSHIP IN 1903. A
CONSISTENT BATTER, HIS DEFENSIVE PLAY
THRILLED FANS OF BOTH MAJOR LEAGUES.

The imprint of two proponents of Jimmy Collins can easily be seen in phrases on his Hall of Fame plaque. "Revolutionized" was popularized by Bob Stedler in his 1943 promotional campaign. "Greatest third baseman" was heralded by John Meahl in the 1920s during his public appearances with Collins and the Buffalo muny league. There is also a bit of irony in the use of "Red Sox," since Collins never actually played for a team by that name, as the name was adopted for the 1908 season after Collins had been traded to Philadelphia. While "defensive play" was to be his lasting distinguishing feature as a ballplayer, he also left a legacy to baseball in other ways related to "Boston" and the "world championship in 1903."

CHAPTER 26

Legacy to Baseball

Although Jimmy Collins was the *first* third baseman to be enshrined in the Baseball Hall of Fame, his tenure as the *only* third baseman lasted less than three years. In 1948 Harold "Pie" Traynor became the second third baseman to be inducted into the Hall of Fame when he was named on 93 of the 121 ballots cast by the baseball writers, two more than the required 91 votes. Traynor quickly supplanted Collins as baseball's "greatest third baseman" in the minds of fans and the media, since he was renowned as both a fielder and a hitter during his 17-year career with the Pittsburgh Pirates.

While Collins and Traynor were both exceptional fielders at third base, Traynor had a distinct edge over Collins in hitting, with a .320 lifetime batting average (versus the .294 average of Collins) and .435 lifetime slugging average (versus .409 for Collins). In many ways it is an unfair comparison, since Collins played in the Deadball Era while Traynor played in the Lively Ball Era, the latter of which produced loftier player statistics. In another sense, though, it is a fair comparison, since Collins paid little attention to statistics unless it would benefit him in salary negotiations. If he knew that having a lifetime batting average over the .300 mark would eventually make a difference, Collins may not have played for the Philadelphia Athletics the last two years in order to preserve that coveted threshold of hitting prowess. His lifetime batting average was at .301 when he left the Boston Americans in June 1907 and was at .299 at the end of the 1907 season. Just one more hit in 1907 would have resulted in Collins having a .300 lifetime batting average if he had retired then and not come back to play the 1908 season. To mid-century baseball observers, the statistical difference in hitting between Traynor and Collins gave Traynor the edge among the game's top two third basemen.

Traynor had another advantage over Collins—he remained in major league baseball after his playing days were over so that his name was recognizable to sportswriters and fans across the nation. After Traynor managed the Pirates for five seasons from 1934 through 1938, he stayed in the Pirates organization in various capacities, which allowed him to maintain contact with the media and expand his name recognition among new writers and fans. Collins' retreat from the game to focus on his real estate interests in Buffalo, while sound from an economic and lifestyle perspective, resulted in dramatically lower name recognition among postwar baseball writers and fans. Beyond Bob Stedler (who died in 1956), few sportswriters in Buffalo were inclined to devote the time to perpetuate Collins' legacy as the game's greatest third baseman at the turn of the century. The Collins family also had little motivation, since Jimmy's wife, Sadie, died in 1947, and his two daughters, Kathlyn and Claire, were busy raising their families.[1]

A third advantage for Traynor was that the BBWAA had elected him to the Hall of Fame, whereas Collins had been elected by the Veterans Committee. Although there is no distinction made on the actual Hall of Fame plaques, the enshrinement method is often a big consideration when comparing various members of the Hall of Fame, with the BBWAA election path considered as the higher standard of excellence. Since the BBWAA did not elect another third baseman to the Hall of Fame for another three decades (Eddie Mathews in 1978), an entire generation of young baseball fans grew up in the 1950s and 1960s thinking that Traynor was the only third baseman in the Hall of Fame. Collins, the old-timer, was relegated to footnote status.

Collins had even become a footnote in Boston Red Sox history. In 1951, when the ballclub celebrated the 50th anniversary of its founding, Collins received scant attention in the Boston newspaper writeups. "Jimmy Collins, the game's greatest third baseman and a Hub favorite, had jumped from the Boston Nationals to take over the managerial reins of the local entry in the new circuit," the *Boston Globe* summarized Collins' contribution to the ballclub's success, glossing over his role in the 1903 World Series.[2] In 1953, for the 50th anniversary of the inaugural 1903 World Series, Collins again received little mention other than having been the player-manager of the Boston team fifty years earlier. Cy Young, then 86 years old, got to throw out the first ball at the opening game of the 1953 World Series at Yankee Stadium.[3]

Fred Lieb, who had written one of the first comprehensive biographical sketches of Collins back in 1923, was Collins' biggest supporter in the postwar era. Lieb devoted a substantial number of pages to Collins in his 1947 book entitled *Boston Red Sox*, as well as prominently mentioning Collins in his comprehensive recap of the 1903 World Series in the September 30, 1953, issue of *The Sporting News*. Lieb also selected Collins to be the third baseman on "*The Sporting News* All-Time All-Star Team" in 1957, the last significant all-time team that named Collins as its third baseman. "While admitting Traynor's many fine attributes, we give the third base position to Jimmy

Collins by a shade," Lieb wrote in the accompanying article. Lieb justified the selection of Collins over Traynor because Collins was the "father of present third base play and opened the possibilities of that position," and had been a target of the American League raiders seeking an inspirational leader.[4] Lieb gave more weight to the intangibles of Collins than to his playing statistics.

By the 1960s, though, Traynor became the automatic nod for the third baseman on any all-time team, given the overwhelming statistical comparison to Collins. The most highly publicized of these all-time teams was the 1969 baseball centennial all-time team. Traynor was picked by the Pittsburgh fans as that ballclub's all-time third baseman; a committee of writers and sportscasters selected Traynor to the centennial all-time team from the pool of third basemen chosen by the fans of each ballclub. "As the only third baseman elected to baseball's Hall of Fame — Jimmy Collins and Home Run Baker were chosen by the Veterans Committee — Pie Traynor was in a class by himself," Bob Broeg wrote about Traynor's selection in an extensive article in *The Sporting News*.[5] Foreshadowing an impending change in the constellation of all-time great third basemen, Brooks Robinson was chosen as runner-up to Traynor on the centennial all-time team. Collins was not even part of that discussion, however, since the Boston fans had failed to name Collins as the Red Sox's all-time third baseman — the fans instead voted that honor to Frank Malzone.[6]

The centennial all-time team was announced on July 21, 1969, at a gala black tie dinner at the Sheraton-Park Hotel in Washington, D.C. the day before the All-Star Game at RFK Stadium on July 22. In addition to Traynor, the other selections to the centennial team were Mickey Cochrane, Lou Gehrig, Rogers Hornsby, Honus Wagner, Babe Ruth, Ty Cobb, Joe DiMaggio, Lefty Grove, and Walter Johnson. All the living Hall of Fame members were invited to the dinner on July 21, as were widows and descendants of deceased Hall of Famers. Traynor and the other members (or their descendents) of the centennial all-time team attended a reception at the White House the next day, which was hosted by President Richard Nixon.[7]

As the descendants of their deceased Hall of Fame father, one or both of Collins' daughters would have been invited to the dinner in Washington celebrating the 1969 centennial all-time team (it is unclear if either daughter actually did attend). As a result of that dinner invitation, his younger daughter Claire decided to attend the Hall of Fame induction ceremony in 1970. "Jimmy Collins, greatest third baseman at the start of the century, is back on the program," the *Utica Observer* reported on descendants of deceased Hall of Famers who were expected to attend the induction ceremony, "thanks to his daughter, Mrs. W. J. Bell, participating in the 1970 gathering."[8] Claire joined Babe Ruth's wife and daughters along with several other descendants of deceased

Hall of Famers. The following year the *Otsego Farmer*, a local Cooperstown newspaper, reported that "Mrs. Claire McCall Bell, daughter of the great third baseman Jimmy Collins" would attend the 1971 induction ceremony.[9]

Claire's second husband, William Bell, was a motivating force in Claire taking a greater interest in her father's legacy to baseball, more than a quarter century after Collins' death. After her first husband, George McCall, died in 1965, Claire moved from suburban Syracuse, New York, to Sarasota, Florida, where she ran into her old high school boyfriend, William Bell, who was then a retired general in the U.S. Air Force.[10] After Bell graduated from South Park High School in South Buffalo in 1927, he attended the United States Military Academy at West Point, where he graduated in 1931 and was commissioned as a second lieutenant in the U.S. Army. He attended flight school and entered the Army Air Corps. After several promotions, Colonel Bell led a Combat Cargo Group in the Pacific Theater during World War II. After the Army Air Corps became the U.S. Air Force in 1947, Bell served in postwar Europe, and in 1956 was promoted to major general. In 1965 he retired from military service.[11] Claire and Bell rekindled their past relationship, married in 1968, and made their home in Longboat Key, Florida, an island in the Gulf of Mexico just off the coast of Sarasota.

Bell likely had a vastly different perspective on Claire's father's years as president of the Buffalo Municipal Baseball Association than did Claire, who may have resented the time her father spent away from home as well as having to suffer the brunt of his income decline in the late 1920s. To Bell and his school chums, the muny league was a welcome diversion from everyday life in South Buffalo and Jimmy Collins was viewed as a hero. To Claire, her father was just a parent, not a public figure who was looked up to by thousands of youngsters. Bell may have reinforced this different perspective of her father by telling Claire the old joke that made its way around the Buffalo school system, in which her father is the punch line: A high school history teacher pointedly asks the school's star athlete to name three famous Buffaloians, to which he hesitantly responds, "Millard Fillmore, Grover Cleveland ... and Jimmy Collins, of course."[12] The joke in an alternative form asks the student to name three famous presidents from Buffalo, but has the same punch line with two U.S. presidents to go with the muny league one.

In Florida, Claire followed in her father's footsteps to pursue public service. Longboat Key underwent rapid development in the 1960s and 1970s as more retired people — like Claire and her husband — moved from colder climates to live in Florida. Claire thought there should be more planned development and controlled growth on Longboat Key, to slow down and put more thought into the commercial development of the island. Claire got involved with a number of civic groups and wrote letters to the editor of the local newspaper, at one point in 1976 railing about a proposed bridge between Longboat Key and Sarasota that would increase traffic on the island. Longboat Key was governed by a town commission, which consisted of seven elected commissioners who then selected a mayor from among themselves. After Claire observed the town commission's interactions with private developers, she was more determined to try to make a difference in the quality of life in Longboat Key. In 1978 she was first elected as a commissioner, and served the citizens of the town in that capacity through 1983.[13]

One of the first issues that Claire tackled as a town commissioner was a proposal to build the island's first major shopping center, to include a Publix supermarket and an Eckerd Drug Store, which the Arvida Corporation proposed to build at the Bay Isles residential complex. Arvida contended that the proposed shopping center wouldn't increase traffic on the island, since it was mainly for Bay Isles residents. Claire, like her father, wasn't bashful about voicing an opinion. "Publix isn't going to come out here to serve Bay Isles and the whole island doesn't want it," Claire told a reporter from the *Sarasota Herald-Tribune*. "I play golf a lot and work in the library so I've been in contact with a lot of people and they tell me they wanted a store and they don't want anything else. They had no idea it would get this big."[14] The project was eventually approved by the town commission, but the size of the building was scaled back.

Claire's tenacity at trying to control growth on the island was rewarded in 1981 when her fellow town commissioners elected her to be mayor. "Claire Bell became the first woman mayor of the Town of Longboat Key Wednesday night," the local newspaper reported, but the outspoken Claire was far from a unanimous choice as "she was elected to that post 4–3."[15] As mayor, she called for a building moratorium on the island. "I feel we are increasingly being painted into a corner," Claire complained. "We're getting hemmed in and still the building goes on and still we do nothing about it."[16] Unsuccessful at marshaling sufficient political support for the building moratorium, Claire served only one term as mayor, as she was not re-elected to the post in 1982.

In the mid–1980s, Claire's older sister Kathlyn also left upstate New York for the warmer climate of the South, when she moved to Atlanta, Georgia, to live with her daughter. When Kathlyn died in 1994 and Claire in 2005, obituaries for both women noted their heritage as the daughter of Hall of Fame third baseman Jimmy Collins.[17]

When third basemen Eddie Mathews and Brooks Robinson were elected to the Hall of Fame in 1978 and 1983, respectively, Collins was further devalued as a worthy member of the third-basemen fraternity in the Hall of Fame. Mathews was a renowned home run hitter, with 512 career homers, while Robinson was a spectacular fielder, with 16 Gold Glove Awards. Robinson, with a .971 lifetime fielding average, was considered to be in a class by himself as an exceptional third baseman. If there was a remote comparison, it was to Pie Traynor, who, the *Baltimore Sun* wrote, was "generally considered the other defensive wizard at third base."[18] There was virtually no mention of Collins at the time of Robinson's election to the Hall of Fame, with most of those references as one of the other third basemen in the Hall that the Veterans Committee had allowed in (as it did with George Kell that year).

In the 1990s, the election of power-hitting third basemen Mike Schmidt (1995) and George Brett (1999) into the Hall of Fame further diminished the luster on Collins' qualifications to be in Cooperstown, which were based on a mix of fielding and hitting achievements in the Deadball Era. It became fashionable to portray Collins as one of the least qualified ballplayers to be in the Hall of Fame. For example, in his 1994 book *The Politics of Glory*, Bill James named Collins as the third baseman on his All Why-Did-They-Elect-*Him* Team.[19]

While Collins had lapsed from the mindset of nearly every baseball fan by the 1990s, he still had instant name recognition within one small segment of baseball fandom — memorabilia collectors. Because the intensely private Collins had signed few items when he was alive, the scarcity of his autograph inflated the value of Collins–signed material into the thousands of dollars among collectors of baseball memorabilia. In 1999 one man resorted to stealing Collins' will from the Erie County Surrogate Court to sell to an unsuspecting collector in the lucrative

Few people held onto this baseball card of minor leaguer Jimmy Collins as the player-manager of the Providence Grays of the Eastern League in the waning days of his professional baseball career. However, since Collins was a Hall of Famer, the value of the card increased exponentially in the memorabilia market of the 1990s, a business result that would have drawn a smile to Collins's face (Library of Congress Prints and Photographs Division, bbc 1540).

memorabilia market.[20] In 2003, a memorabilia expert estimated that a Collins-signed postcard would sell for $2,500, a handwritten letter on Buffalo Municipal Baseball Association letterhead would fetch at least $4,000, and the value of a personal cancelled check could not be estimated since none had ever made their way into the hobby.[21]

In the first decade of the twenty-first century, the value of any baseball item associated with Jimmy Collins soared following the book publication and media publicity celebrating the 100th anniversaries of the 1901 founding of the Boston Red Sox and the 1903 inaugural World Series. A Collins baseball card in the T205 series, originally issued in 1911, routinely sells for several hundreds of dollars, even in poor condition. Among Hall of Famers in the set, the Collins card is the scarcest because he was playing for Providence in the minor leagues that year and few people bothered to hold on to that card compared to a card of Ty Cobb or Christy Mathewson.

Where does Jimmy Collins stand within the pantheon of third basemen in the Baseball Hall of Fame? Unfortunately, this is a useless question to debate. Collins was the best third baseman during the 1895–1904 timeframe, when he was a superior fielder and an above-average hitter on four championship teams. Arguably, he was also the best third baseman for the entire Deadball Era and even the entire first half-century of professional baseball from 1871 to 1920. However, all these conclusions combined with three dollars will get you a mocha iced coffee at Dunkin' Donuts. The times have changed. What observers valued in Collins during his playing days no longer carries nearly as much weight as do other factors today. Every third baseman that the BBWAA elected to the Hall of Fame since Collins' enshrinement in Cooperstown in 1945 is a legitimate choice as a better third baseman than Collins. It is irrelevant, though, where Jimmy Collins stands within the pantheon of third basemen in the Baseball Hall of Fame.

The legacy of Jimmy Collins to baseball is not defined by his admirable exploits as a ballplayer more than a hundred years ago. His legacy is defined by his substantial contribution in establishing the foundation of the Boston Red Sox franchise as its manager and public face during its formative years. The legacy of Jimmy Collins is being the patron saint of today's Red Sox Nation.

While Ban Johnson was the visionary and Charles Somers the financier, Collins was the man on the front lines that made the inaugural 1901 Boston Americans a success and turned it into a World Series champion in 1903. Officially, Collins' position consisted of three jobs (manager, captain, and player) but due to absentee-owner Somers he was also the public face of the Americans. The astute, soft-spoken, but headstrong Collins was perhaps the only man who could have pulled it off; certainly, he was one of only a select few who was willing to take the risk of the position. Johnson couldn't even convince Boston businessmen to invest in the ballclub, causing Somers to step up to front the money, due to fear over the ostensibly entrenched National League team in Boston. Even with a willing Collins, Somers had to offer him a three-year guaranteed contract to take the position. Collins used the money to fund his nascent real estate business in Buffalo, so the possible failure of the enterprise was not a big risk to the 31-year-old Collins. He could simply retire as a ballplayer. There were not many major league ballplayers of a similar mindset with the goods to handle the position.

Not only did he lead the team to victory in the inaugural 1903 World Series — his best-known accomplishment a century later — he also was instrumental in establishing the Red Sox–Yankee rivalry, which in its nascent years of 1903 and 1904 was known as the Americans–Highlanders battle — his least-known achievement. His friendship with Clark Griffith, the confederate leader of the jumpers from the National League to the American League, helped make the vaunted season-ending series in 1904 even more palpable in the public eye.

Because baseball to Collins was a means to another end — his real estate business in Buffalo — he never reveled in his glory or attempted to create a lasting image that would be immediately recognizable to members of today's Red Sox Nation. On the contrary, he seems to have purposely destroyed his goodwill with the fans by deserting the ballclub during the 1906 season. However, without the entrepreneurship of Collins to take the risk of the managerial position and his operational fortitude to make it work, the building of Fenway Park — now "America's Most Beloved Ballpark" — and the assembling of associated Red Sox teams would never have materialized. That Red Sox–Yankee rivalry would have been different. No trade of Babe Ruth in 1920 to institute the Curse of the Bambino. No Williams–DiMaggio debate in the 1940s. No heart-breaking homer by Bucky Dent in the 1978 playoff game. No walkoff homer by David Ortiz in the ALCS as a prelude to World Series victory in 2004, 86 years after the team's last championship in 1918.

A lesser driven man could not have accomplished what Collins did for the Boston Americans ballclub; a lesser driven man couldn't be found to do it, never mind a more driven person. Collins was the ideal man for the job because baseball was not his ultimate motivation. Baseball men couldn't see the potential in the new American League ballclub. Cold-blooded business acumen with a talent to forecast the future, tempered with some knowledge of baseball, was the requirement to succeed. Collins was building houses in a flood plain in Buffalo, but he could foresee the future potential when the area was flood-controlled. Establishing a ballclub to appeal to both Brahmin and Irish-American patrons in an ethnically stratified Boston society was a similar task. As he navigated the upper and lower strata of Boston society during his days as a ballplayer with the National League team, Collins could envision the future of a more socially diverse Boston once the Irish-Americans acquired greater political power.

The foundation for the Boston Red Sox franchise, valued at $912 million in 2011 by *Forbes*, began with a $10,000 contract in 1901 that Jimmy Collins negotiated with an out-of-town financier to perform what many considered to be an impossible job. Collins succeeded. By delivering a knockout punch to the smug owners of the Boston ballclub in the National League, Collins ensured that the Boston ballclub in the American League would always be number one among baseball fans in Boston. Without Collins' efforts, the Boston Red Sox would not be the iconic ballclub that it is today. Jimmy Collins truly is the patron saint of Red Sox Nation.

Chapter Notes

Preface

1. Nigel Hamilton, *How to Do Biography* (Cambridge: Harvard University Press, 2008), 109, 209.

Chapter 1

1. *Buffalo News*, March 20, 1999.
2. Glenn Stout and Richard Johnson, *Red Sox Century: One Hundred Years of Red Sox Baseball* (Boston: Houghton Mifflin, 2000), 11.
3. Louis Masur, *Autumn Glory: Baseball's First World Series* (New York: Hill and Wang, 2003), 5, 10.
4. Roger Abrams, *The First World Series* (Boston: Northeastern University Press, 2003), 182.
5. Cy Kritzer, "Late Jimmy Collins, the 'King of Third Sackers,' Became Hot Corner Star by Ability to Handle Bunts," *The Sporting News*, March 11, 1943.
6. *The Sporting News*, March 16, 1901.
7. Kritzer, "Late Jimmy Collins."
8. *Sporting Life*, March 2 and September 21, 1895; Kritzer, "Late Jimmy Collins."
9. *Boston Globe*, April 3, 1896; *Sporting Life*, October 24, 1896.
10. *Boston Globe*, February 9, 1897; *Sporting Life*, October 23, 1897; *Brooklyn Eagle*, December 22, 1897.
11. *Boston Globe*, March 13, 1898, and October 21, 1898.
12. *Sporting Life*, February 11, 1899.
13. Kritzer, "Late Jimmy Collins"; *The Sporting News*, March 16, 1901; Reed Browning, *Cy Young: A Baseball Life* (Amherst: University of Massachusetts Press, 2000), 111; *Boston Globe*, October 1, 1901.
14. *Boston Globe*, February 10, 1902, and October 19, 1903.
15. *Boston Globe*, October 15 and 19, 1903.
16. *Sporting Life*, November 14, 1903; Kritzer, "Late Jimmy Collins."
17. *Boston Globe*, October 18, 1905.
18. *Boston Globe*, January 18, 1906; *Sporting Life*, June 22, 1907.
19. *Washington Post*, February 16, 1908.
20. *Worcester Telegram*, February 6, 1906.
21. *Worcester Telegram*, February 5, 1912.
22. *Niagara Falls Gazette*, March 1, 1943.

Chapter 2

1. U.S. Census, 1870, New York, Niagara County, Niagara Falls, Suspension Bridge (Series M593, Roll 1055, Page 409).
2. U.S. Census, 1900, New York, Erie County, Buffalo, Ward 22 (Series T623, Roll 1031, Page 31).
3. *Buffalo City Directory*, 1862, 1865.
4. Mark Goldman, *High Hopes: The Rise and Decline of Buffalo, New York* (Albany: State University of New York Press, 1983), 56.
5. David Doyle, "The Remaking of Irish America, 1845–1880," in *Making the Irish American: History and Heritage of the Irish in the United States*, edited by J.J. Lee and Marion Casey (New York: New York University Press, 2006), 215.
6. Mathew Jordan's obituary ("uncle of captain Anthony Collins of the third precinct"), *Buffalo Express*, September 7, 1883.
7. *Commercial Advertiser Directory for the City of Buffalo*, 1851–1852.
8. *Buffalo City Directory*, 1873.
9. *Buffalo City Directory*, 1882, 1883.
10. Laurence Glasco, *Ethnicity and Social Structure: Irish, Germans, and Native-Born of Buffalo, N.Y., 1850–1860* (New York: Arno, 1980), 18.
11. Cindy Diem and Michael Kaska, "Buffalo Police Department History," Buffalo Police Then and Now website, <www.bpdthenandnow.com>.

12. *Buffalo Courier*, November 18, 1872.
13. *Buffalo City Directory*, 1883; Jerrold Casway, *Ed Delahanty in the Emerald Age of Baseball* (South Bend: University of Notre Dame Press, 2004), x.
14. Allan Nevins, *Grover Cleveland: A Study in Courage* (New York: Dodd, Mead, 1932), 30.
15. James Richardson, *Urban Police in the United States* (Port Washington, NY: National University Publications, 1974), 47.
16. *Buffalo Express*, June 2, 1879.
17. Nevins, *Grover Cleveland*, 84–85.
18. *Buffalo Express*, July 31, 1885.
19. *Buffalo Express*, December 1, 1883.
20. *Buffalo Express*, July 31, 1885.
21. Ibid.
22. John Thelin, *A History of American Higher Education* (Baltimore: Johns Hopkins University Press, 2004), 97.
23. *Buffalo Courier*, September 28, 1885.
24. Correspondence to author from Scott Burns, director of alumni relations at the St. Joseph's Collegiate Institute, dated March 31, 2011.
25. *Buffalo Express*, June 30, 1888.
26. *Buffalo Express*, May 5, 1891.
27. *Buffalo Courier*, June 23, 1886; *Buffalo Express*, June 18, 1890.
28. *Buffalo Courier*, June 25, 1884.
29. *Buffalo Courier*, June 30, 1888.
30. *Buffalo City Directory*, 1888, 1889.
31. *City of Buffalo Atlas*, 1894.
32. Jay Dolan, *The Irish Americans: A History* (New York: Bloomsbury, 2008), 87.
33. *Buffalo Express*, April 30, 1891.
34. *Buffalo Courier*, September 1, 1910.
35. Kritzer, "Late Jimmy Collins."
36. *Buffalo City Directory*, 1890.

Chapter 3

1. Tim Murnane, "His Winter Pastime Collecting Rents," *Boston Globe*, January 15, 1905.
2. *Buffalo Express*, June 16, 1889.
3. *The Sporting News*, December 25, 1897.
4. "Buffalo Bisons History," Official Web Site of Minor League Baseball, <minorleaguebaseball.com>.
5. David Fleitz, *The Irish in Baseball: An Early History* (Jefferson, NC: McFarland, 2009), 18.
6. Ibid., 25, 178.
7. Casway, *Ed Delahanty*, x.
8. Murnane, "His Winter Pastime."
9. "Buffalo Bisons History."
10. Charlie Bevis, *Sunday Baseball: The Major Leagues' Struggle to Play Baseball on the Lord's Day* (Jefferson, NC: McFarland, 2003), 283.
11. Goldman, *High Hopes*, 177.

12. *Buffalo Express*, March 11, 1924.
13. *Buffalo Express*, March 3, 1889.
14. *Buffalo Express*, June 30, 1890.
15. *Buffalo Express*, July 20, 1891.
16. *Buffalo Express*, September 28, 1891.
17. *Buffalo Express*, July 4, 1890.
18. *Buffalo Express*, July 4, 1891.
19. *Buffalo Express*, September 28, 1891.
20. *Buffalo Express*, March 28, 1893.
21. *Buffalo Express*, October 3, 1892.
22. *Buffalo Express*, March 14, 1893.
23. Charlie Bevis, "Rocky Point: A Lone Outpost of Sunday Baseball in Sabbatarian New England," *NINE: A Journal of Baseball History & Culture* (Fall 2005).
24. Kritzer, "Late Jimmy Collins."
25. *Buffalo Express*, May 24, 1893.
26. *Buffalo Express*, May 26, 1893.
27. Ernest Lanigan, "Hall of Famer Collins Made Debut With Buffalo," *Syracuse Post-Standard*, December 29, 1946, in Collins' player file at the A. Bartlett Giamatti Research Center at the Baseball Hall of Fame.
28. *Buffalo Express*, June 5, 1893.
29. *Sporting Life*, June 24, 1893.
30. *Sporting Life*, July 8, 1893.
31. *Buffalo Express*, September 4, 1893.
32. *Buffalo Express*, October 9, 1893.
33. *Buffalo Express*, April 20, 1894.
34. *Sporting Life*, September 16 and 30, 1893.
35. *Sporting Life*, January 13, 1894.
36. *The Sporting News*, February 10, 1894.
37. *Sporting Life*, June 2, 1894.
38. *Buffalo Express*, August 21, 1894.
39. *Providence Journal*, August 27, 1894.
40. "Daguerreotypes: James J. (Jimmy) Collins," *The Sporting News*, July 27, 1933.
41. *Boston Globe*, September 8, 1894.
42. *Buffalo Express*, September 8, 1894.
43. *Ft. Worth Morning Register*, August 5, 1900.

Chapter 4

1. *Boston Globe*, November 15, 1894.
2. Fleitz, *Irish in Baseball*, 178.
3. Casway, *Ed Delahanty*, x.
4. *Boston Globe*, November 15, 1894.
5. *Sporting Life*, February 23, 1895.
6. *Sporting Life*, March 2, 1895.
7. *Boston Globe*, February 28, 1895.
8. Kritzer, "Late Jimmy Collins."
9. *Boston Globe*, January 13, 1896.
10. *Louisville Courier-Journal*, May 20, 1895.
11. *Boston Globe*, August 8, 1895, and January 12, 1897.
12. Stanley Hamlet, "Jimmy Collins," in *Deadball Stars of the American League*, edited by David Jones (Cleveland: Society for American Baseball Research, 2006), 403–404.

13. *Louisville Courier-Journal*, June 1, 1895.
14. *Baltimore Sun*, June 1, 1895.
15. Hugh Jennings, "Collins, Leader at Third, Wanted to Play Outfield," *Atlanta Constitution*, January 5, 1926.
16. Kritzer, "Late Jimmy Collins."
17. *The Sporting News*, March 28, 1951.
18. *Boston Globe*, January 13, 1896.
19. *Louisville Courier-Journal*, June 14, 1895.
20. *Brooklyn Eagle*, June 16, 1895.
21. *The Sporting News*, November 21, 1940.
22. *Boston Globe*, January 13, 1896.
23. *Louisville Courier-Journal*, July 13, 1895.
24. *Boston Globe*, August 8, 1895.
25. *Louisville Courier-Journal*, July 29, 1895.
26. Kritzer, "Late Jimmy Collins."
27. *Sporting Life*, August 17, 1895.
28. *Boston Globe*, August 29, 1895.
29. *Boston Globe*, September 6, 1895.
30. *Sporting Life*, September 21, 1895.
31. *Louisville Courier-Journal*, September 13, 1895.
32. Kritzer, "Late Jimmy Collins."
33. *Sporting Life*, October 5, 1895.

Chapter 5

1. *Boston Globe*, November 13, 1895.
2. *Boston Globe*, November 14, 1895.
3. *Boston Globe*, December 16, 1895.
4. Harold Kaese, *Boston Braves* (New York: G.P. Putnam's Sons, 1948), 22–23.
5. Ibid., 24, 75.
6. Thomas O'Connor, *The Hub: Boston Past and Present* (Boston: Northeastern University Press, 2001), 86–87.
7. Ibid., 153.
8. *Boston Globe*, January 13, 1896.
9. *Boston Globe*, January 19, 1896.
10. *Boston Globe*, April 3, 1896.
11. *Boston Globe*, April 17, 1896.
12. *Boston Globe*, April 21, 1896.
13. Arthur Dixwell's obituary, *Boston Globe*, September 17, 1924.
14. *Boston Globe*, April 24, 1896.
15. *Baltimore Sun*, April 24, 1896.
16. *Boston Globe*, April 25, 1896.
17. *Boston Globe*, April 27, 1896.
18. *Boston Globe*, March 17, 1895.
19. Philip Lowry, *Green Cathedrals* (New York: Walker, 2006), 23–26.
20. *Boston Globe*, June 5, 1896.
21. "Veteran Groundskeeper Knew All the Old Baseball Stars," *Boston Globe*, September 19, 1921.
22. *Sporting Life*, September 19, 1896.
23. *Sporting Life*, October 24, 1896.
24. *Boston Globe*, October 3–4, 1896.
25. *Baltimore Sun*, October 13, 1896.
26. *Boston Globe*, February 9, 1897.
27. Kritzer, "Late Jimmy Collins."
28. *Boston Globe*, March 19, 1897.
29. *Boston Globe*, June 6, 1897.
30. *Boston Globe*, June 9, 1897.
31. *Boston Globe*, April 20, 1897.
32. *Boston Globe*, September 24, 1897.
33. Peter Nash, *Boston's Royal Rooters* (Charleston: Arcadia, 2005), 19; Abrams, *The First World Series*, 94.
34. Bill Felber, *A Game of Brawl: The Orioles, the Beaneaters & the Battle for the 1897 Pennant* (Lincoln: University of Nebraska Press, 2007), 5.
35. Ibid., 39.
36. *Boston Globe*, September 25, 1897.
37. *Sporting Life*, October 23, 1897.

Chapter 6

1. Kaese, *Boston Braves*, p. 89.
2. *New York Times*, September 13, 1897.
3. *Boston Globe*, October 11, 1897.
4. *Buffalo Express*, October 2, 1897.
5. *Boston Globe*, October 5, 1897.
6. Ibid.
7. *Boston Globe*, October 7, 1897.
8. *Boston Globe*, October 10, 1897.
9. *Boston Globe*, October 11, 1897.
10. *Boston Globe*, October 12, 1897.
11. *Sporting Life*, October 23, 1897.
12. *New York Times*, October 13, 1897.
13. *Sporting Life*, November 13, 1897.
14. *New York Times*, August 21, 1897.
15. *Brooklyn Eagle*, December 22, 1897.
16. *Boston Globe*, October 3, 1897.
17. *Sporting Life*, October 30, 1897.
18. *Baltimore Sun*, October 20, 1897.
19. *Sporting Life*, January 1, 1898.
20. *Brooklyn Eagle*, December 22, 1897.
21. Ibid.
22. Ibid.
23. *Sporting Life*, January 1, 1898.
24. *Brooklyn Eagle*, December 22, 1897.
25. *The Sporting News*, November 13, 1897.
26. *Brooklyn Eagle*, December 22, 1897.
27. *Sporting Life*, November 20, 1897.
28. *Brooklyn Eagle*, December 22, 1897.
29. Ibid.
30. *New York Times*, November 13, 1897.
31. *Brooklyn Eagle*, December 22, 1897.
32. Ibid.

Chapter 7

1. *Boston Globe*, March 13, 1898.
2. Kaese, *Boston Braves*, 113.
3. *Boston Globe*, May 23, 1898.

4. *Chicago Tribune*, March 3, 1898.
5. *Boston Globe*, March 21, 1898.
6. *Sporting Life*, October 29, 1898.
7. *Sporting Life*, October 22, 1898.
8. Ibid.
9. *Sporting Life*, February 25, 1899.
10. *Sporting Life*, March 11, 1899.
11. *Buffalo Express*, October 9, 1898.
12. Kaese, *Boston Braves*, 55.
13. *Boston Globe*, July 17, 1898.
14. *Boston Globe*, September 6, 1898.
15. *Boston Globe*, September 30, 1898.
16. *Boston Globe*, February 27, 1899.
17. *Boston Globe*, October 1, 1898.
18. *Boston Globe*, October 21, 1898.
19. *Boston Globe*, October 18, 1898.
20. *Boston Globe*, October 21, 1898.
21. *Philadelphia Inquirer*, February 5, 1899.

Chapter 8

1. *Sporting Life*, August 20, 1898.
2. Peter Morris, *A Game of Inches: The Stories Behind the Innovations that Shaped Baseball: The Game on the Field* (Chicago: Ivan R. Dee, 2006), 79–81, 218–219.
3. Ibid., 86–88.
4. *Boston Globe*, August 14, 1899.
5. *Sporting Life*, September 11, 1897.
6. *The Sporting News*, May 28, 1898.
7. *Chicago Tribune*, August 29, 1898.
8. *Sporting Life*, March 4, 1899.
9. *The Sporting News*, May 28, 1898.
10. *Buffalo Express*, February 26, 1898.
11. *The Sporting News*, March 1, 1934.
12. *Sporting Life*, October 28, 1899.
13. Steve Geitschier, ed., *Complete Baseball Record Book* (St. Louis: Sporting News, 2008), 74.
14. *The Sporting News*, December 25, 1897.
15. *The Sporting News*, May 28, 1898.
16. *Sporting Life*, August 20, 1898.
17. "Daguerreotypes: James J. (Jimmy) Collins," *The Sporting News*, July 27, 1933.
18. *Amsterdam (NY) Recorder*, May 6, 1936.
19. *The Sporting News*, May 28, 1898.
20. *Buffalo Express*, October 9, 1898.

Chapter 9

1. *Sporting Life*, February 11, 1899.
2. *Boston Globe*, January 22, 1900.
3. *Boston Globe*, January 20–21, 1900.
4. Howard Chudacoff, *The Age of the Bachelor* (Princeton, NJ: Princeton University Press, 1999), 48.
5. Ibid., 54.
6. Ibid., 67–68.

7. U.S. Census, 1900, Massachusetts, Suffolk County, Boston, Ward 12 (Series T623, Roll 681, Page 34).
8. Chudacoff, *The Age of the Bachelor*, 98.
9. U.S. Census, 1900, New York, Erie County, Buffalo, Ward 5 (Series T623, Roll 1025, Page 8).
10. "William H. Fitzpatrick History," William H. Fitzpatrick Institute of Public Affairs and Leadership, Canisius College, <www.canisius.edu/fitzpatrick/history.asp>.
11. *Boston Globe*, July 29, 1900.
12. *Sporting Life*, May 1, 1897; *Washington Post*, April 3, 1900.
13. *Sporting Life*, June 16, 1900.
14. *Washington Post*, July 30, 1900.
15. *Washington Post*, September 10, 1900.
16. *Boston Globe*, November 12, 1900; *The Sporting News*, March 1, 1934.
17. Geitschier, *Complete Baseball Record Book*, 74.
18. *Boston Globe*, October 14, 1900.

Chapter 10

1. *Washington Post*, December 15–17, 1900.
2. Eugene Murdock, *Ban Johnson: Czar of Baseball* (Westport, CT: Greenwood, 1982), 46–47.
3. *Boston Post*, March 12, 1901.
4. *Boston Globe*, January 4, 1901.
5. Ibid.
6. *Boston Globe*, March 8 and May 9, 1901.
7. *Sporting Life*, May 18, 1901.
8. *Chicago Tribune*, January 24, 1901.
9. *Boston Globe*, January 4, 1901.
10. *Boston Globe*, January 7, 1901.
11. *The Sporting News*, January 26, 1901.
12. *Chicago Tribune*, January 12, 1901.
13. *Washington Post*, March 8, 1943.
14. Murdock, *Ban Johnson*, 47.
15. *Boston Globe*, January 26, 1901.
16. *Chicago Tribune*, January 23, 1901.
17. *New York Times*, February 9, 1901.
18. *Boston Globe*, February 10, 1901.
19. *Washington Post*, February 12, 1901.
20. *Chicago Tribune*, February 17, 1901.
21. *Buffalo Express*, February 14, 1901.
22. *Boston Globe*, February 24, 1901.
23. *Boston Globe*, March 2, 1901.
24. *Chicago Tribune*, March 3, 1901.
25. *Buffalo Express*, March 10, 1901.
26. *New York Times*, August 13, 1901.
27. *The Sporting News*, March 16, 1901.
28. *Sporting Life*, March 16, 1901.
29. Kritzer, "Late Jimmy Collins."
30. *Boston Globe*, March 10, 1901.
31. *Boston Globe*, March 8, 1901.
32. *Boston Globe*, March 11, 1901.

Chapter 11

1. *Boston Globe*, March 11, 1901.
2. *Boston Globe*, March 17, 1901.
3. *Boston Globe*, March 11, 1901.
4. *Boston Globe*, March 6, 1901.
5. *Boston Globe*, March 22 and 30, 1901.
6. *Boston Globe*, March 29, 1901.
7. *Boston Globe*, April 21, 1901.
8. *Boston Globe*, April 29, 1901.
9. Ted Leavengood, *Clark Griffith: The Old Fox of Washington Baseball* (Jefferson, NC: McFarland, 2011), 17, 38; Gustaf Axelson, *Commy: The Life Story of Charles A. Comiskey* (Chicago: Reilly & Lee, 1919), 186.
10. *Boston Globe*, April 27, 1901.
11. *Boston Globe*, February 3, 1901, and March 11, 1951.
12. *Boston Globe*, March 3, 1901.
13. *Boston Globe*, March 10, 1901.
14. *Boston Globe*, May 9, 1901.
15. *Boston Journal*, June 18, 1901.
16. *Chicago Tribune*, June 19, 1901.
17. Leavengood, *Clark Griffith*, 40.
18. *Boston Globe*, May 24, 1901.
19. *New York Times*, August 13, 1901.
20. *Boston Globe*, January 30, 1902.
21. *Buffalo Express*, September 22, 1901.
22. *Boston Post*, September 28, 1901.
23. *Boston Globe*, October 1, 1901.
24. *Boston Globe*, October 2–5, 1901.
25. Browning, *Cy Young*, 111.
26. *Boston Globe*, November 15, 1901.
27. *Buffalo Express*, November 11–12, 1901.
28. *Boston Globe*, January 5, 1902.

Chapter 12

1. *Chicago Tribune*, February 10, 1902.
2. *Boston Globe*, October 19, 1903.
3. History of the home mortgage provided in W.R. Huff, "FHA Succeeds in Breaking Down Legal and Educational Checks to Its Program," *Wall Street Journal*, July 9, 1935.
4. *Buffalo Express*, September 29, 1902.
5. *Buffalo Express*, September 21, 1902.
6. Murnane, "His Winter Pastime."
7. Ibid.
8. *Sporting Life*, December 30, 1905.
9. *Sporting Life*, July 12, 1902.
10. James Collins, "The Champion Baseball Team of the World," *The Illustrated Sporting News*, April 16, 1904.
11. Jake Morse, "The Story of Cy Young," *Baseball Magazine*, September 1908.
12. "Jim Collins' New Methods: Chick Stahl Attributes Boston's Success to Buffalo Boy's Generalship," *Pittsburgh Post-Gazette*, December 1, 1903.
13. *Sporting Life*, December 30, 1905.
14. "Collins' New Methods."
15. Fred O'Connell, "Boston's Baseball Idol: Jimmy Collins, Manager and Captain of the World's Champion Club," *Washington Post*, September 11, 1904.
16. Ibid.
17. Collins, "Champion Baseball Team."
18. O'Connell, "Boston's Baseball Idol."
19. Murdock, *Ban Johnson*, 74.
20. *Boston Globe*, September 19, 1901.
21. *Boston Globe*, March 6 and 13, 1902.
22. *Boston Globe*, August 12, 1902.
23. *Boston Globe*, July 30, 1902.
24. *Chicago Tribune*, October 12–13, 1902.
25. *Boston Globe*, September 30, 1902.

Chapter 13

1. *Sporting Life*, December 26, 1903.
2. *New York Times*, January 11–12, 1903.
3. *Philadelphia Inquirer*, February 22, 1903.
4. *Boston Globe*, October 19, 1903.
5. *Boston Globe*, March 1, 1903.
6. *Boston Globe*, March 9, 1903.
7. *Boston Globe*, April 2, 1903.
8. *Boston Journal*, April 21, 1903.
9. Lieb, *Boston Red Sox*, 38.
10. Browning, *Cy Young*, 125.
11. *Sporting Life*, August 8, 1903.
12. Ibid.
13. Ibid.
14. *Chicago Tribune*, August 28, 1903.
15. Masur, *Autumn Glory*, 15.
16. *Boston Transcript*, September 25, 1903.
17. *Chicago Tribune*, September 25, 1903.
18. *New York Times*, September 19, 1903.
19. *Chicago Tribune*, September 24, 1903.
20. *Boston Transcript*, September 25, 1903.
21. *Philadelphia Inquirer*, September 16, 1903.
22. *Chicago Tribune*, September 24, 1903.
23. *Boston Transcript*, September 25, 1903.
24. *Chicago Tribune*, September 24, 1903.
25. *Boston Transcript*, September 25, 1903.
26. Ibid.

Chapter 14

1. Stout and Johnson, *Red Sox Century*, 38.
2. Ibid., 38–39.
3. *Boston Post*, October 2, 1903.
4. *Boston Globe*, October 2, 1903.
5. Stout and Johnson, *Red Sox Century*, 42.
6. *Boston Globe*, October 3, 1903.
7. *New York Times*, February 18, 1905.
8. Kritzer, "Late Jimmy Collins."
9. *Boston Globe*, October 3, 1903.
10. Frank Sleeper, "The Series That Almost

Never Got Played," *Sports Illustrated*, September 30, 1968.
11. Stout and Johnson, *Red Sox Century*, 44.
12. *Pittsburgh Press*, October 9, 1903.
13. *Sporting Life*, October 17, 1903.
14. *Boston Globe*, October 10, 1903.
15. *Boston Globe*, October 15–16, 1903; *Sporting Life*, October 24, 1903.
16. *Meridan* (Conn.) *Journal*, October 16, 1903.
17. *Pittsburgh Press*, October 14, 1903.
18. *The Sporting News*, October 31, 1903.
19. *Boston Globe*, October 11, 1903.
20. *Sporting Life*, October 31, 1903.

14. *New York Times*, July 16, 1904.
15. Ed Linn, *The Great Rivalry: The Yankees and the Red Sox 1901–1990* (New York: Ticknor & Fields, 1991), 29.
16. *Boston Journal*, October 8 and 10, 1904.
17. *Boston Journal*, October 6, 1904.
18. Linn, *The Great Rivalry*, ix.
19. *Boston Globe*, October 18, 1904.
20. Kritzer, "Late Jimmy Collins."
21. *Sporting Life*, October 22, 1904.
22. Kritzer, "Late Jimmy Collins."
23. *Boston Globe*, November 16, 1904.
24. *Boston Globe*, November 28, 1904.
25. *Boston Globe*, October 17, 1904.

Chapter 15

1. *Sporting Life*, November 14, 1903.
2. Kritzer, "Late Jimmy Collins."
3. *Sporting Life*, September 10, 1904.
4. *Boston Post*, March 27, 1904.
5. Charles Fountain, *Under the March Sun: The Story of Spring Training* (New York: Oxford University Press, 2009), 17.
6. William Ross, "Spring Training in Georgia," in *The National Pastime: Baseball in the Peach State*, ed. Ken Fenster and Wynn Montgomery (Cleveland: Society for American Baseball Research, 2010), 117.
7. *Macon Telegraph*, January 17, 1904.
8. *Boston Post*, March 27, 1904.
9. *Macon Telegraph*, March 8, 1904.
10. *Sporting Life*, April 2, 1904.
11. *Boston Post*, March 21, 1904.
12. *Macon Telegraph*, March 18, 1904.
13. *Boston Globe*, March 28, 1904.
14. James Collins, "The Champion Baseball Team of the World," *The Illustrated Sporting News*, April 16, 1904.
15. *Boston Post*, March 27, 1904.
16. *Macon Telegraph*, March 28, 1904.
17. *Boston Globe*, April 11, 1904.

Chapter 16

1. *Boston Globe*, April 19, 1904.
2. Lieb, *Boston Red Sox*, 50.
3. *Sporting Life*, April 2, 1904.
4. *Sporting Life*, April 30, 1904.
5. Lieb, *Boston Red Sox*, 50.
6. Edward Woolley, "The Business of Baseball," *McClure's Magazine*, July 1912.
7. *Boston Globe*, April 19, 1904.
8. Stout and Johnson, *Red Sox Century*, 57.
9. *Boston Globe*, June 19, 1904.
10. Ibid.
11. *Boston Globe*, July 10, 1904.
12. *National Police Gazette*, July 8, 1905.
13. *Sporting Life*, December 17, 1904.

Chapter 17

1. Murnane, "His Winter Pastime."
2. Ibid.
3. *Buffalo Express*, February 19, 1905.
4. *Macon Telegraph*, March 13, 1905.
5. *Macon Telegraph*, March 16, 1905.
6. James Collins, "Why Boston Will Again Win the Championship," *The Illustrated Sporting News*, April 22, 1905.
7. Collins, "Champion Baseball Team."
8. Collins, "Why Boston Will Again Win."
9. *Boston Globe*, September 11, 1905.
10. *The Sporting News*, January 20, 1906.
11. *Boston Globe*, July 11, 1905.
12. *Boston Globe*, September 12, 1905.
13. *Boston Globe*, July 25 and 29, 1905.
14. *Boston Globe*, August 8, 25, and 27, 1905.
15. *Boston Globe*, August 1, 1905.
16. *Boston Globe*, August 29, 1905.
17. *Boston Globe*, October 18, 1905.
18. *Boston Globe*, October 15, 1905.
19. O'Connell, "Boston's Baseball Idol."
20. *Sporting Life*, December 23, 1905.
21. *Chicago Tribune*, December 22, 1905.
22. *Boston Globe*, December 30, 1905.
23. *New York Times*, December 31, 1905.
24. *Chicago Tribune*, January 10, 1906.
25. Murdock, *Ban Johnson*, 74.
26. *Chicago Tribune*, December 22, 1905.
27. *Boston Globe*, January 18, 1906; *Sporting Life*, June 22, 1907.
28. *Boston Globe*, January 25, 1906.
29. *Chicago Tribune*, January 27, 1906.
30. *Sporting Life*, February 3, 1906.

Chapter 18

1. *Washington Post*, November 27, 1905.
2. *Boston Globe*, December 31, 1905.
3. *Boston Globe*, January 27, 1906.
4. *Worcester Telegram*, February 6, 1906.
5. *Boston Globe*, March 31, 1906.

6. *Worcester Telegram*, February 5, 1912.
7. Ibid.
8. *Fall River Globe*, May 18, 1906.
9. *Boston Globe*, September 12, 1907.
10. *Worcester Telegram*, September 10, 1907.
11. *Worcester Telegram*, February 5, 1912.
12. Ibid.

Chapter 19

1. Lieb, *Boston Red Sox*, 66.
2. Geitschier, *Complete Baseball Record Book*, 157.
3. *Boston Globe*, May 24, 1906.
4. *Washington Post*, May 16, 1906.
5. Ibid.
6. *Boston Globe*, May 18–21, 1906.
7. Murdock, *Ban Johnson*, 74.
8. U.S. Census, 1880, Massachusetts, Suffolk County, Boston, Ward 22 (Series T9, Roll 560, Page 405).
9. *Boston City Directory*, 1896–1898.
10. U.S. Census, 1900, Massachusetts, Suffolk County, Boston, Ward 19 (Series T623, Roll 685, Page 39); *Boston City Directory*, 1906.
11. *Boston Globe*, June 11, 1906.
12. *Boston Globe*, July 1, 1906.
13. *Washington Post*, July 16, 1906.
14. *Boston Globe*, August 1, 1920.
15. *Boston Globe*, July 17, 1906.
16. *Sporting Life*, July 28, 1906.
17. *Boston Globe*, July 17, 1906.
18. *The Sporting News*, July 28, 1906.
19. *Boston American*, July 26–27, 1906.
20. *Boston Globe*, August 16–17, 1906.
21. *Boston Globe*, August 29, 1906.
22. *Boston Post*, August 29, 1906.
23. *Sporting Life*, October 20, 1906.
24. *Sporting Life*, January 5, 1907.
25. *Sporting Life*, October 6, 1906.
26. *Sporting Life*, September 22, 1906.
27. Ibid.
28. *Washington Post*, September 13, 1906.
29. *Providence Journal*, August 5–6, 1906.
30. *Providence Journal*, November 10, 1906.
31. *Providence Journal*, December 16, 1911.
32. *New York Times*, October 24, 1906.
33. *Sporting Life*, December 31, 1906.
34. *Sporting Life*, January 7, 1905.
35. *Buffalo Express*, October 23, 1906.
36. *Sporting Life*, October 20, 1906.
37. *Washington Post*, November 4, 1906.
38. *Philadelphia Inquirer*, November 14, 1906.
39. *Sporting Life*, October 13, 1906.
40. *Sporting Life*, January 5, 1907.
41. *Buffalo Express*, September 27, 1906.
42. *Boston Globe*, November 20 and December 5, 1906.
43. *Boston Globe*, December 14, 1906.

Chapter 20

1. *Boston Globe*, January 13 and 18, 1907.
2. *Boston Globe*, January 26, 1907.
3. *Buffalo Express*, February 20, 1907.
4. *Boston Globe*, March 4, 1907.
5. *Boston Globe*, March 8, 1907.
6. *Chicago Tribune*, March 29, 1907.
7. *Washington Post*, March 29, 1907.
8. Dennis Auger, "Chick Stahl," in *Deadball Stars of the American League*, edited by David Jones (Cleveland: Society for American Baseball Research, 2006), 420.
9. *Sporting Life*, June 22, 1907.
10. *Boston Globe*, November 15, 1906.
11. *Boston Globe*, November 14, 1906.
12. Stout and Johnson, *Red Sox Century*, 65.
13. *Boston Globe*, January 11, 1907.
14. *Boston Globe*, June 12, 1907.
15. *Boston Post*, June 12, 1907.
16. *Boston American*, June 12, 1907.
17. *Boston Herald*, June 13, 1907.
18. *Boston Herald*, June 14, 1907.
19. Correspondence dated June 1, 2011, to author from Our Lady of Hope Church in Buffalo, which holds the records for the now-closed parish of the Church of the Annunciation; Telephone call on July 18, 2011, with the archives of the Archdiocese of Boston, which holds the records for the now-closed parish of St. Francis de Sales Church.
20. *Boston Globe*, April 28, 1907.
21. *Boston Globe*, June 7, 1907.
22. *Boston Globe*, June 8, 1907.
23. Norman Macht, *Connie Mack and the Early Years of Baseball* (Lincoln: University of Nebraska Press, 2007), 496–497.
24. *Sporting Life*, June 22, 1907.
25. *Boston Globe*, June 8, 1907.

Chapter 21

1. *Philadelphia Inquirer*, June 9, 1907.
2. *Washington Post*, June 14, 1907.
3. *Philadelphia Inquirer*, June 24, 1907.
4. *Philadelphia Inquirer*, September 3, 1907.
5. *Washington Post*, September 4, 1907.
6. Macht, *Connie Mack*, 396.
7. *Philadelphia Inquirer*, October 1, 1907.
8. *Washington Post*, February 16, 1908.
9. *Worcester Telegram*, February 5, 1912.
10. *Washington Post*, October 28, 1907.
11. *Providence Journal*, April 14, 1908.
12. *Philadelphia Inquirer*, February 2, 1908.
13. *Boston Globe*, April 19, 1908.
14. *Buffalo Evening News*, March 13, 1943.
15. *Boston Globe*, August 14, 1908.
16. Birth date listed on the death certificate of Agnes Collins, dated May 2, 1909, Buffalo, New York, Bureau of Vital Statistics.

17. *Philadelphia Inquirer*, September 11, 1908.
18. Jack Coombs, "From My Diary," *Baseball Magazine*, May 1909.

Chapter 22

1. *Sporting Life*, November 28, 1908.
2. *Chicago Tribune*, December 8, 1908.
3. *Philadelphia Inquirer*, December 12, 1908.
4. *Chicago Tribune*, January 6, 1909.
5. *Chicago Tribune*, December 7, 1908.
6. *Sporting Life*, February 1, 1909.
7. *Philadelphia Inquirer*, December 13, 1908.
8. *Chicago Tribune*, January 26, 1909.
9. *New York Times*, January 31, 1909.
10. *Minneapolis Tribune*, January 30, 1909.
11. *Minneapolis Tribune*, January 31, 1909.
12. *Minneapolis Tribune*, February 7, 1909.
13. *Boston Globe*, March 8, 1909.
14. *Washington Post*, March 10, 1909.
15. *Minneapolis Tribune*, March 13, 1909.
16. *Sporting Life*, March 20, 1909.
17. Buffalo, New York, Bureau of Vital Statistics, certificate of death #97 in 1909.
18. Collins family plot records, Holy Cross Cemetery, Lackawanna, New York.
19. U.S. Census, 1910, Massachusetts, Suffolk County, Boston, Ward 19 (Series T624, Roll 622, Page 16).
20. *Chicago Tribune*, May 5, 1909.
21. *Washington Post*, June 9, 1909.
22. *Washington Post*, June 26, 1909.
23. *Minneapolis Tribune*, September 27, 1909.
24. Boston birth records, 1909, Book 585, Page 223, in the Massachusetts Archives.
25. *Minneapolis Tribune*, September 28, 1909.
26. *Sporting Life*, October 16, 1909.
27. *Providence Journal*, October 31, 1909.
28. *Chicago Tribune*, October 20, 1909.
29. *Providence Journal*, October 31, 1909.
30. *Boston Globe*, August 19, 1909.
31. *Chicago Tribune*, January 22, 1909.
32. *Buffalo Express*, November 16, 1909.
33. *Sporting Life*, January 29, 1910.
34. *Boston Globe*, April 13, 1910.
35. *Providence Journal*, April 22, 1910.
36. *Buffalo Express*, May 10, 1910.
37. *Chicago Tribune*, May 23, 1910.
38. *Buffalo Courier*, September 1, 2, and 6, 1910.
39. *Baltimore Sun*, October 19, 1910.
40. *Sporting Life*, June 17, 1911.
41. *Providence Journal*, June 11, 1911.
42. Kritzer, "Late Jimmy Collins."
43. *Sporting Life*, August 5, 1911.

Chapter 23

1. *Baltimore Sun*, February 15, 1912.
2. *Sporting Life*, December 10, 1910.
3. *Providence Journal*, December 16, 1911.
4. *Worcester Telegram*, February 5, 1912.
5. *New York Sun*, April 7, 1912.
6. Boston birth records, 1912, Book 609, Page 23, in the Massachusetts Archives; *Boston City Directory*, 1912.
7. *Sporting Life*, October 5, 1912.
8. *Washington Post*, March 30, 1913.
9. *Sporting Life*, July 6, 1912.
10. *Boston Globe*, July 25, 1912.
11. *Washington Post*, September 25, 1912.
12. *Brooklyn Eagle*, December 13, 1912.
13. *Boston City Directory*, 1913.
14. "Diamond Romance Culminates in Engagement Announcement," *Boston Globe*, May 4, 1925.
15. Thomas O'Connor, *The Hub: Boston Past and Present* (Boston: Northeastern University Press, 2001), 186.
16. *Boston Globe*, January 9, 1914.
17. O'Connor, *The Hub*, 191.
18. Honora Murphy's obituary, *Boston Globe*, November 25, 1913.
19. *New York Times*, March 24, 1914.
20. *Buffalo Express*, March 24, 1914.
21. U.S. Census, 1920, New York, Erie County, Buffalo, Ward 5 (Series T625, Roll 1100, Page 223).
22. *Boston City Directory*, 1914; *Buffalo City Directory*, 1915.
23. *Sporting Life*, December 12, 1914.
24. Harry Collins' World War I military draft registration card, Ancestry website, <www.ancestry.com>.
25. "Diamond Romance."
26. U.S. Census, 1920, New York, Erie County, Buffalo, Ward 5 (Series T625, Roll 1100, Page 223).
27. "Curtiss Aeroplane Now Speeding Up Production," *Wall Street Journal*, February 25, 1918.
28. Stout and Johnson, *Red Sox Century*, 67.
29. Tim Murnane's obituary, *Boston Globe*, February 8, 1917.
30. "Jake Morse," The Baseball Biography Project website, <http://bioproj.sabr.org/>; Morse died in 1937.

Chapter 24

1. *Buffalo Express*, March 12, 1922.
2. *Buffalo Express*, February 23, 1922.
3. *Buffalo Express*, October 26, 1922.
4. *Buffalo Express*, November 4, 1922.
5. *Buffalo Express*, December 6, 1922.
6. *Buffalo Express*, April 24, 1922.
7. *Boston Globe*, April 20, 1924.
8. *Buffalo Express*, April 24, 1922.
9. Harold Seymour, *Baseball: The People's*

Game (New York: Oxford University Press, 1990), 74–75.
10. *Buffalo Express*, June 5, 1922.
11. *Boston Globe*, September 12, 1922.
12. *Boston Globe*, January 16, 1930.
13. *New York Times*, October 2, 1920.
14. *Niagara Falls Gazette*, January 26, 1926.
15. Goldman, *High Hopes*, 214–215.
16. Goldman, *High Hopes*, 218.
17. Correspondence to author from Grace Jackson at Mt. Mercy Academy in Buffalo, dated May 9, 2011.
18. *Buffalo City Directory*, 1927.
19. Tom Nicholas and Anna Scherbina, "Real Estate Prices During the Roaring Twenties and the Great Depression," UC Davis Graduate School of Management Research Paper No. 18-09, March 21, 2011.
20. U.S. Census, 1930, New York, Erie County, Buffalo, Ward 25 (Roll 1433, Page 11B).
21. *Boston Globe*, August 9, 1931.
22. *Boston Globe*, September 2, 1929.
23. Thomas Goode's obituary, *Boston Globe*, January 24, 1933.
24. Fred Lieb, "Jimmy Collins, Game's Greatest Third Baseman," *Hartford Courant*, March 4, 1923, II: 21.
25. George Trevor, "Boston Jimmy Collins Shines Among All Third Basemen of Modern Era," *Brooklyn Eagle*, April 1, 1926.
26. *Boston Post*, September 9, 1930.
27. "Daguerreotypes: James J. (Jimmy) Collins," *The Sporting News*, July 27, 1933.
28. Goldman, *High Hopes*, 226–228.
29. Kritzer, "Late Jimmy Collins."
30. *Buffalo City Directory*, 1935.
31. Kritzer, "Late Jimmy Collins."
32. *New York Times*, December 24, 1935.
33. *Amsterdam (NY) Recorder*, May 6, 1936.
34. Ibid.
35. Warren Spahn's obituary, *Buffalo News*, November 25, 2003.
36. *Buffalo Evening News*, February 28, 1943.
37. *Buffalo Evening News*, March 6, 1943.
38. *Buffalo Evening News*, March 9, 1943.
39. Collins family plot records, Holy Cross Cemetery, Lackawanna, New York.
40. *Boston Globe*, March 10, 1943.

Chapter 25

1. Bob Stedler, "Sport Comment," *Buffalo Evening News*, January 1943, and other material in Jimmy Collins' player file at the A. Bartlett Giamatti Research Center at the Baseball Hall of Fame.
2. *Amsterdam (NY) Recorder*, January 12, 1943.
3. *New York Times*, January 16, 1943.
4. *Boston Globe*, January 11, 1943.
5. BBWAA voting results, Baseball Hall of Fame website.
6. *New York Times*, January 31, 1938; *Boston Globe*, July 12, 1939; *The Sporting News*, August 3, 1939.
7. Cooperstown *Otsego Farmer*, March 12, 1943.
8. *New York Times*, January 16, 1945.
9. *New York Times*, January 29, 1945.
10. *New York Times*, January 30, 1945.
11. *New York Times*, April 26, 1945.
12. *The Sporting News*, May 3, 1945.
13. *Boston Globe*, April 26, 1945.
14. *The Sporting News*, March 1, 1945.
15. *New York Times*, June 14, 1946.

Chapter 26

1. Collins family plot records, Holy Cross Cemetery, Lackawanna, New York; Kathlyn Walsh's obituary, *Buffalo News*, September 14, 1994; Claire Bell's obituary, *Syracuse Post-Standard*, October 4, 2005.
2. *Boston Globe*, May 31, 1951.
3. *New York Times*, October 1, 1953.
4. *The Sporting News*, January 2, 1957.
5. *The Sporting News*, August 2, 1969.
6. *Boston Globe*, July 6, 1969.
7. *Washington Post*, July 22–23, 1969.
8. *Utica Observer*, July 19, 1970.
9. Cooperstown *Otsego Farmer*, August 5, 1971.
10. William Bell's obituary, *Sarasota Herald-Tribune*, August 16, 1996.
11. William Bell's biography, U.S. Air Force website, <www.af.mil/information/bios/bio.asp?bioID=4657>.
12. Kritzer, "Late Jimmy Collins."
13. Claire Bell's obituary, *Sarasota Herald-Tribune*, October 5, 2005.
14. *Sarasota Herald-Tribune*, June 27, 1978.
15. *Sarasota Herald-Tribune*, March 19, 1981.
16. *Sarasota Herald-Tribune*, February 17, 1982.
17. Kathlyn Walsh's obituary, *Buffalo News*, September 14, 1994; Claire Bell's obituary, *Syracuse Post-Standard*, October 4, 2005.
18. *Baltimore Sun*, January 13, 1983.
19. Bill James, *The Politics of Glory: How the Hall of Fame Really Works* (New York: Macmillan, 1994), 178.
20. *Buffalo News*, March 20, 1999.
21. "Autograph Analysis and Signing Habits of Hall of Fame Third Baseman James Joseph 'Jimmy' Collins," Professional Sports Authenticator website, <www.psacard.com/articles/article_view.chtml?artid=3991>.

Bibliography

Print Material

Abrams, Roger. *The First World Series*. Boston: Northeastern University Press, 2003.
Browning, Reed. *Cy Young: A Baseball Life*. Amherst: University of Massachusetts Press, 2000.
Chudacoff, Howard. *The Age of the Bachelor: Creating an American Subculture*. Princeton: Princeton University Press, 1999.
Collins, James. "The Champion Baseball Team of the World." *The Illustrated Sporting News*, April 16, 1904.
_____. "Why Boston Will Again Win the Championship." *The Illustrated Sporting News*, April 22, 1905.
Dabilis, Andy, and Nick Tsiotos. *The 1903 World Series*. Jefferson, NC: McFarland, 2004.
"Daguerreotypes: James J. (Jimmy) Collins." *The Sporting News*, July 27, 1933.
Doyle, David Noel. "The Remaking of Irish America, 1845–1880." In *Making the Irish American: History and Heritage of the Irish in the United States*, edited by J.J. Lee and Marion Casey. New York: New York University Press, 2006.
Fleitz, David. *The Irish in Baseball: An Early History*. Jefferson, NC: McFarland, 2009.
Fountain, Charles. *Under the March Sun: The Story of Spring Training*. New York: Oxford University Press, 2009.
Glasco, Laurence. *Ethnicity and Social Structure: Irish, Germans, and Native-Born of Buffalo, N.Y., 1850–1860*. New York: Arno, 1980.
Goldman, Mark. *High Hopes: The Rise and Decline of Buffalo, New York*. Albany: State University of New York Press, 1983.
"Greatest Third Baseman." *Buffalo Express*, October 9, 1898.
Hamlet, Stanton. "Jimmy Collins." In *Deadball Stars of the American League*, edited by David Jones. Cleveland: Society for American Baseball Research, 2006.
Jenkins, William. "In the Shadow of a Grain Elevator: A Portrait of an Irish Neighborhood in Buffalo, New York, in the Nineteenth and Twentieth Centuries." *Eire–Ireland: Journal of Irish Studies*, Spring-Summer 2002.
Jennings, Hugh. "Collins, Leader at Third, Wanted to Play Outfield." *Atlanta Constitution*, January 5, 1926.
Kaese, Harold. *Boston Braves*. New York: G.P. Putnam's Sons, 1948.
Kritzer, Cy. "Late Jimmy Collins, the 'King of Third Sackers,' Became Hot Corner Star by Ability to Handle Bunts." *The Sporting News*, March 11, 1943.

Leavengood, Ted. *Clark Griffith: The Old Fox of Washington Baseball.* Jefferson, NC: McFarland, 2011.
Lieb, Fred. *Boston Red Sox.* New York: G.P. Putnam's Sons, 1947.
____. "Jimmy Collins, Game's Greatest Third Baseman." *Hartford Courant*, March 4, 1923.
Macht, Norman. *Connie Mack and the Early Years of Baseball.* Lincoln: University of Nebraska Press, 2007.
Masur, Louis. *Autumn Glory: Baseball's First World Series.* New York: Hill and Wang, 2003.
Morris, Peter. *A Game of Inches: The Stories Behind the Innovations that Shaped Baseball: The Game on the Field.* Chicago: Ivan R. Dee, 2006.
Morse, Jake. "The Revolution in the Local American Club: Young Taylor Down and Out and Jimmy Collins in Complete Control." *Sporting Life*, February 10, 1906.
Murdock, Eugene. *Ban Johnson: Czar of Baseball.* Westport, CT: Greenwood, 1982.
Murnane, Tim. "His Winter Pastime Collecting Rents." *Boston Globe Magazine* section. *Boston Globe*, January 15, 1905.
Nicholas, Tom, and Anna Scherbina. "Real Estate Prices During the Roaring Twenties and the Great Depression." UC Davis Graduate School of Management Research Paper No. 18-09. March 21, 2011.
O'Connell, Fred. "Boston's Baseball Idol: Jimmy Collins, Manager and Captain of the World's Champion Club." *Washington Post*, September 11, 1904.
O'Connor, Thomas. *The Hub: Boston Past and Present.* Boston: Northeastern University Press, 2001.
Overfield, Joseph. "James Joseph Collins." In *Baseball's First Stars*, edited by Frederick Ivor-Campbell, Robert Tiemann, and Mark Rucker. Cleveland: Society for American Baseball Research, 1996.
Ross, William. "Spring Training in Georgia." In *The National Pastime: Baseball in the Peach State*, edited by Ken Fenster and Wynn Montgomery. Cleveland: Society for American Baseball Research, 2010.
Sleeper, Frank. "The Series That Almost Never Got Played." *Sports Illustrated*, September 30, 1968.
Stedler, Bob. "Jimmy Collins, Buffalo's Baseball Immortal, Dies." *Buffalo Evening News*, March 6, 1943.
Stout, Glenn, and Richard Johnson. *Red Sox Century: One Hundred Years of Red Sox Baseball.* Boston: Houghton Mifflin, 2000.
Trevor, George. "Boston Jimmy Collins Shines Among All Third Basemen of Modern Era." *Brooklyn Eagle*, April 1, 1926.

ARCHIVAL MATERIAL

Baseball Hall of Fame, A. Bartlett Giamatti Research Center, Cooperstown, NY. Jimmy Collins' player file.
Boston Public Library, Boston, MA. *Boston City Directory* and *Buffalo City Directory*.
Buffalo, New York, Bureau of Vital Statistics. Marriage and death records of the city.
Holy Cross Cemetery, Lackawanna, NY. Collins family plot records.
Our Lady of Hope Church, Buffalo, NY. Marriage records for the now-closed parish of the Church of the Annunciation.
Massachusetts Archives, Boston, MA. Birth, marriage, and death records of the state prior to 1921.
U.S. Census Bureau, Washington, DC. Federal census records of 1870, 1880, 1900, 1910, 1920, and 1930.

BASEBALL PERIODICALS

Baseball Magazine
Sporting Life
The Sporting News

GENERAL NEWSPAPERS

Baltimore Sun
Boston Globe
Boston Herald
Boston Journal
Boston Post
Brooklyn Eagle
Buffalo Courier
Buffalo Evening News
Buffalo Express
Chicago Tribune
Cooperstown *Otsego Farmer*
Louisville Courier-Journal
Macon Telegraph
Minneapolis Tribune
New York Times
Niagara Falls Gazette
Philadelphia Inquirer
Providence Journal
Sarasota Herald-Tribune
Washington Post
Worcester Telegram

Index

Numbers in **bold italics** indicate pages with photographs.

All-America Baseball Team 49, 52–57, ***53***, 114
American Association 177–178, 182
American League 75, 78–84, 103, 106–107, 194
Armbruster, Charlie 143, 152

Baker, Frank 176, 215
Baltimore NL ballclub 31, 33, 45, 47–48, 49–57, 62, 69, 124, 204
Bannon, Jimmy 32, 33
Barnie, Billy 49, 53, 54–55, 57
Bell, Claire *see* Collins, Claire
Bergen, Marty 43, 51, 54, 71
Boston, Massachusetts 41–42, 45–47, 89, 92, 127, 138–139, 145, 155, 159, 192–193, 220
Boston AL ballclub 78, 79, 83, ***90***, 91, 95, 107–108, 129, 130–131, 136, 141–142, 152, ***154***, 169, 174, 186, 191, 192, 203, 212, 214, 219, 221
Boston NL ballclub 31–32, 41, 58, 62, 70, 74, ***75***, 76–77, 80, 94, 107, 144, 182, 186, 220
Brett, George 218
Brouthers, Dan 20, 35, 127
Buffalo, New York 10–14, 21–22, 73, 99–100, 195, 197, 201–202, 204–205
Buffalo AL ballclub 78–79
Buffalo City League 21–24, 200
Buffalo EL ballclub 21, 25, 107, 128, 150, 156, 159–160, 161, 178, 186, 194, 199
Buffalo Municipal Baseball Association 9, 197–200, 205–206, 209, 216, 219
Buffalo NL ballclub 20, 21, 203
Burkett, Jesse 54, 142, 147–149, 151, 156, 161

Callahan, Jimmy 76, 178, 179, 180
Cantillon, Joe 91, 162, 178, 180–181, 182, 185
Cantillon, Mike 178, 179–181, 185
Chapman, Jack 21, 26–27, 30, 31, 72
Chesbro, Jack 131, 135, 136
Clarke, Bill 55, 74, 82
Clarke, Fred 35, 116, 119, 211
Collins, Agnes (daughter) 175, 181, 184, 187, 206
Collins, Alice (mother) 10, 99, 140, 167, 181, 206
Collins, Anthony (father) 10–17, 70, 71, 91, 95, 96, 118, 141, 158, 181, 187, 206
Collins, Anthony, Jr. (brother) 10, 17
Collins, Claire (daughter) 190, 202, 203, 205, 214, 215–217
Collins, Henry (brother) 10, 17, 72, 73, 100, 195
Collins, Jimmy: All-America Baseball Team tour 53, 57; all-time team selection 203–204, 214–215; amateur 19, 22–26, 28; bachelorhood 28, 59, 72–73, 140–141, 151, 166, 170; as baseball scout 190–191, 192; birth 10, 27; Boston AL ***90***, 91, 96, ***101***, 105, ***111***, 142, 152, ***154***, 155, 169, 213; and Boston AL ownership 82–83, 85, 95; Boston NL 31–33, 42–48, ***45***, 59–62, ***61***, 67–69, ***67***, ***75***, 76–77; as boxing judge 201; Buffalo EL 26–30; bunt fielding, legend 33–35, 37, 68–69, 204, 205, 208; captain 74, 83, 89, 91, 100, 108, 151; championships 48, 51, 62–63, 108, 120, 130, 136–138, 219; children 175, 181, 183, 190, 202; as city employee 63, 71, 74, 205; as college baseball coach 193; compensation and contract negotiations 6–8, 26–27, 29, 32, 33, 38, 40–42, 45–46, 51, 58–59, 63,

235

71, 79, 83–87, 96, 98, 107, 123–124, 137–138, 144, 146, 162–163, 179–180, 184–185, 187; compensation guarantees 6, 85–86, 123, 146, 158–159, 162, 220; death 206; desertion 156, 157–158, 161, 220; education 13, 15–16, 19–20, 21, 70; executive 145–146, 151–154; failed attempts at ownership 9, 130, 145, 150–151, 156–157, 159–161, 163, 175–178, 182, 186, 189–190; fielding 24, 27–28, 34–35, 37, 45, 46, 64–66, 68, 77, 96, 101, 105, 203, 207, 211, 213, 219; friends 19, 46, 50, 73, 140, 160, 168, 169, 197; Hall of Fame 1–2, 196, 199, 204, 205, 207, 208–212, 213, 214, 215, 218, 219; hitting 46–47, 48, 59–60, 61–62, 69, 91, 96, 105, 169, 204, 211, 213, 219; injuries 43–44, 48, 104, 152, 155, 158, 161, 172, 174, 183, 188; in-laws 157, 167, 182, 190, 192, 203; jumping leagues 5, 79–87, 219–220; legacy 203, 212, 214, 216, 219–221; leisure activities 28, 40, 55, 56, 59, 66, 70, 72, 73, 77, 140, 141, 155, 157, 164, 176, 188, 203; Louisville NL 33–38, 40; manager 83–87, 88–89, 91–92, 95, 96, 100–103, 104, 108, 124, 127–128, 130–132, 141–142, 151–152, 155–156, 179–181, 184, 187, 189; marriage 3, 28, 163, 166–168, 169; memorabilia 5, 218–219; Minneapolis EL 179–184, *183*; as municipal baseball league president 9, 197, 198, 200, *200*, 205–206, 216; nephews 192, 195; old-timer games 200–201, 204, 209; Philadelphia AL 171–173, 175, 178, 213; physical appearance 60, 61, 119, 140, 164; postseason series 45, 49–57, 96, 110, 121–122, 137, 144; profit-sharing 7, 123–124, 130, 138, 141, 144, 146; Providence EL 184–188, *218*; as railroad clerk 17, 24, 29; real estate investments 73–74, 77, 83, 86–87, 98–100, 121, 139, 140, 146, 190, 194, 195, 201–203; records set 67–68, 77, 152; religion 59, 168, 206; residences 12, 16–17, 72–73, 170, 181, 182, 190, 192–193, 194, 202, 203, 205, 206; salary cap in NL 46, 58, 71, 74; signature 5, 70, 218–219; spring training 40, 46, 74, 91, 104, 107, 124–128, 141, 164–165, 180, 186; Temple Cup series 49, 52; third baseman, greatest 5, 58, 64, 94, 135, 199, 203–204, 210, 211, 213; union representative 74; wealth 8, 122, 174, 179, 190, 192, 205, 206; and Worcester NEL 8, 147–150, 174, 190; World Series 6, *7*, 109–121, 137, 192, 205, 214, 220; youth 13, 19

Collins, Jimmy, attributes: blunt 20, 179, 191, 192, 201; bosses, disdain for 61, 95, 104, 130, 139, 153, 190; business mindset 3, 8, 16, 23, 25, 26, 63, 70, 81, 90, 103, 121, 140, 160, 178, 190, 195, 198, 209, 213, 220; death, coping with 169, 182, 187; father, influence of 13, 17, 24, 141, 179, 195; hubris 141, 145, 154, 157, 161, 163, 179; humor 176; insubordination 156–159, 220; integrity 70, 85, 135, 143, 189; Irish heritage and values 11–12, 17–18, 20–21, 22–23, 24–25, 36, 127, 192, 195, 197; leadership 61, 70, 83, 91, 100–103, 108, 116, 126, 152, 156, 184, 187; private 1, 116, 132, 165, 167, 175, 195, 205, 207; public service 198–199, 209; relationship with ballclub owners 63, 71, 85–86, 95, 104, 108, 130, 139–139, 143–145, 153, 158, 161–162, 180–181, 186; relationship with league executives 38, 87, 105, 106–107, 131, 145, 153–154, 156, 163; relationship with sportswriters 68, 84, 88–89, 91–92, 127, 135, 155, 160, 191–192, 195–196, 207, 209; reluctance 103, 152; soft-spoken 50, 70, 92, 94, 100, 118, 119, 138, 144, 159, 168, 184, 219; strong-minded 32, 38, 40, 78, 90, 131, 220

Collins, Kathlyn (daughter) 183, 202, 205, 206, 214, 217
Collins, Margaret (sister) 16, 167, 168, 181
Collins, Sadie (wife) 166–168, 181–182, 188, 190, 203, 214; *see also* Murphy, Sadie
Comiskey, Charles 75, 83, 91, 184, 185
Criger, Lou 90, 91, 108, 115, 126, 136, 143, 152
Crowley, Timothy 139, 174, 185, 186, 187
Cuppy, Nig 90, 91

Dinneen, Bill 73, 89, 97, 104, 108–109, 116, 120, 126, 130, 136, 184
Dixwell, Arthur 43, 47, 63, 72, 80–81, 86, 94, 130
Doe, Fred 141, 147, 148, 150, 156, 160–161, 174, 186
Dougherty, Pat 96, 104, 108, 116, 126, 131–132, 136
Dowd, Tom 90, 91, 96, 104
Dreyfuss, Barney 36, 38, 109–111, 120–121
Duffy, Hugh: ballplayer 32, 66, 71, 74, 76, 211; college coach 195; investor in ballclubs 147, 156–157, 160, 174, 186, 189; manager 78, 79, 80, 81, 88, 95, 103, 184, 185

Eastern League 25–26, 148, 160, 161, 177–178, 182, 189

Farrell, Charley 108, 118, 126, 143
Ferris, Hobe 89, 91, *101*, 108, 115, 126, 152, 204
Fitzgerald, John 51, 81, 92, 129–130, 145, 155, 192
Fitzpatrick, William 73, 99–100
Franklin, James 25, 29, 78

Index

Freeman, Buck 73, 89, 91, 96, *101*, 108, 118, 126, 152

Gibson, Norwood 103, 108, 126, 130
Godwin, John 143, 152, 155
Goode, Thomas 157, 182, 190, 191, 192, 203
Griffith, Clark 74, 76, 78, 82, 91, 95, 103, 105, 131, 135, 161, 190, 220
Grimshaw, Moose 142

Hamilton, Billy 40, 43, 44, 71, 72, 74
Hemphill, Charlie 90, 91, 96, 104
Hornsby, Rogers 200, 215
Hughes, Tom 104, 108, 117, 131, 183
Huntington Avenue Grounds 44, 80, 82, 87, 93, 104, 107, 124, *134*, 191

Irish-Americans 11–13, 17, 20–21, 31, 41–42, 63, 73, 81, 92, 99–100, 126–127, 155, 159, 192–193; *see also* Collins, Jimmy, attributes: Irish heritage and values

Jennings, Hughey 34–35, 43, 54, 55, 69, 82, 127, 171, 204
Johnson, Ban 75–76, 78–80, 82, 89–90, 102, 105, 106–107, 112, 129, 131, 137, 144–145, 153–155, 158, 162–163, 180, 219
Johnson, Walter 172, 175, 191, 209, 215, 219

Kane, Ambrose 91
Keeler, Willie 24, 34, 37, 62, 105
Kell, George 218
Kelley, Joe 31, 37, 45, 54, 55, 124, 127
Kellum, Win 90, 91
Killilea, Henry 6, 95, 98, 104, 105, 106, 107, 108, 110–113, 117, 120, 123–124, 129, 162, 177
Knight, John 169, 170
Kuhns, Charlie 66–67

LaChance, Candy 96, 104, 108, 118, 126, 142, 204
Lajoie, Nap 60, 84, 93, 94
Lavis, Charlie 47, 81, 135, 136, 139, 174, 184, 185, 186, 187
Lewis, Ted 90, 91, 104
Lieb, Fred 108, 129, 203, 214–215
Long, Herman 32, *67*, 71, 74, 105
Louisville NL ballclub 26, 33, 36, 38, 42
Lowe, Bobby 32, 37, 41, 48, *67*, 71, 74

Mack, Connie 21, 72, 80, 83, 103, 104, 108, 145, 162, 169–170, 172, 175, 176, 178, 204, 211
Macon, Georgia 107, 124–128, 141
Malzone, Frank 215
Mathews, Eddie 214, 217

McAleer, Jim 162, 191
McCall, Claire *see* Collins, Claire
McCarthy, Tommy 32, 40, 63
McCloskey, John 33, 35, 36, 69, 183
McGraw, John 31, 34, 37, 48, 52, 63, 78, 104, 105, 127, 137, 191
McGreevey, Mike 47
McKenna, Kit 91
McLean, Larry 91
Meahl, John 197–198, 199, 212
Minneapolis AA ballclub 178, 183, 185
Mitchell, Fred 91, 96
Morgan, Red 155
Morse, Jake 32, 38, 66, 86, 88, 123, 141, 146, 159, 185, 196
Murnane, Tim 58, 77, 84, 88, 92, 116, 140, 141, 147, 155, 196
Murphy, Honora 155, 167, 182, 190, 194
Murphy, Sadie 139, 155, 157, 166; *see also* Collins, Sadie
Murray, Billy 30, 31

Nash, Billy 32, 40, 42, 43, 54, 55, 56
National League 58–59, 74, 78–79, 84, 94–95, 106–107, 109, 194
New York AL ballclub 105, 106, 128, 131–137, 203, 220
Nichols, Charley 50, 71, 103

O'Brien, John 103, 108, 118
O'Connell, Fred 89, 92, 102, 126–127, 141, 196
O'Neil, Tip 126, 132, 183, 184
O'Rourke, Jim 20, 62–63, 96, 127

Parent, Fred 89, 91, *101*, 108, 118, 126, 136, 204
Philadelphia AL ballclub 78, 79, 104, 108, 145, 171–173
Phillippe, Deacon 114, 118, 119
Pittsburgh NL ballclub 109, 114–120, 213–214
Players Protective Association 74, 76, 79, 82, 83, 85, 106
Powers, Pat 147, 159, 160, 161, 189
Preston, Walt 33, 34, 35, 68
Providence EL ballclub 25, 30, 45, 147–148, 156, 159–160, 174, 184, 185, 186
Pytlak, Frankie 206

Regan, Mike 138, 139, 141
Robinson, Brooks 215, 217–218
Royal Rooters 47, 80, 81, 114, 118–119, 135, 136, 138, 139, 141, 191
Ruth, Babe 131, 136, 192, 195, 201, 203, 204, 215, 220

Schmidt, Mike 218
Schreckengost, Ossee 90, 91, 96

Selbach, Al 132, 142
Selee, Frank 30, 31, 36, 40, 44, 46, 49, 53, 57, 61, *75*, 85, 88, 97, 100, 105, 108
Soden, Arthur 31, 41, 46, 58, 71, 79, 81, 85, 94, 129–130, 182
Somers, Charles 79, 80–85, 89–90, 95–96, 98, 104, 106, 179, 219
South End Grounds 44, 60, 80, 94
Spahn, Warren 206
spectators at ballparks 36, 43, 47, 59, 81, 93–94, 145; transportation used 20, 28, 44–45, 92–93
Stahl, Chick 46, 48, 49, 54, 57, 73, 74, 76, 89, 91, 96, 101, 105, 108, 118, 120, 126, 139, 152, 155, 156, 158, 162, 164–167, *167*
Stahl, Jake 108, 191
Stedler, Bob 206, 208, 209, 210, 212, 214
Stivetts, Jack 30, 51, 52
Sunday baseball laws 21, 25–26, 36, 51, 52, 55, 56–57, 59, 76, 119, 128, 132, 148, 172, 180–181, 186, 203

Tannehill, Jesse 126, 130
Taylor, Charles 119–120, 129, 145, 153, 154, 158, 161, 162

Taylor, Harry 76, 82, 85, 160, 161
Taylor, John I. 129–130, 131, 137, 138, 141, 143–146, 151, 162, 169–170, 174, 191
Temple Cup 45, 49–53, 57, 106, 112, 114
Tenney, Fred 46, 49, *67*, 71, 74, 200, 207
Traynor, Pie 205, 213–215, 218
Tucker, Tom 32, 46

Unglaub, Bob 131, 144, 165, 169

Wagner, Honus 115, 204, 215
Walsh, Kathlyn *see* Collins, Kathlyn
Webb, Mel 186, 211
Williams, Jimmy 68, 77
Winter, George 108, 126, 130, 131, 175
Wolfe, Roland 126
Worcester NEL ballclub 147–150, 186, 190
World Series, 1903 5–6, 106–107, 109–113, 114–121
World Series, 1904 137

Yeager, George 51, 66
Young, Cy 90, 91, 93, 96, 101, 104, 108–109, 115, 117–118, 120, 126, 128, 130, 135, 143, 152, 169, 175, 204, 214

www.ingramcontent.com/pod-product-compliance
Ingram Content Group UK Ltd.
Pitfield, Milton Keynes, MK11 3LW, UK
UKHW041942140426
5217IPUK00014B/615